AUP 23

The Lost Rib

Female Characters in the
Spanish-American Novel

Sharon Magnarelli

Lewisburg
Bucknell University Press
London and Toronto: Associated University Presses

Associated University Presses
440 Forsgate Drive
Cranbury, NJ 08512

Associated University Presses
25 Sicilian Avenue
London WC1A 2QH, England

Associated University Presses
2133 Royal Windsor Drive
Unit 1
Mississauga, Ontario
Canada L5J 1K5

Library of Congress Cataloging in Publication Data

Magnarelli, Sharon, 1946–
    The lost rib.

    Bibliography: p.
    Includes index.
    1. Spanish American fiction—20th century—History
and criticism.   2. Women in literature.   I. Title.
PQ7082.N7M29   1985   863'.009'352042   83-46157
ISBN 0-8387-5074-5

Printed in the United States of America

Contents

Acknowledgments

There can be little doubt that the most difficult page one must write in any book is this one. Surely during the seven years of this project, everyone with whom I had contact had some influence on it, for better or worse. Since I cannot acknowledge them all, I mention only a few of the many people who might be listed here and beg indulgence from the others.

First, I gratefully acknowledge the financial assistance which came from the National Endowment for the Humanities in the form of a summer research stipend and from Yale University in cooperation with the Mellon Foundation and the Lily Foundation, which provided several summer stipends and several years of library privileges. I would also thank Roberto González Echevarría, who read parts of the manuscript and made many useful suggestions, as did Manuel Durán. Many of the ideas developed in this study were first tried out on students in my classes at Albertus Magnus College, and I thank them for their patience. I would also thank my husband, Lou, and the faculty of the Department of Foreign Languages at Albertus Magnus College for their encouragement and support throughout the project. I also owe special thanks to Sr. Juliana D'Amato for her assistance in proofreading.

The Lost Rib

Introduction:
Adam's Rib

ONCE upon a time, in the beginning of time, according to the Bible, Adam lost a rib. From that rib, we are told, God fashioned woman, Eve, to serve as Adam's helper: "So the Lord God caused a deep sleep to fall upon the man, and while he slept took one of his ribs and closed up its place with flesh; and the rib which the Lord God had taken from the man he made into a woman and brought her to the man" (Gen. 2.21–22).[1] Thus reads one of the earliest Judeo-Christian views of the female. How literally we are meant to understand this vision we shall never know for sure, but paradoxically, this rendition of the creation of woman directly contradicts the one espoused merely one chapter earlier where we are told: "Then God said, 'Let us make man in our image, after our likeness; and let them have dominion! . . . So God created man in his own image, in the image of God he created him; *male and female he created them*" (Gen. 1.26–27). Unfortunately, it is not this earlier version of the simultaneous creation of man and woman which has been most often remembered and reiterated throughout history, but rather the rib story.[2] Doubtlessly, to the extent that Western civilization and society as we know them are based on the fundaments of Christianity and the Bible, the rib story, by virtue of its endless repetition, has provided one of the principal sources for today's perception of women and one of the principal sources of concern for feminists, as evidenced by the frequent references to the question by feminist scholars and critics.[3]

While the females portrayed in Spanish-American novels would ostensibly appear to be only peripherally related to the female sketched in Genesis, the distance is not so great. Essentially, the rib story heralds two ideological stances with regard to the female, stances which continue to prevail even today. On one level (that of the *énoncé*) the story insidiously posits that woman has always been a by-product of man. According to this account, the first man never intended to create Eve; there was no design or forethought, malicious or otherwise, on Adam's part. It was the will of God; Adam was merely the instrument. The story might be viewed, then, as an inadvertent parable of what has occurred throughout history. Surely woman has often been a by-product of man, who traditionally has been

11

charged with writing civilization's sacred books, history books, and epics. Many of these male writers may never have meant to perpetuate either a favorable or an unfavorable vision of the "little woman"; she merely formed a peripheral part of that society he was describing or shaping, so he included some marginal references to her—references which may have been as superfluous as Adam's rib apparently was.

On another level, however (that of the *énonciation*), such fortuity is extremely doubtful. It appears that the Jahvist writers, creators of the rib story, consciously and intentionally rewrote the earlier Elohist story of creation.[4] To this extent, we might view their activity, too, as a parable of the other stance which has been repeated throughout history. Temporally, the Jahvist writers postdated the Elohist writers, and their rendition of the creation story clearly underlines their calculated reshaping of the story so that it would satisfy their own purposes. Thus, the formulation of a new version of the story, which changes the creation of the two sexes from a simultaneous gesture to one which is temporally successive and then "proves" the "natural" superiority of the male, reflects a tendency to use language to create a new reality (or at least a new perception of reality), to reshape an ideology by replacing old beliefs with a series of new concepts created merely by language. Insofar as there is no biological reason to presume that one gender chronologically preceded the other, it is most logical to view the Jahvist story as wishful thinking on the part of its creators. The story, indeed, reflects the mythic gesture, as studied by Elizabeth Janeway, whereby "myth opposes belief [desire] to facts in order to change the facts or obscure them,"[5] or the "self-fulfilling prophecy" explicated by Mary Daly (*Church*, p. 193).

Nonetheless, because our overall view of the female has generally been so much more reprobative than that of the male, it is perhaps all too easy to accuse the entire masculine gender of hostility or a negative attitude toward all females. While I certainly would not suggest that misogyny has not existed or does not continue to exist, nor that the Jahvist writers had women's best interests at heart, it is possible that much of the pejorative image of the female which has emerged from our literature (both sacred and profane)[6] may have been less malevolent than has often been supposed. After all, within the framework of what we call the history of Western civilization, the male has always been in power, and surely it has rarely occurred to anyone in authority to share that prestige with the powerless group or to make any special effort to improve the image of that other group. Since it would seem to be the instinct of all animal species to seek power and guard it zealously, perhaps one has no right to suggest that the males of society, charged with the creation and perpetuation of "civilization," should have been noble enough to share that position or to improve the female's image. Indeed, the group in authority definitively risks undermining its own prestige if its praise of the other group is too approbatory. It would seem more fruitful then to view the portrayal of the female in literature, sacred and profane, as a combination of the intentional and the unintentional, overlaid with a greater or lesser degree of wishful thinking. Most authors probably have just mirrored what they think they have seen. Ultimately, their intentions, whether malevolent or beneficent, are outside of the scope of this study, which will examine what Spanish-American authors have said, explicitly or implicitly, and the implications of those statements, while leaving to others an analysis of their intentions.

Theodor Reik *(Creation)* has done a most interesting study of the psycho-historical foundations and implications of this creation story. My approach will be different, although my conclusions are not necessarily incompatible with his. He sought to discover how the myth, the confusion, and the subsequent disparity between the two versions came to be. I, on the other hand, shall endeavor to analyze the product of these presentations of the female's origins, to see where we have been led as a result. That is, Reik has examined the prehistory, the cause of this explanation of woman's creation; I shall study its posthistory or effects.

What becomes clear as one examines the biblical versions of the creation of woman and what Reik has unsuspectingly underscored in his study of these is one essential point: from what has been posited as her very first moment, her origins, woman has been created, invented, unwittingly though it may be, by and for man. From the beginning she was already repetition, re-creation, reshaping, in a word, translation from one format to another, from one form to another, from one language to another. And perhaps herein lies the problem and the confusion.[7]

To begin a study of female characters, several points must be borne in mind. First, one must recognize that the principal preoccupations of any writer (historical, fictional, sacred, etc.) are threefold: language, the act of writing, and time. Language must be the writer's first concern since he must transfer or translate certain aspects of his world (real or imaginary) into language, choosing just the right words to convey just the right meaning. At the same time, he must be continually aware of the act of writing itself inasmuch as he must necessarily select what he will include and what he will omit, order those selections, and be ever aware that he is selecting and ordering as he constantly faces the problem of whether to share this activity (and his problems with it) with his reader or hide it from him. Finally, time, which can never be identical inside and outside of the text, must be an eternally present concern. Now, these three main preoccupations do not eliminate the possibility of others: religious, sociological, political, psychological, and so forth, but these three concerns are ever present, always interrelated, and often related to the subject of the female. On an extraliterary level the reasons for the connections between language, writing, time, and women are multiple. First, since most texts are written by the male, the female necessarily represents that intriguing, mysterious

Other and thus embodies many of the same mysteries and enigmas as language. Additionally, the creative aspects of writing and language provide an easy and perhaps inevitable psycholingual metaphoric association between these two and the "reproductive," "procreative" female.

At the same time, the rib parable further illustrates a link between women and language: the search for origins. Language, by its very nature, implies a continual search for the referent, which is always missing and which, as Derrida has suggested, may never have existed.[8] Similarly, we continually search for Adam's rib, the origins of women, but the stories of creation, with their duplicity, contradictions, and juxtaposition, obliquely suggest that woman too may have always been supplement, added to, reshaped. As a result, vast bodies of mythology have grown up around both women and language, threatening to engulf them both. This study will attempt to disentangle some of that mythology while recognizing that Adam's lost rib metaphorically assimilates both woman and language (inasmuch as Adam was charged with naming all of the creatures of the Garden, which is a type of creation/re-creation), although woman may have formed merely an incidental part of that mythology. As Reik has suggested, myths were probably created by men for men:

> The first myths are, it seems to me, produced by, and meant for, men. They often become, it is true, old wives' tales, but only after they have been contemptuously dismissed by the men of the tribe. Women are more often occupied than preoccupied with the creation of man. Their imagination is not involved with the solution to the question of how the first human being was created. This is no problem for them: they know. It could not have been very different, they feel, from the manner in which their own children are born. The myths and legends of creation, including those of the Bible, presuppose an audience of men. (P. 17)

Equally applicable here, no doubt, is Elizabeth Janeway's definition of myth to which I have already referred:

> For it is the nature of myth to be both true and false, false in fact, but true to human yearnings and human fears. . . . Myth is born out of psychological drives. What we do not have, that is what we need; and that is what we present to ourselves as desirable. . . . We strengthen this mythic structure by projecting our fears out onto the world, whence they return as threats. (P. 26)

The result of this vast mythology which envelops the female of our species is that throughout history she has been alternately praised and disparaged. We see her exalted during certain historical eras; at those moments she has been idealized beyond recognition and worshiped in a form which ultimately had little or no bearing on her concrete being in the world. Antithetically, during other periods, she has been disparaged and scorned for many of the same reasons for which she was previously admired, reasons again which had equally little to do with her essence. In so many ways, then, women have always been personae, characters, literary creations, both inside and outside of fiction, continually fantasized, fabricated, and counterfeited. We have alternately believed them to be a great deal more or considerably less than what they are.

The study which follows examines the portrayal of women in the context of the Spanish-American novel, recognizing fully that the image of females we find in these novels is also a by-product, perhaps not consciously intended by the authors. The study began as an effort to answer three basic questions: (1) Why is the Spanish-American novel so nearly devoid of memorable female protagonists? (2) How do the novels portray their female characters, and how do these portrayals, in many instances, create the novels' audiences? (3) Why is it that even those novels whose titles promise female protagonists ultimately focus on other topics or characters?

In response to the first two questions, there is a tendency to postulate hastily that most of the Spanish-American novelists are male, and, therefore, it is only logical that they should create male protagonists and secondary female characters. However, the fact that most of the notable female characters in world literature have been created by males belies the accuracy of such a simplistic response. Madame Bovary, Temple Drake, Daisy Miller, and Moll Flanders are just a few of the well-known female characters that have been created by men. Certainly, then, the answer to the question is more complex and involves several other considerations. In addition, and perhaps more importantly, the lack of memorable females imposes a set of standards and expectations on the novels' audiences, for surely there can be little doubt that literature, like other art forms (both popular and those considered more "cultured," more elite), have influenced, as much as they have been influenced by, social mores. Literature, whether it takes the form of novels, the Bible, or fairy tales, is like song, television, myth, and film in that all reflect shared beliefs while they perpetuate and spread those beliefs. Such, of course, is precisely what has occurred with the image of women over the years.

More recently, the mass media have led us to anticipate excitement, adventure, and superhuman events in the media lives of both males and females. If, in spite of the reputed exaggeration and stimulation, the novel still presents dull or forgettable women, what are we to hope for from our everyday life, which must necessarily be less exhilarating? I suggest that such a portrait influences the novels' audiences, their expectations, and the way they view themselves and others.

I further recognize fully that we cannot hope to "know" what women were like at any given point in history. No single novel can be understood as an accurate reflection of how women were perceived in that historical period. Whatever sources we might study, we would be left with only a generalization which at best *might* tell us something about society's perception of *some* women of that time. Instead I propose to examine a series of novels published over a period of one hundred years, and show how some Spanish-American authors have perceived women (at least some women) over the century. I shall presume that since all the novelists studied acquired some degree of fame and financial success and that since I have generally selected their better-known works, read by thousands if not hundreds of thousands of readers, the image of the female presented cannot be completely alien to the image held by much of the reading public. It is presumed that readers in large numbers do not continue to read what is alien or contradictory to their own ideology and system of values.

The third question posed underlines a curious phenomenon that does not seem unique to Spanish-American letters. As early as the middle of the nineteenth century, in Spanish America, one encounters titles which suggest and seem to promise novels about women: *Amalia, María, Doña Bárbara* (whose title character is one of the few notable female characters), *La traición de Rita Hayworth, El beso de la mujer araña,* and others. Paradoxically, each of these titles is a misnomer; each ultimately fails to center on the promised protagonist, and each turns its attention, instead, to a male character who becomes the true protagonist. *María,* for example, is not really about María at all. Contrary to what the title implies, the text focuses on Efraín, the male narrator-protagonist, and on his morose psychological state (as the genre of the love story generally does). María is only the catalyst of his sorrows. In fact, she is a total absence, a nonentity in the text, to the extent that she has already died before the start of the narration of the story, a narration which forms a part of that fiction and which serves to re-create and/or make her present again. It is most significant that in this presumably feminine genre (the love story, a genre supposedly written for and about women), the woman is fantasized and re-created even within the fiction. Similarly, *Doña Bárbara* is far more preoccupied with Santos Luzardo and thus creates more reader empathy for him than for Bárbara herself. In a parallel fashion, Rita Hayworth never appears in the novel which bears her name; she is spoken of but is never a part of the action.

In the process of answering these questions, I hope to demonstrate the direct and immediate relationship between the depiction of the female and the attitude of society toward language insofar as the novel (i.e., writing) inevitably reflects an attitude toward the medium of its text—language. One can find the beginnings of an underlying skepticism toward language as early as *María,* in spite of the fact that the text was produced in a period apparently filled with confidence in the ability of language to reproduce, re-create, and recapture that which is past. Already, then, one encounters doubts and the early signs of an overt loss of innocence with respect to language and the signifier. From that point onward, the novel "progresses" to the overt "mistrust" of language as epitomized in the prose of the last twenty years. One of the principal topics of the "new" novel, of course, has been the total inadequacy of language to say or reproduce anything—an inadequacy which has resulted from the separation of the signifier from its signified.

There is little doubt that a parallel phenomenon has occurred in the portrayal of the role of the female. Within the novel the female is, of course, totally created by language, as is any literary character, but we have yet to discover how much and to what extent we ourselves are influenced and shaped by that language. In *María*, for example, one finds an apparently placid acceptance of predetermined adjectives and a willingness on the part of Efraín to assign those adjectives with a naïveté indicative of his faith in their ability to encompass "reality." This perspective changes, however (as does the faith in a golden age past), by the middle of the twentieth century. Thus, in *La ciudad y los perros*, one notes a subtle questioning of the dichotomous manner in which women and all aspects of the environment are perceived (a dichotomy which is directly produced by language), while *La traición de Rita Hayworth* goes one step further and allows the distinctions between male and female to become blurred, nebulous, and ultimately insignificant. It is patent that not only do the changes in the portrayal of the female within the text parallel the changes in society's view of language, but, indeed, her depiction is directly dependent upon that change in perception.

In this manner, I shall not only show that the answers to these questions are directly linked to language, but I shall also investigate the possibility that, contrary to popularly held beliefs that our cognizance of the world affects our language, it is our language which to a greater or lesser extent molds our vision of the world. Along the same lines, I shall also examine how literature, as a linguistic product, directly and indirectly affects the role and status of women in the "real world."

The selection of texts studied here is admittedly somewhat arbitrary. I have tried to span the time period from the publication of *María* in 1867 to the publication of *El gato eficaz* in 1972. As I have indicated, the specific novels were chosen for the most part because of their relatively widespread popularity, on the theory that those texts which are more widely read are (1) more likely to express a philosophy or point of view shared by a significant number of readers, and (2) (in turn) more apt to influence and affect social attitudes. The growing popularity of *El gato eficaz* attests that it too meets these criteria.

My approach has been eclectic. I have chosen for each work those methods which seemed most appropriate and most productive for the analysis of that particular work and have attempted not to force any approach on the text. Thus, in the coming pages the reader will find linguistic analyses, textual explications, mythological studies, and sociological views. The type of material being discussed has at times forced me to speak of characters as if they were people rather than verbal entities, conglomerations of words. I not only acknowledge but in fact insist that they are but linguistic creations, and not people. However, validly or not, the novel is often understood as a reflection of the world around the author, and most readers do undergo a willing suspension of disbelief and read *as if* the characters were indeed people. It is especially the more naïve reader who reads in this fashion, and he/she is precisely the one most likely to be influenced by this reading material. Thus, even when I do speak of characters as if they were people, I have not lost sight of the fact that they are but a series of metaphors which *seem* to have certain characteristics in common with Homo sapiens.

Some readers may well protest that my analyses of the individual texts are incomplete. They are; such has been my intention. Most of the novels have been dealt with at length by a multitude of critics and scholars, and I see no need to repeat what has been well expressed elsewhere. My intention has been, very specifically, to examine only one aspect of the texts: the female characters. Nevertheless, I do insist that my focal point is essential to the comprehension of the texts and has far too often been ignored by others. Furthermore, I suggest that the portrayal of the female in these novels has significant bearing on other elements of the texts and that a reconsideration of the female's role must necessarily lead to new readings of the novels and our relationship to them.

Throughout the coming chapters I have offered the readers parenthetical English translations of the citations of the texts studied. On occasion, since any text can be translated in more than one manner, I have made significant changes in the translated material in order that my point would be as apparent in the English translation as it is in the Spanish text. Whenever I have found it necessary to do this, I have indicated the same by including my translation in brackets.

But enough generalization. The texts, with a little prodding, will speak for themselves.

1
The Love Story:
Reading the Writing in Jorge Isaacs's
María

La espesa rueda de la tierra
su llanta húmeda de olvido
hace rodar, cortando el tiempo
en mitades inaccesibles.

Pablo Neruda

PUBLISHED in 1867 by Jorge Isaacs (Colombia, 1837–95), *María* is one of the earliest Spanish-American novels still widely read today. Generally relished by adolescents, *María* has been successively highly esteemed and discredited because of its maudlin romanticism. Numerous critics have demonstrated its close affiliation with European romanticism, and many have considered it but a poor copy of French works such as *Atala* and *Paul et Virginie*.[1] Nevertheless, some of the most important aspects of the text, especially those related to the title female, have been neglected. In the following pages, I shall examine *María* in terms of the dramatized narrative process and its portrayal of women. To date, scholars have focused principally on the story, analyzing it either as a reflection of Isaacs's own life or in terms of its rather insipid and terribly commonplace love story.[2] What has all too often been overlooked (and what is both most interesting and most important) are the facts that, first, *María* is much more than a love story, and, secondly, the genre of the love story in and of itself is much more significant than we have previously acknowledged. That *María* is more than a simple love story is evidenced by the textual presentation and dramatization of the very important acts of reading and writing. *María* is not simply a tale of love, told in the third person; rather the story is developed within a framework which includes its own narration. We watch not only the unfolding of the story (the *énoncé*) but also the narrational process of that story (the *énonciation*) which forms a part of the

19

fiction, and, as I shall demonstrate, this narration is but the reading and rewriting of a prior *énoncé*, those past and earlier signs.[3]

Recounting in the first person, Efraín focuses on a few months of his youth, on a significant pause between two of his journeys. The novel opens as he recalls his first departure from the family embrace. When he returned from that first educational journey, he found a paradise which apparently was even superior to the one he had remembered leaving behind four years before. A pure and innocent love unfolded between Efraín and María, although they both knew that his sojourn at home (and consequently his proximity to her) would be but the brief span of time before his next voyage. Having said goodbye to María and having promised to marry her upon his return, he departed on that second journey. Later, receiving urgent word to return home, he did so, expecting to repeat his previous return to paradise, but María had already died and the paradise had disintegrated.

The story, then, is trite—one of thousands of love stories told in countless languages. My interest in it stems not from the story itself, not from what it overtly tells us about the epoch in which it was written (its *costumbrismo*), nor from the character development. Instead, my curiosity about the text derives from its apparent misnomer and from its *énonciation;* the dramatized narrative gesture suggests very different conclusions about the novel from those of many of its earlier critics.

What is perhaps most intriguing about *María* is that its title, like that of so many Spanish-American novels, is misleading. Although the novel's title page promises a tale of a woman named María, in the final analysis, the novel is not essentially about María. Rather, it is an examination of the psychological state of Efraín, and, more importantly, a portrayal of his attempts to recapture those fleeting moments, already past, of childhood innocence and happiness. María may be the instrument and the stimulus of this innocence and happiness, much as she is portrayed as the inspiration for Efraín's narration, but she certainly is not the protagonist in the usual sense of the term.

Perhaps before one can consider the implications of the title of the novel, one needs to examine the significance of having baptized the young girl with the name María, rather than Juanita, Carmen, or some other suitable appellation. The name *María*, of course, evokes an affiliation with the Virgin Mary and all the connotations of the religious virgin mother. In Western literature from the Middle Ages through the twentieth century, we find that many of the literary converts adopt the name María upon baptism, suggesting the belief or hope that the adoption of the name presumes the annexation of the characteristics associated with that name. Such is certainly the case with Isaacs's María.

However, María, born of Jewish parents, Salomón and Sara,[4] was originally named Ester. Ester, or Esther, is a particularly relevant name since it derives from the Hebrew Ishtar, who was the chief goddess of the Babylonians and the Assyrians. According to M. Esther Harding, Ishtar was a moon goddess and a goddess of fertility, "personification of that force of nature which shows itself in the giving and the taking of life."[5] She was a cyclic goddess who, like the Romans' Proserpina, spent part of the year in the sky giving life and part of the year in the underworld taking it away. Harding notes that during the period when Ishtar was in the land of no-return, or the underworld, the "whole world is described as being sunk in a kind of hopeless inactivity, mourning for her return" (p. 159).[6] In addition, Ishtar, because of her cyclic nature, is the goddess of time.

Now, the evolution of the Christian Virgin Mary and her affiliation with the earlier moon goddesses, Ishtar and Isis, have been demonstrated by numerous scholars. Isaacs, however, overtly assigns both names to his character, thereby endowing her with what we might colloquially call the best of both worlds. The merging of the two goddess figures is patent in the fact that throughout the novel María is depicted in terms of both nature and motherhood (terms inexorably linked in earlier times but not necessarily considered related in Christianity); she is consistently found in Efraín's mother's room, and frequently acts as proxy mother to Juan. And she is always portrayed by Efraín in relation to nature—she brings the flowers, prepares the bath with flowers, etc.:[7] "María estaba bajo las enredaderas que adornaban las ventanas del aposento de mi madre" (p. 12) ("María was behind the creeper that climbed up by the windows of my mother's room," p. 2); "Soñé que María entraba a renovar las flores" (p. 16) ("I dreamed that María came in to renew the flowers on my table," p. 7).[8] In this respect María represents all that is fertile and life-giving but is refined by the Christian concept of purity, virginity, and holiness. She is, thus, the very representation of the "civilized" (some may call it patriarchal) progress from the more primitive mother goddesses to the contemporary Christian concept of perfect woman. This "progress" is echoed in her religious conversion from Judaism to Christianity and directly influences our reading of this text.

Although this seemingly simple and irrelevant modification of María's name may not appear to be of great significance, it does reflect and become a synecdoche for the attitude toward the portrayal of the female. First, the very fact that Isaacs felt it necessary to provide María with two names reflects an interest in language, naming, and finding just the right word or phrase to express the situation as he sees it, to which I referred in the introduction to this study. At the same time it also reflects the author's concern with time as I have discussed it. Just as the Bible provides two creation stories, one succeeding the other in time, the female character here is provided with two successive names (and, in some sense, births): she is first Ester and then María. As the later rib story persists, so does the name María. But even more importantly, the permutation highlights and

underlines the primary concern in this study: the re-creation and supplementation of the female. María is born Ester, Hebrew. That is, her first
presence in the world (within the confines of the fiction, of course) is a
Jewish presence, but that "origin" is erased and reshaped by her conversion to Christianity. The re-creation of her being is thus reflected in her
name as she apparently willingly gives up her original religion and name in
exchange for the socially acceptable Catholicism and Catholic name. Sug-
gestively, however, this "voluntary" conversion occurs when María is far
too young to give what we would call today "informed consent."

In this regard, then, the female character here (on the level of the *énoncé;*
I shall discuss the *énonciation* later) is a supplement, a mask, a negation of
her former being, or carried one step further, she becomes a nonentity, a
projection of another. After the name change, she is no longer Ester but
assumes the prefabricated name and characteristics of the Virgin Mary,
which the patriarchal society has deemed appropriate. Ironically, however,
one must wonder how we are meant to interpret María's final illness and
death. On some level it would seem that her new identity was inadequate
to disguise and extinguish the old completely, for she does die from the
weakness and illness inherited, significantly, from her mother, Sara.
Somehow, the old family traits have persisted in spite of the name change.

At the same time, the substitution of the name becomes particularly
relevant to the creation of an audience for the novel. As I suggested in the
introduction, a novel frequently creates its own audience. There can be
little doubt that a novel entitled *Ester* would attract and create quite a
different audience than one entitled *María.* Ester would necessarily be
"other" and alienated within the Catholic society that surrounds her, but
María, via the change in appellation, on some level and to some extent
eradicates, negates, or at least partially disguises her otherness.

Also important is the parallel between the relation of María to this text
and that of the Virgin to Christianity or the Bible. The Virgin Mary, of
course, maintains a curiously contradictory position. She is not one of the
protagonists of the Christian text, for the main characters are all male:
Father, Son, Holy Spirit.[9] But the Virgin is the instrument, the mediator,
the stimulus in much the same way as María.[10] She cannot directly grant
heavenly favors, but she can intercede and thus be the instrument of those
favors. She has no power except that of intercession; she cannot act directly, but she can influence the acts of the male trinity.[11]

On another level one might understand the entire novel in terms of that
"hopeless inactivity, mourning for her return" that occurs when Ishtar
goes to the land of no-return (death), for what is the novel but a form of
mourning for the return of María? The novel is clearly an obituary monument to her, and only at the conclusion of the narration can Efraín now
begin some type of fruitful activity, for only then does the mourning period
cease and life resume. Only at the conclusion of the text is the goddess or

María in some sense returned, at least in the fictionalized form of a novel which presumably re-creates, re-presents, and depicts her anew. Her existence, literally and metaphorically, depends upon the reading of the novel.

Inasmuch as the novel attempts to recapture the pause between two journeys, the novel itself is a pause, a static product which arrests (or gives the illusion of arresting) the motion of time and life, the continuum. The novel thus signals a mythic view of life as a series of static medallions; one "journeys" from one medallion or stage to the next, but once there, all is basically and essentially static, unmoving, and unchanging until the moment arrives to travel on to the next medallion. Clearly, such a credence is a direct effort to deny or negate the continual movement of life, and this negation, although also mythic in origin, is contrary to the myth of Ishtar— a myth which inherently encompasses this motion.[12] But mankind's inability to cope with changes and unexpected contingency is a frequent theme in literature, and Efraín is not different from don Jerónimo of José Donoso's *El obsceno pájaro de la noche*, who not only tried to negate all that did not conform nicely with his perfect "medallón de piedra eterna" ("medallion of eternal stone")[13] but who also hired Humberto to write the history so that it would comply. Donoso even notes that it is the ritual which fixes life as in a medallion. Efraín, however, did not have to employ Humberto; he will write the story and make it static himself. Efraín, himself, will play the priestly role and perform that ritual (writing) which will inscribe the figures on the medallion.

Thus one can explain the name assigned to the female character and Efraín's role and goal as writer, but how does one explain the allocation of her name to the title of a book which might better be named *Efraín* or perhaps *Efraín y María*? As I have noted, *María* is only one of many Spanish-American novels whose titles belie their contents. José Mármol's *Amalia*, for example, written in approximately the same historical period as *María*, centers even less than does *María* on the female character whose name is evoked in the title. *Amalia*, a voluminous work, originally published in serial form, principally criticizes the atrocities of the Rosas regime in Argentina. The "love story" encompassed in *Amalia* forms a very loose and, in effect, superficial unifying factor for the rest of the novel. It is not gratuitous to consider *Amalia* in relation to *María*, and the former may indeed shed some light on the latter, for the two novels have several facets in common.

One of those common denominators is the temporal stance. *María* is narrated after the death of its heroine; in other words, the fictionalized present of the narration or *énonciation* affords a vantage point from which to look back upon the past of the story, or *énonce*. In a similar manner, *Amalia* pretends to be narrated *ex post facto*. Although the novel is written during the dictatorship of Rosas, the author specifically states in the "Explicación," "Pero el autor, *por una ficción calculada*, supone que escribe su obra con algunas generaciones de por medio entre él y aquéllos" ("But the author, *through a calculated fiction,* imagines that he is writing the work with several generations between himself and them").[14] He continues, "El autor ha creído que tal sistema convenía tanto a la mejor claridad de la narración" ("The author has believed that such a system contributes as much to the clarity of the narration"). In this respect, then, both novels focus on what is past and absent even though in *Amalia* the extranovelistic existence of the point of focus overtly underlines the fictionalization of that absence and nonexistence as they become products of that fiction. Through the process of fictionalization the center is thus distanced, removed, relegated to the past and in that sense made impotent and subsequently harmless.

But perhaps what is most important in the two novels is that they both embrace the underlying theme of language itself. Each is concerned with the problems of expression, of converting ideas, emotions, and events into language. In *María* this preoccupation is reflected in Efraín's early acknowledgment of the paucity of his language to express the depth of his emotions. As he notes, "Las grandes bellezas de la creación no pueden a un tiempo ser vistas y cantadas; es necesario que vuelvan al alma empalidecidas por la memoria infiel" (p. 13) ("The great beauties of nature cannot be sung at the same time they are seen; they must return to the soul, made dim by a faulty memory," p. 4); "su acento, sin dejar de tener aquella música que le era peculiar, se hacía lento y profundo al pronunciar palabras suavemente articuladas, que en vano probaría yo a recordar hoy: porque no he vuelto a oírlas, porque pronunciadas por otros labios no son las mismas, y escritas en estas páginas parecerían sin sentido. Pertenecen a otro idioma" (p. 35) ("her tones, without ceasing to have their peculiar music, would grow slow and solemn as she spoke words which it would be vain for me to try to recall now: I cannot hear them any more, and when they are uttered by other lips they are not the same; if they were written on this page they would seem meaningless. They belong to another language," p. 32); and "nuestra voz es impotente" (p. 13) ("our voices are powerless," p. 3). Similarly in *Amalia* the reader is repeatedly presented with reproduction or pseudo-reproduction of prior texts: letters, edicts, speeches, newspaper clippings, etc., in which the word is shown in its full ability to distort the facts, resuscitate emotions (especially inappropriate ones), and support the power structure. Consider, for example, the Rosas regime's repeated use of "¡Mueran los inmundos salvajes asquerosos unitarios!" ("Death to the filthy, savage, disgusting Unitarians!") and similar expressions. In this manner, the novel demonstrates how the Rosas regime uses language to distort, again signaling the distance between the word and the world. Thus, in both novels one finds a basic philosophy that Truth exists independently of language and that language is incapable of expressing or capturing the Truth.[15] And yet, ironically, one presumes that the "Truth" of María is reflected in her name.

In addition, while both titles are delusive to some degree, it appears that

the title of *Amalia* is not only more misleading but also intentionally decep-
tive, for María certainly plays a greater role in the novel of her name than
does Amalia in hers. Doubtlessly, the title of *Amalia* is designed to attract
attention and readership—an audience which would not even begin to
read a novel entitled *The Atrocities of Rosas* or something similar. Furthermore, I suspect that the love story buried in *Amalia* is also merely an artifice
to entice readers and hold their interest in what is otherwise a prosaic,
expository collection of political essays. In both novels the titles serve to
distract attention from the true focus of the novel—political dissertations
on one case, Efraín in the other.

It takes little imagination to understand why Mármol would want to shift
the focus from the political writings, but might one assume a similar mo-
tive in Isaacs's novel? Certainly, the title *María* would captivate (at first,
anyway) quite a different audience from that which would be attracted to
the title of *Efraín*. *María* is most likely going to enjoy a predominately
female audience, which would probably be Christian; when it tempts a
male audience (usually adolescent) there remains nonetheless the underlying assumption that it is still a "girls' book," and in this respect, not to be
taken too seriously. It is not fortuitous that throughout our Western literary tradition, the novels whose titles name males are those works which
narrate the adventures of an appropriately "manly" protagonist—
adventures of courage, conquest, and heroic feats. Consider, for example,
Amadís de Gaula, Gulliver's Travels, Guzmán de Alfarache,[16] *Doctor Faustus,
Nazarín, Zalacaín, Don Segundo Sombra,* and *Tom Jones.*[17] Patently, then, the
feminine title does not announce the focus of the novel but rather functions, first, to attract a certain audience (perhaps the *lector hembra* or *de-
socupado*), secondly, to establish from the outset a certain attitude toward
the text, and thirdly, to shift the attention away from the masculine actor
and center. This final function suggests a strong social imposition of the
ideal of what is suitably masculine and feminine. While Efraín may represent an adolescent ideal, he certainly cannot (and perhaps must not) reflect
an adult male prototype.

Seen in this matter, then, *María* in specific and the love story in general
must be recognized for what they truly represent: a rite of passage. *María*
is still read, as noted above, for its story of youthful, pure love and devo-
tion. Although the love story no doubt forms the basis for a large portion of
popularly read "literature" (the majority of the rest of that "literature"
probably revolves around the mystery or detective story), to my knowledge the love story per se (and particularly in terms of the rite of passage it
becomes) has never been analyzed.[18] Northrop Frye has examined the notion of the hero-quest pattern which indubitably forms the nucleus of the
love story, but there are distinctions.[19] Because the love story is the basis for
so much literature for, about, and by women, it is an integral step in an
analysis of their portrayal.

The basic ingredients of a love story are a male and a female, preferably young, who meet and try to overcome a series of obstacles to their love (social class, parental disapproval, geographical distance, rival loves, etc.). Although Frye defines the general category of romance in terms of three steps or stages: conflict, struggle, and discovery (p. 187), it seems that the love story, for the most part, evolves through five phases:

1. ENCOUNTER
2. CONQUEST
3. LOSS
4. STRUGGLE / PROOF
5. DEATH OR MARRIAGE

The first of these steps is the encounter; that is, boy meets girl, but for one reason or another, the relationship seems hopeless, bound to failure (without this basic futility or frustration there would be no story). The second stage is what I shall call the mini-conquest; the initial problems or obstacles are overcome or speciously eliminated. Girl appears to love boy, and the other barriers to their love are ostensibly resolved. Granted, some stories stop here, but most of them (in the interest of heightened emotion and reader involvement) continue. In phase three there is a new (real or imagined within the fiction) loss of the loved one. Owing to some development in the plot new obstacles are placed between the lovers: the new rival intervenes, a fortuitous event results in new geographical separation or parental disapproval. Whatever the circumstances, the new privation is felt much more acutely because it stands in contrast to the recent happiness and apparent fulfillment. Step four then involves the resurgent efforts to overcome these new problems (the labors or proofs), while step five is the conclusion, the result of these efforts. Clearly, there are only two possible conclusions to the love story: the difficulties are surmounted so boy and girl marry and "live happily ever after"; or, the impediments are not eliminated, and boy and girl (or the survivor, if one dies, as one often does) are relegated to a life of eternal isolation and separation from the loved one—at the very least, a symbolic form of death.

While this may seem simple enough, the true significance of the love story lies much deeper and is far more complex. First, the love story as I have already discussed in relation to *Amalia* and *María* is generally narrated *ex post facto* (as indeed are most stories). The story tells how boy won or lost the love of girl after that love has already been won or lost. In this sense, then, *María*, like fiction in general and love stories in particular, reflects an absence. Efraín writes of his sweetheart only after she has ceased to exist (even within the fiction)—only when she has become an absence. While each literary character is covertly an absence insofar as he is fictional and nonexistent, María is overtly so. María has already died before Efraín begins to narrate, so even within the text she has already been converted to a word, a sign whose referent can never be made present. And, the word here is static; its significance is already determined and cannot alter. There is no development of characters in the novel (as there rarely is in the love story), and even the evolution of a love between them is perhaps illusory in that not only is their love already past, but also it does not truly develop—it merely rises up from its latent state.

It is perhaps most interesting that in the stereotype of the love story, it is the male who pursues, woos, proves himself a worthy male, while the female sits back and watches. In other words, he is all activity, she unmoving. In general, the portrayals of men and women in this novel are equally oppositional (speaking of men and women within the same social class). While men are shown as taking care of women, and women are represented as caring for men (each obviously in a different fashion), men are also portrayed as attending to the hunt and business, while women concern themselves with the home and religion. Men are physically stronger, while women are weak, although moral strength seems independent of gender. Men are better educated, more well-traveled, and thus more worldly and knowledgeable than women. Somewhat over simplified, it might be said that the men in this novel go out and do things (are active) while the women sit home and wait. Although Efraín's writing demonstrates a strong predilection for nouns, adjectives, and inactive verbs, we might surmise that men are principally portrayed by active verbs whereas women tend to be depicted by nouns, adjectives, and inactive verbs. Compare, for example, these two passages: "Las mujeres parecían vestidas con más esmero que de ordinario. Las muchachas, Lucía y Tránsito, llevaban enaguas de zaraza morada y camisas muy blancas. . . . Las trenzas de sus cabellos, gruesas y de color de azabache, les jugaban sobre sus espaldas. . . . Me hablaban con suma timidez. . . . Entonces se hicieron más joviales y risueñas; nos enlazaban amistosamente los recuerdos de los juegos infantiles" (p. 28) ("The women were dressed with more than usual care. Lucía and Tránsito, the girls, wore petticoats of violet-colored chintz, and fine white chemises. . . . Their thick, jet-black hair was arranged in braids, which danced upon their shoulders. . . . They addressed me with the greatest timidity. . . . Then they became more smilingly at ease; we were drawn to each other in the most friendly manner by the remembrance of games together as children," pp. 23–24); "José me condujo al río y me habló de sus siembras y cacerías, mientras yo me surmergía en el remanso diáfano desde el cual se lanzaban las aguas" (p. 29) ("José led me to the river, and talked to me about his crops and his hunting while I was taking a plunge in the transparent pool whence the stream fell over a small cascade," p. 24). This is not to suggest that the physical appearance of José is not described with the same detail as that of the girls, but the description of the girls is almost totally lacking active verbs; in fact, the most active verb in the entire passage, which is applied to the girls, is *servir*, the one activity definitely allowed women. And, the procedure is typical of the novel. (As Emigdio so pointedly expresses it, "¡Como si pudiera convenirme a mí el casarme con una señora para que resultara de todo que tuviera que servirle yo a ella en vez de ser servido!" [p. 63] ["How could I ever persuade myself to marry a lady, when it would simply result in my becoming her servant instead of her becoming mine?" p. 63].) What active verbs are present, for the most part are applied to masculine characters. As in other love stories, here too, the women wait while the men prove themselves.[20] Thus, many of the major portraits of María in the novel are static memories. Each is like a painting; in one Efraín remembers María standing, still as in a picture, by the window of their house as he departs on one of his journeys.[21] These memories, reiterated within the text, parallel the artistic capture of a fleeting instant, made eternal by the artist's presentation of it.

María then, even within the fiction, is never anything but a group of words, a conglomerate of adjectives, which are not even proper, not specific, insofar as they must be shared with the rest of humanity. For this reason Efraín mourns the paucity of his language to describe his love. She becomes for him, as well as for the reader, but a composite of nouns modified by adjectives. And ultimately, María, even within the fiction, functions in much the same way as any mass of written words, at once passive as they simply "lie" there, unmoving on the page, while simultaneously they act as agents, stimulating the reader to emotions and/or actions, just as María provided Efraín with the stimulus to write. In all these aspects, then, *María* reflects the genre of the love story.

Finally, since the protagonists of the love story are almost always youthful (in fact, the story very often centers on first love), the narration of the story reflects a nostalgia, a yearning for that past golden age of perfect and pure love. Thus, the end of the story, whether happy or sad, is inevitably a point of division and symbolic death, which, to paraphrase Neruda, cuts the duration of life into separate segments which can never meet. In this sense, the *énoncé* (like the *énonciation*) is inevitably a rite of passage. If the loved one dies, then, of course, the survivor dies in the symbolic sense that a "part of him" dies with her. It is the moment of her death and his realization or psychological acceptance of that death that signal his passage from an old state to a new state. That is, the youthful, idealistic dreamer (adolescent) gives way to the mature, wise man of the world who clearly can never again repeat the childlike innocence of the first love. In a similar manner, if the tale has a happy ending, then its conclusion is accordingly the ritual of marriage. While superficially marriage may appear a contradiction of the symbolic death, the fact is that the rite of marriage implies a similar death insofar as the marriage ceremony is the symbol of leaving one state and being reborn into another. That is, through the ritual the young man and woman leave the home of the parents (e.g., the father who "gives away" the bride), leave their childhood behind to become mature man and woman, heads of their own household and future parents. Clearly, whether the love itself succeeds or fails, the ritual has been performed, and the young man moves on to the next phase of life.

However, what is most significant, if indeed paradoxical, in *María* is that the passage is Efraín's and not hers, in spite of the title of the novel. If she matures, progresses, or "passes" at all, it is in the prehistory of the *énoncé* when she transforms from Ester to María. The writing freezes her in her innocent (i.e., prepassage) state.

Thus, we circle back to the notion that *María* in particular and the love story in general necessarily evoke that prepassage golden age, that ostensibly static period that precedes the journey. In evoking that golden age, two symbols, both female, emerge: the mother and the beloved. The idealized mother unquestionably symbolizes that golden age most perfectly, for she gives life and also affords protection, love, and nourishment. The beloved, on the other hand, maintains a more ambiguous position, for although she is closely related to the mother image, sometimes to the extent of providing a mother substitute (at the very least she is the future mother of his children), she encompasses a negative side also. She has the power to reject the suitor.[22] And, more importantly, her acceptance of the suitor necessarily separates him from his mother as, in effect, does the primitive rite of passage. That Efraín perceives María in direct relation to his mother, I have already shown; he even says at one point, speaking of María's welcome upon his return, "sus ojos [los de María] estaban humedecidos aún al sonreír a mi primera impresión afectuosa, como los de un niño cuyo llanto ha acallado una caricia materna" (p. 13) ("her eyes were yet moist when she smiled at my first affectionate word, like those of a child whose tears have been dried by a mother's caress," p. 4). The interrelationship and perhaps confusion between the two is further emphasized at the end of the novel; Efraín has returned after María's death and cruelly chastises his mother for having called him home when it was already too late. He hurls at her, "Así me engañaron . . . ¿A qué he venido?" ("So they deceived me! What have I come for?"), and she responds, "¿Y yo?" (p. 268) ("Haven't I suffered, too?" p. 289).

(This rite of passage which necessitates a break with the parents and the establishment of a new relationship between parent and child is perhaps nowhere more evident than in Erich Segal's *Love Story*, paradigm of contemporary, popular love stories. In this novel, Oliver's dilemma revolves not only around his love for Jenny but also around his antagonism toward his father—and consequently toward his mother insofar as they form a single unity. *Love Story* ends with the death of Jenny *and* the establishment of a new rapport between Oliver and his father—a rapport based on a man-to-man rather than parent-child relationship.)

Clearly, then, the evocation and re-creation of the lost paradise is the goal of the love story. While Frye has noted that the romance in general reflects a wish-fulfillment dream in which "the perennially childlike quality of romance is marked by its extraordinary persistent nostalgia, its search for some kind of imaginative golden age in time or space" (p. 186), the significant facet of the love story is that this golden age, while evoked, is simultaneously and necessarily depicted as no longer attainable. The love story indubitably centers on the inability to return, as is demonstrated in the story of Nay and Sinar, interpolated within *María*. It is not coincidental that the tale of Nay and Sinar follows basically the same structure (story and narration) as the novel. The only difference is that the golden age evoked by Nay is remote not only in time but also in space. Nay, however, like Efraín, cannot return and cannot be reunited with the loved one; she, too, must resort to narrating her memories of this lost paradise. Her only consolation is her creation, her son, Juan Angel. In a similar manner, Efraín's only consolation will be his creation, the novel.

Earlier I noted that *María* begins with an apparently successful return which is never to be repeated. Clearly, the novel itself, that is the fictionalized *énonciation*, is an overt effort to repeat that return.[23] But what is most significant is not the desire to repeat a return, but the fiction of the return itself, for the first "return" of the novel is, in fact, not a reversion at all but the *illusion* of a regression. Efraín is disguising his forward movement in the pseudo return, much as he disguises the true focus of the novel with its feminine title. The fact that María and Efraín later feel an erotic love as opposed to the fraternal love they had previously experienced only underlines the illusory nature of this regression.[24]

The appeal of the love story, then, seems to rest in the dialectical nature of the text which simultaneously pulls us forward as it pushes us back (both temporally and spatially). In some sense, again one finds that the love story is the "best of both worlds," for one concurrently experiences all that is advantageous in the utopia while one continues to hold on to the positive attributes of progress, of moving ahead. There is little doubt that the nostalgia for any golden age is at least partially based on the knowledge that one is not locked into that phase. But María, unfortunately, is imprisoned in that stage. Just as she stayed behind as Efraín ventured off on his various educational journeys, so also she remains quiescent at the conclusion of the book, a static, fixed portrait, unchangeable for all eternity.

In addition, the evocation of the lost utopia, with its dialectical pseudo-movement, is directly related to the acts of reading and writing: acts of great importance throughout the text. The novel, in many ways, is the dramatization of the processes of reading and writing. There are many overt ways in which reading and writing are emphasized and shown to be among the prime concerns of the text. Not only does Efraín act as secretary for his father, in effect doing all his reading and writing for him, but also there are references to his interest in reading and writing poetry while away at school (p. 85). In fact, the act of reading is one of the most fre-

quently repeated activities in the story. For example, early in the course of
the action, Efraín appoints himself teacher for Emma and María. Curiously, and no doubt significantly, these "lessons," during which he reads
and explains to the girls, become intricately identified with a nascent eroticism: María's "aliento, rozando mis cabellos, sus trenzas al rodar de sus
hombros, turbaron mis explicaciones" (pp. 34–35) ("María's breath, graz-
ing my hair, her braids, tossed on her shoulders, confused my explanations," omitted in English translation), and "mi corazón palpitaba fuer-
temente" (p. 35) ("my heart was beating hard," omitted in English
translation). Thus, Efraín "gives" the lessons as much for what he receives
in sensual pleasure as for any more noble goal of enlightening the girls.
The objective for "teaching" María, then, must be the development of her
feminine sensuality, since little concern is demonstrated for the refinement
of her intellect. In many ways, this whole question of the lessons reminds
one of the writing lesson to be described by Lévi-Strauss nearly a century
later. Intentionally or not, like the primitive described by Lévi-Strauss,
Efraín uses the lessons as a means of establishing and reinforcing the
power hierarchy.[25] And, like the origin of writing as explained by Jacques
Derrida, these lessons respond to a need which is more sociological than
intellectual,[26] as they cause both of the characters (and especially María,
since she has less experience with books) to associate books and reading
with physical awakening and desire. It is little wonder, then, that in a later
chapter María suggests that reading is an activity which must be shared by
two people. When asked by Efraín if she had read during his absence, she
answers, " 'No, porque me da tristeza leer sola' " (p. 135) (" 'No, it makes
me sad to read alone,' " p. 158).

Efraín continues in the following chapter to explain the effect his reading
of Chateaubriand has had on María, an explanation which merits an attentive analysis:

> Las páginas de Chateaubriand iban claramente dando tintas a la ima-
> ginación de María. Ella, tan cristiana y tan llena de fe, se regocijaba al
> encontrar bellezas por ella presentidas en el culto católico. Su alma to-
> maba de la paleta que yo le ofrecía los más preciosos colores para her-
> mosearlo todo, y el fuego poético, don del cielo que hace admirables a los
> hombres que lo poseen y diviniza a las mujeres que a su pesar lo revelan,
> daba a su semblante encantos desconocidos para mí hasta entonces en el
> rostro humano. Los pensamientos del poeta, acogidos en el alma de
> aquella mujer tan seductora en medio de su inocencia, volvían a mí como
> eco de una armonía lejana y conocida cuyas notas apaga la distancia y se
> pierden en la soledad. (P. 35)

> (The pages of Chateaubriand were clearly coloring María's imagination.
> So Christian and so full of faith, she delighted in finding the beauty
> which her religion had promised her. Her soul took the most precious

colors from the palette I offered her in order to beautify everything, and
the poetic fire, gift from Heaven which makes the men who possess it
admirable and which sanctifies the women who reveal it in spite of
themselves, gave her countenance charms which for me were heretofore
unknown in the human face. The poet's ideas, received in the soul of
that seductive but innocent woman, returned to me like the echo of a
distant, familiar harmony whose notes are silenced by distance and lost
in solitude. [Omitted in the English translation])

This passage, like many others in the book, simultaneously and discretely
reflects the attitude of the narrator toward his subject, María, while it
underlines the importance of reading within the novel. The first sentence
of the passage clearly implies that María's mind is something of a tabula
rasa, a blank, white space, waiting to be filled in and colored by Efraín (by
the materials selected by him at the very least). Each sentence of the paragraph, through some type of reference to her faith, purity, and innocence,
reinforces this image of a blank, white space insofar as these qualities are
traditionally, metaphorically associated with whiteness. When we think of
white spaces to be filled in, we immediately think of the blank white page,
which, filled with suitable markings, will become a great work of literature.
I suspect, in this regard, that it is not gratuitous that Isaacs (or Efraín, if you
prefer) has chosen to use the word *"tintas"* (inks) rather than *matices, colores, tonos,* or some other suitable term. Thus, one is left with the impression that as he reads to her, Efraín will "write" on María's mind and
imagination, and/or that the print of these literary works will become reim-
printed on her. Thus, she is created.

One of the main ideas that surface in this passage is the influence of
literature on life (a concept later to be posited by Borges). The implication is
that the markings of one page can somehow magically be transposed
(through the mediation of Efraín) onto María's blank or white imagination.
Previously, the writings of Catholicism had influenced, become "imprinted" on, and helped to form the personality of María, and now, Romantic literature is completing the task. While alone, María read Christian
writings (presumably offered her and encouraged by Efraín's parents),
and, under the auspices of Efraín, she is now being offered the French
Romanticists. Significantly, however, she does not, in fact, "read" the latter; rather they are read to her. Efraín, the teacher, molder, shaper, reader,
and writer, is the "priest" of this cult called literature. This interpretation is
reinforced a paragraph later when María is described, listening to Efraín
read *Atala:* "medio arrodillada cerca de mí, no separaba sus miradas de mi
rostro" (p. 36) ("half kneeling, close to me, she did not take her eyes off my
face" omitted in English translation)—a portrayal which might be a verbal
description of any one of dozens of paintings of biblical women kneeling
before Christ. (Such a movement away from the source as a result of
limitless repetitions clearly reflects the textual procedure in this novel, too.)

Efraín, the priest, selects the literary works to which she is to be exposed, then reads or offers them to her (as he metaphorically expresses it), and, finally, provides the exegesis as he reads so that the less enlightened may comprehend a small part of the great mysteries. It further appears that she has been warned not to attempt to read or understand it all, for she complains, "'Iba a volver a leer *Atala* [significantly, the work he had been reading to her]; pero como me has dicho que tiene un pasaje no sé como...'" (p. 135) ("'I was going to read some more of 'Atala,' but as you told me there is a passage in it not exactly—'" p. 158).

But, one must ask, why this combination of Catholic and Romantic readings? On the surface, these two bodies of literature would seem to be worlds apart. What do they have in common that allows them to be the only ones offered by the patriarchal society which surrounds the title character? The answer, undoubtedly, rests in the manner in which both of these great bodies of literary accomplishment present females. Each presents two distinctly dichotomous views of woman. In each, one possible portrayal is one of contempt (covert or overt) coupled with outright misogyny. Think, for example, of the early Judaic tradition and of St. Paul, to mention only two examples within biblical writings. In romanticism a similar misogyny and contempt is demonstrated by the Romantic figure par excellence, don Juan.[27] At the other extreme, we find an idealization of woman that distorts her beyond recognition as anything human (e.g., the Virgin Mary or the typical Romantic heroine)[28]—a distortion which ultimately may simply mask a latent misogyny inasmuch as such deification or wishful thinking may well be another expression of a contempt for the reality.[29] There is little doubt that most love stories, *María* included, are structured around the latter characterization—that is, an overidealization of the female character, a deification which demands of her the impossible, while maintaining her in a position totally divorced from reality. It is these love stories which, unfortunately, and as overtly demonstrated by *María*, provide the principal reading material for the adolescent in her formative years and which, thus, introduce each girl to the model (absurd though it is) that she is to try to follow in the coming years.

Thus, first, María (perhaps like any adolescent girl) is a product of literature, and secondly, this literature is controlled by males, both in the sense that they have written it and in the sense that they have selected for her just what she will read or, more likely, have read and explicated to her by them. The patriarchal control, then, is very nearly complete, and the attitude expressed in the novel is not very different from that of the European anthropologists in their relations with the "primitives." Efraín's patronizing egoism and sense of superiority are patent in the cited passage; here, as in the rest of the novel, although the subject would ostensibly appear to be (and perhaps, in light of the title, should be) María, it is, in fact, Efraín. She may take only the possibilities he offers; to this extent her development and improvement are implemented by him and must be credited to him. He is, in every respect, then, her creator.

It is perhaps in the third sentence of the quoted passage that Efraín's sense of masculine superiority becomes most overt. In the previous paragraph he referred to the writing of the text we are reading and thus overtly accepted himself as a writer, a poet. In this paragraph, speaking of the *fuego poético,* a gift from heaven, he notes that it makes men admirable and deifies women who reveal it *"a su pesar."* "In spite of themselves" implies that such talent will either go unrecognized by women or was meant to be kept hidden and not revealed by them, although men, clearly, should manifest such abilities. At the same time, this phrase coupled with the next sentence which refers to María as simultaneously *seductora* and *inocente* suggest a superior (poetic) vision on the part of Efraín; he can see what others cannot—the *fuego poético* in María as well as the mixture of seductress and innocent virgin.

But, the final sentence of the paragraph brings together the principal leitmotifs of the novel. Here one sees not only that Efraín, his life, and his writings are also influenced by literature but that María provides something of a sounding board from which to reverberate the "notes" of the poet. As he explains, she absorbs the poet's thoughts and then echoes them back to him, thus projecting to him a harmony that time and distance have made dim. The terminology of the text, certainly, encourages one to think of the myth of Narcissus and Echo. Echo, of course, loved Narcissus but, much like María, was unable to initiate a conversation; she could only repeat what others said—María seldom says anything in the novel and seems to be a reflection (as the quotation suggests) of the thoughts of the poet (Efraín or Chateaubriand). Narcissus, on the other hand, fell in love with his own reflection and pined away. Are *María* and María not, in effect, the reflections of Efraín insomuch as he has created both, and does he not pine away because of an unrequited love that is only a reflection of himself? And is the novel itself not an echo of romanticism and other works of fiction just as it is an echo of the past golden age?

Thus, the reading of the French Romanticists forms an integral part of the novel as Efraín and María indubitably identify with the protagonists of these novels and unquestionably see all that surrounds them in terms of, or as a reflection of, these novels. The conclusion of *María* is clearly already written in *Atala,* and since Efraín's narrative task is to rewrite a Romantic novel, it is apropos that *María* dates from a moment in which romanticism was no longer considered stylish.

The book further portrays reading insofar as Efraín is continually "reading" signs or what he interprets as signs. He tries to read the meaning of certain looks or gestures on the part of María. He reads the absence of flowers in his room as an absence of love (p. 30, p. 27 in English); later he interprets her smile: "aquella sonrisa castísima que revela en las mujeres como María una felicidad que no les es posible ocultar" (p. 33) ("that most pure smile which reveals in women like María a happiness impossible to conceal," p. 31)—again, the priestly Efraín can see what is below the surface of María and that over which she presumably has no control. Also, he notes, "la luz de sus ojos . . . me decían . . . que en aquél era tan feliz como yo" (p. 134) ("The light in her eyes . . . told me, as they often had, that she was happy," p. 157). He also reads María's presence in nature and reads the blackbird as an evil omen. For Efraín, in fact, nature itself is but another language to be read and interpreted, a language which merely awaits his priestly, poetic intervention to tell us all. For example, during his final return to his homeland, he comments that the trees "parecían con sus rumores dar la bienvenida a un amigo no olvidado" (p. 252) ("with their sounds seemed to welcome a friend who had not been forgotten," omitted in English translation). Thus, there is nothing which is not open to his interpretation. Everything is comprehensible to one who reads, and the possibility that his "reading" might be erroneous is never considered within the text—the "priest" never errs.

What he seems to overlook in all of his reading, however, is the inevitable supplementation involved in the act; he reads María in nature only because he supplements nature with her—imposes her on nature. It is his own subjective state which allows him to see her there, and no form of presence or any purposefulness on the part of nature. One must wonder, then, if the enjoyment of the text, *María*, on the part of readers today is not similarly a function of reader supplementation. Does one not enjoy *María* because in some manner one is able to read oneself into the text? And does not this imposition of the self on the text directly parallel the gesture of the chroniclers as they "read" the New World and then "wrote" it for their contemporaries? The book in this sense is a monument to María in much the same way as the stone over her grave is a monument to her. Like the written text, the latter is a white pedestal with black engraving.

If we accept, then, that the love story is essentially a rite of passage, we must at this point recognize that the narration or the writing of the story (especially when that *énonciation* forms an overt part of the fiction) is also a rite of passage. Writing is, indeed, a ritualistic, ceremonial sort of activity and like any ritual is subject to very definite, prescribed rules and formulae. Also like any other rite, it dramatically makes present that which is absent. In *María*, however, the writing is very specifically a rite of passage as the narrator dramatizes his leaving behind of the past, female-dominated world. In fact, as Theodor Reik has noted, "one of the most important purposes of the puberty rites is to loosen the ties between boys and their mothers and to bind the novices to the society of men. This part of primitive education, marking the growth of boys into maturity, is accomplished by drastic means" (*The Creation of Woman*, p. 123).

The narration or writing of *María* thus serves as a rite of passage for

Efraín, who might be seen as both initiate and priest, and as a purification or exorcism of the past. María, now converted into a single, simple signifier, is immortalized and made permanent, impervious to the failings of future memory lapses. But, at the same time, she is distanced and made into an object, now separated from the subject. She can never change after she has been converted into the word, and that conversion distances her; she now forms a part of and, in fact, represents that golden age, fixed in the past, and paradisiacal because it is static, past, and unthreatening.

The very notion of a ritualistic or ceremonial writing is paralleled by another ritualistic activity directly portrayed in the text: the cutting of hair. As early as the second paragraph of the text the reader is presented with the first ceremonial haircut. Efraín is remembering the eve of his first departure when his sister entered his room "y sin decirme una sola palabra cariñosa . . . cortó de mi cabeza unos cabellos" (p. 11) ("without saying a single word . . . cut off a lock of my hair," p. 1). In the next paragraph he labels that hair "esa precaución del amor contra la muerte delante de tanta vida" ("that precaution of love against death, even in the presence of abounding life"). Toward the end of the novel a similar ritual is performed, again by the same agent, his sister. Apparently, María had requested that Emma cut her braids after her death and give them to Efraín. Superficially, both of these acts appear gratuitous or excessively emotional. Nevertheless, the repetition of the act implies significance, and I would suggest that the acts are symbolic. María's braids are her postmortuary gift to him. She was very vain about her hair, and the braids themselves are a sign of her femininity (men, of course, supposedly are neither vain about their hair nor do they wear braids). Interestingly, that the hair is indeed symbolic of femininity is demonstrated by the fact that in certain Greek rites, the women no longer sacrificed their virginity to the gods as had been the custom, but rather their hair, "as a sort of symbolic surrender of their womanhood" (Harding, p. 136). Most relevant is perhaps the supplemental nature of the hair to these later women and of virginity to the earlier woman. In both cases, the sacrificed matter is viewed as something not essential to the inherent being, something additional, extra, and thus expendable.[30] María's braids are cut from her and separated from her essence, although they stand as a symbol of that essence in much the same way Efraín's writing is separated from that essence, that referent, although it too stands as a symbol of that paradise lost. The very biological fact that hair itself is dead matter reinforces the notion of the cutting of hair, like writing, as the separation from the vital, the essential, the living.

What one is left with then is narration and writing which are ritualistic attempts to simultaneously underline and negate the separation, while attempting to fill the void left by that separation. The ritualistic attempts in turn lead one directly back to the story of the creation of woman, which, like the rite of passage, attempts to negate the very real biological fact that man is born of woman, and not vice versa as the biblical story would like to imply. And, according to the story, that creation of woman left a void (which presumably can only be filled by man's reuniting with woman in the form of sacred matrimony). María and Eve, signs of past golden ages which no longer exist, never were anything but reflections, echoes, creations. Efraín writes to recapture this past, to reconquer this paradise. Thus, inexorably, the writing, itself fictionalized within the text, becomes a supplement of a supplement. To the extent that writing is inevitably supplemental, since it replaces, substitutes, and adds to a nonpresence, writing which portrays itself as it writes, writing which fictionalizes its own process of writing, must become doubly supplemental—just as even within the fiction, María is a supplement of a supplement, ultimately eternal absence.

2
Women and Nature: In Man's Image Created

IN the approximately sixty years which elapsed between the printing of *María* and the publications of *La vorágine* (1924) by José Eustacio Rivera (Colombia, 1888–1928) and *Doña Bárbara* (1929) by Rómulo Gallegos (Venezuela, 1884–1969), the image of the woman would be expected to alter somewhat. And indeed it did, but, unfortunately, it changed for the worse if we are to assume that *Doña Bárbara* and *La vorágine* are typical of the period. While the female in *María* was an established, customary portrait, almost a nonentity because of its conventionality, and little more than a projection of the "poet's" ego, in these two novels of the 1920s, the female is depicted principally as a malevolent being in collaboration with the evil forces of the universe, an image which does not differ greatly from that of the first female, Eve, who conspired with the Devil in the form of a serpent. Nature, too (the Garden) has lost its charm in these works; no longer the *locus amenus* of classicism and romanticism, it is now viewed, like the female and barbarism, as a threat to the very existence and continuity of man and civilization. While in either of these two historical periods the female of literature is definitely prosaic, at least in romanticism she tended to be a less unpleasant stereotype.

Classified as *novelas terrígenas*, *Doña Bárbara* and *La vorágine* have been studied by a multitude of critics and scholars, most of whom have tended to focus on the use of nature and the opposition between barbarism and civilization within the novels.[1] To date, however, no one has carefully considered the fact that in these texts as well as in most of the other *novelas terrígenas*, women and nature are not only closely linked but often presented as mirror reflections of each other. Nature, of course, has traditionally been perceived as female, but in the coming pages we shall examine woman's role in relationship to nature, how the female corresponds to and functions within the entire dichotomy between civilization and barbarism, and some of the changes that seem to have occurred in society's view of both woman and nature during the time lapse between romanticism and the early twentieth century, when these texts were published.

Although it is not my purpose here to examine the historical reasons for the transfigurations in the portrayal of the female, a brief look at the events of those sixty years may afford some insight into the changes themselves and help us to understand them better. During the period in question, naturalism and then modernism had prevailed in European literature; Spain had lost most of her holdings in the New World; the First World War had been fought; feminists had gained women the right to vote in the United States; and two scholars had made major contributions to our image of ourselves and our world: Freud and Darwin.[2] Although it would be difficult to ascertain the specific extent of the influence of each of these factors on the literature of the early twentieth century, there is little doubt that each played a part in the development of the novelistic material. It is conceivable, however, that Darwin's theory of the "survival of the fittest," which portrayed the universe (nature) as hostile and threatening, coupled with Freud's patriarchal stance (often labeled misogyny), which presented the female as antagonistic and castrating, particularly damaged the world's perception of the female.

Most relevant to the topic and most frequently overlooked by scholars and critics as they analyze these two novels, however, is the direct and immediate dependency of the portrayals of both the female characters and nature on the fictionalized "psyches" of the protagonists. Significantly, what one finds when one carefully considers the portrayals of women and nature in both *Doña Bárbara* and *La vorágine* are some striking similarities, and perhaps even a pattern of myth making which may not be greatly distanced from the extratextual world. That Gallegos was possibly influenced by Rivera and *La vorágine* has already been shown (Añez), but what has not been analyzed in detail is that the depiction of the female and nature is directly dependent upon, and shaped or misshaped by, the perception of the main character in each work. Thus her depiction cannot be analyzed except in relationship to him. Furthermore, the contingency of her image upon him becomes especially significant as one recognizes the unreliability and/or dubious position of each of these main characters. Let us begin with Cova.

Although the unreliability of Cova's narration and his incompetence as a trustworthy narrator would seem self-evident to the careful reader and in need of no further discussion, a review of criticism to date underlines the fact that Cova has all too often been viewed by readers quite amicably as a Romantic or epic hero.[3] For example, in exaltation of Cova and his endeavor one is apt to encounter statements such as "La acción de *La vorágine* es calificable de *épica* porque representa la lucha *heróica* del hombre contra la naturaleza,"[4] and "Arturo Cova, hombre impulsivo, contradictorio, espectácular y un tanto fanfarrón, sin apegos, pero *de sentimientos nobles y hasta*

románticos."⁵ Yet another critic has referred to Cova's journey as "la odisea
más grandiosa, interesante, y aterradora que haya realizado el hombre en
tierras de America" (Posada Delgado, "El paisaje," p. 882). I insist, however, and it is basic to any further discussion of women or nature in this
text, that Cova is neither a hero, of heroic proportions, noble, nor presented as such within the text. Rather, *La vorágine* is a mixture of diary,
confession, and memoirs of a character whose "vision" and competence to
judge, within the fiction, is neither valid nor to be trusted. From the very
beginning Cova himself demonstrates the dubious quality of his perception and of his ability to grasp with lucidity the significance of the world
around him.⁶ Yet it is he who shapes our vision of the female within the
text.

Cova's dubious reliability is already evident on the title page of the
Rivera novel, for the title has either been misunderstood or is delusive.
Readers have often understood *la vorágine* as the jungle, but if one does so,
then it is difficult to explain the inclusion of Part 1 of the text, which takes
place in the plains. Clearly, one of the principal justifications for interpret-
ing the *vorágine* in this fashion is that Cova himself advocates this
metaphoric link as he makes two direct references to the *vorágine* in this
context: "Y por este proceso—¡oh, selva!—hemos pasado todos los que
caemos en tu vorágine" (p. 185) ("And that, oh jungle! is how all who have
fallen into your vortex have been transformed," p. 234), and "Tengo el
presentimiento de que mi senda toca a su fin, y, cual sordo zumbido de
ramajes en la tormenta, percibo la amenaza de la vorágine" (p. 256) ("I
have the feeling that my trail is nearing its end, and I hear, like the swirl of
foliage in a storm, the looming threat of the vortex," p. 316).⁷ However, it is
pertinent here to consider the "source" (within the fiction) of these statements—Arturo Cova.

Richard Ford has already suggested the dubious veracity of Cova's statement regarding Ramiro Estevánez's position as recipient of the text,⁸ and
one can detect this duplicity far earlier in the text without great difficulty.
For example, how much confidence shall we place in a character who in the
very first paragraph informs his reader that he seeks ideal love, "que me
encendiera espiritualmente" (p. 11) ("that would fire me spiritually,"
p. 17), but that in a love relationship he must always be the dominator,
"cuyos labios no conocieron la súplica" (p. 11) ("whose lips never begged
or implored," p. 17)? Obviously, the second statement negates the notion
of ideal love as proposed in the first; his language is self-contradictory.
With equally fallacious reasoning, two pages later he tells of his intimate
desire to be *captured* so that he can be *free* (of Alicia). This is not poetic
paradox; it is the reasoning of a seriously demented character. These two
examples, in addition, demonstrate not only a perverse concept of women
and his potential relationship with them but also a serious linguistic prob-
lem.⁹ It seems that he does not understand the conventional meanings of

the words he employs. He is using language in a sense other than the one we all understand, for to his reading public, freedom cannot be found in captivity. From, the beginning, then, one must recognize that the language Cova is using (a language used in large part to describe women and nature) is not at all innocent, but fraught with meanings one does not generally attribute to it. Thus, we cannot accept at face value what is said, but instead must be on guard and not allow ourselves to be seduced, by the apparent innocence of the words, into believing that they mean only what they superficially suggest.

Cova's attitude toward the other characters in the text (particularly the female characters) also betrays his duplicity. Throughout the diary, he repeatedly censures Alicia and denigrates her for personality traits that are as much (if not more) his as hers. Shortly after fleeing Bogotá, he criticizes her for not being "más arriscada, menos bisoña, más ágil" (pp. 12–13) ("more daring, more venturesome and agile, less of a tenderfoot," pp. 18–19), but the later scene at the ranch underlines the fact that these same disparagements of her might well have been directed toward him. That is, with apparent ease and innocence, Cova, like Santos Luzardo as I shall demonstrate, shifts the referent of his words, and with it the focus of his narration, from himself to another. As one progresses through the text one discovers that he blames first her and later the *selva* for all that is wrong with his life—predicaments for which only he is responsible. At Alicia he even hurls the accusation, "Por ti dejé todo" ("For you I left everything") when in fact he left all in order not to be incarcerated. Similarly, he accuses the jungle, "Tú me robaste el ensueño" (p. 97) ("You stole from me the dreams," p. 127), while at still other moments he disparages the jungle for being inhuman (suggesting, of course, that one could expect it to be human). In both cases he accepts and intends for his reader to accept his own metaphor as literal reality. In addition, he reproaches the *selva* by saying, "la selva trastorna al hombre, desarrollándole los instintos más inhumanos" (p. 139) ("the jungles change men. The most inhuman instincts are developed," p. 177); once again, either he fails to understand the meaning of the term "inhuman," or he is making the *selva* the referent for those qualities that can apply only to man, and, thus, he casts on the external the guilt for what is surely internal.[10]

Cova's complete confusion between the two is perhaps most apparent in Part 3. Part 2 had ended in the midst of Clemente's narration (in quotation marks). While Part 3 appears to be a continuation of this narration, the quotation marks are missing, and it is difficult to identify the *I*—is it Clemente or Cova? The issue is further complicated by the fact that Cova himself gratuitously becomes a part of the Clemente story, taking on some of the characteristics of the protagonist of that story and later declaiming *as if* he had experienced Clemente's adventures. In addition, at various points in the text, one watches Cova imagining himself retelling the story (each time greatly embellished), and one must wonder if the text itself does not embody this very same activity: Cova watching Cova tell his story. Thus, he is not different from the narrator of Luisa Valenzuela's *El gato eficaz*, who some fifty years later is to say, "Yo no trepo: me trepan, desde aquí me observo jugar a ser mirada con mi propia mirada que me guarda cariño" ("I don't climb; they climb me, from here I watch myself play at being watched by my own gaze which is affectionate toward me").[11]

Thus it is manifest that the narrator of *La vorágine* is portrayed as a theatrical individual who has left his native city and ventured out into the "wilds"—that is, as a foreigner or alien in a new and unknown territory. His vision of the plains and the jungle is that of a character who is already removed from his native land, who is slowly becoming more and more alienated from reality, and who cannot understand what he observes because he is an outsider, totally influenced by literature and by his preconceived notions of what he should find in this new land. As Bull has noted, "Perhaps no author . . . has ever presented an extensive study of nature through the eyes and emotions of characters so incapable of describing nature in an objective fashion" (p. 307). In this sense Cova is not different from the Europeans who discovered the New World or even the European anthropologists of the late nineteenth and early twentieth centuries, whose entire comprehension of the world they encountered was based on, inseparable from, and a projection of themselves and their old world. And yet it is Cova who formulates our image of the female and apparently provided the basis for that image as it was continued in *Doña Bárbara*.

Thus, returning circularly to the notion of the *vorágine*, one must by association question the validity of his conception of the *vorágine* as the jungle and begin to understand the *vorágine* in a manner which sheds more light on the meaning of the text and its portrayal of both women and nature. Surely, we must comprehend the *vorágine* as the whirlpool of irrationality which slowly takes control of Arturo's life. I have mentioned several instances of Arturo's unreliability, and there are other moments of the text which point to his mental instability or dementia. For example, at the end of Part 1, during the burning of Franco's house, he reports, "¡En medio de las llamas empecé a reír como Satanás!" (p. 96) ("In the midst of the flames I laughed like a devil!" p. 124). The fact that he reports this about himself highlights his instability. Similarly, in Part 2 he witnesses the violent death of two of his companions and observes, "La visión frenética del naufragio me sacudió con una ráfaga de belleza. *El espectáculo fue magnífico*" (p. 130, emphasis added) ("The disaster overwhelmed me with a sense of beauty. *The spectacle was magnificent*," p. 167, emphasis added). Again, the spectacle of a violent death cannot be magnificent by our standards. Clearly, then, the *vorágine* which seems to be "devouring" him (like the *selva* which, according to Rivera, did devour him) is his own mind and is more internal than external.[12] Thus, one might effectively summarize

Cova's proclivity by noting that he consistently takes what is internal and threatening from within, transposes it, and regards it as something external and threatening from the outside—often metaphorically transposing it into some aspect of nature or a woman.

Without a doubt, one of the principal structuring factors in this text (as well as in *Doña Bárbara*, as I shall discuss later) is the discrepancy between the character's vision and what are presented or implied as the "facts" within the text, that is, between two different levels of *énoncé*.[13] But, what is even more important, I believe, is that from the very beginning Cova is depicted by Rivera as a Romantic poet. Our very first glimpse of Cova, in the epigraph, which is supposedly a fragment of the letter Cova writes to the consul, underlines what appear to be the two major themes of the novel, both directly linked to the female and nature: time and the conflict between a Romantic and a naturalistic view of the world (a disparity in many ways also related to time and the notion of progress). In this letter, Rivera affords us our first exposure to the Romantic vision and rhetoric of Cova; then, in the early pages of the text we are again presented with the romanticism of Cova, who, like the Romantic poet, eternally seeks freedom and ideal love, must forever chase after chimeras, and rarely demonstrates the wisdom of acknowledging that the fantasies are within.

In this sense, one is led to wonder if it is not the lyrical vision of Cova which forms the basis of his unreliability, for one soon recognizes the discrepancy between what he expects to discover (and what he sometimes *thinks* he finds), and what he does encounter, again a problem echoed in his perception of the female. In fact, the basis of the text might well be defined as the tension between romanticism and naturalism (or realism), and the suggestion is that the naturalistic view is ultimately more valid since Cova and his Romantic view are unable to survive.[14] What Rivera and the text seem to ignore, however, and what is especially pertinent to our discussion of women, is that contrary to the beliefs of the period, the naturalistic vision is as slanted and subjective as the Romantic vision. Certainly, the very notions implied in the opposition between romanticism and naturalism are directly related to the notions of internal and external and again parallel our perception of the female as either Madonna or prostitute.[15] That is, romanticism characterizes itself and is accepted as a subjective vision; the inner self is overtly projected onto the outer world, and thus the external world is recognized as a projection of that ego. On the contrary, realism and naturalism, like the scientific method, proffer themselves as objective, extrinsic visions, which are in no way dependent upon or related to the subject, but which are totally conditioned on the object. They pretend to be external, but ultimately, of course, the very possibility of objectivity is but a myth—an innocent belief that mankind is capable of understanding (or re-creating) anything except in relation to himself. Although there are certainly varying degrees of subjectivity, most scholars now recognize that any supposedly objective analysis is still contingent upon the mediation of the viewer. The real danger here, as with the symbol or the signifier, arises the moment the realist begins to take his enterprise seriously and forgets that what he sees is only a projection of himself to a greater or lesser extent. Clearly, what I have said here about the realist must also be posited about the scientist and his presumable objectivity. We shall indeed never know how much of Freud's findings about the psychological "nature" of woman are merely subjective projections.

Returning specifically to the two texts in question, we must now examine the development of a pattern which is established in *La vorágine* and continued in *Doña Bárbara*. *La vorágine* presents a negative image of both women and the jungle, but the careful reader can recognize the portrait as the fantastic weavings of an unstable madman who is nonetheless a poet (which may be a comment on the role of literature in shaping society's view of women). Thus although her portrayal is pejorative, its negativity is mitigated to some degree (minimal though it may be) by the unreliability of the narrator. If Gallegos was indeed influenced by Rivera as Añez suggests, then the impact of this negative model is particularly pertinent, for in spite of the perfidy of Cova, his vision of both the female and the jungle has been accepted as valid in *Doña Bárbara*. The satanic, menacing connotations which Cova projects on both women and nature are now the rhetorical propositions upon which the Gallegos novel is based. Perhaps the average reader can recognize Cova's instability and the untrustworthiness of his perception, but few can discern the same in Gallegos's novel, although as I shall show, deception also pervades the latter.

As one examines the presentation of women and nature in *Doña Bárbara*, one must bear in mind two significant deceptions upon which the text is based, neither of which has been fully acknowledged. As in *La vorágine* and *María*, the first deception is found on the title page. The title of the novel promises the story of a woman, doña Bárbara, but carefully considered, the novel is not the story of her but focuses on Santos Luzardo's "heroic" journey, his successes in the hostile world. The novelistic material is presented principally from his point of view (even though he is not the narrator), and he is the center of both the text and our reader identification and sympathies, not doña Bárbara. In spite of the fact that the narrator does provide the background information (the story of doña Bárbara and Asdrúbal) which would allow or perhaps encourage the reader to identify and empathize with the title female, doña Bárbara is portrayed predominantly as Santos would perceive her—as part of the periphery and/or as the enemy who collaborates with that other enemy, nature—a depiction established in *La vorágine* by a deranged narrator. Only at scattered, isolated, and brief moments is one afforded insight into doña Bárbara's fictional psychology and motivated to any sense of compassion for her. And clearly, one is offered this insight and motivated to compassion for both Santos and Lorenzo.

In this sense, the female character here, as in romanticism, does little more than provide the dramatic stimulus and background against which the hero can perform his virtuous deeds and reign supreme. In this respect the novel seems to be structured around that void or absence so frequently spoken of in regard to the *nueva novela* of the 1960s and 1970s. In a parallel manner, although the term *doña Bárbara* may be understood as a signifier for nature, and although nature has often been referred to as the protagonist of the *novela terrígena*, nature here also serves only as background and stimulus which allow the hero to demonstrate his moral and physical strength. Nature's position as absence is also underlined by the fact that although Gallegos writes as if he knew the *llano* well, he actually spent only eight days there (Englekirk, "*Doña Bárbara*").

But, what about the moral and physical strength of the hero? Is Santos the perfect, moral hero who represents civilization and all that is good in the world? Perhaps not, for the second discrepancy to which I have referred, like the one in *La vorágine*, is that between the main character's perception of the situation and what are presented as the "facts" within the text. Although Santos perceives doña Bárbara as a totally evil being, and although one tends to accept his view of her, the text itself (Gallegos, the narrator?) frequently suggests that she is not really as malevolent as she is believed to be, that much of what is said about her is pure creation, even within the fiction. However, as readers we tend to forget this aspect all too quickly. Of this I shall have more to say, but first let me note that Santos Luzardo is not the paragon of virtue one tends to envision as one remembers this novel. It is imperative to recognize that he initiated his journey for less than completely estimable and magnanimous reasons. To begin with, it is germane that Santos, like Lorenzo, is referred to as a misanthrope (p. 19), suggesting that his incentive cannot be completely philanthropic. Furthermore, he had demonstrated no interest in Altamira until it gradually ceased producing sufficient capital to maintain his desired life-style. Altamira and the *llanura*, in fact, held no attraction for him at all: "La tierra natal ya no lo atraía" (p. 20) ("His native soil had no attraction for him," p. 26). Thus, his motivation is financial interest, desire for property, and his main objective is to sell Altamira, convert the land into an exchange medium, and gather enough money to go to Europe in search of a more perfect civilization—that is, the European rather than the American. At the same time, he wished to leave Caracas because, as the text explicitly states, the Venezuelan city was "algo muy distante todavía de la ciudad ideal, complicada y perfecta como un cerebro, a donde toda excitación va a convertirse en idea" (p. 20) ("far from being that ideal city, intricate and perfect as a mind, in which all movement becomes converted into ideas," p. 26).

Clearly, what is highlighted in this passage is the idealistic, that is, unrealistic nature of Santos's endeavor and thus its close affiliation with Cova's undertaking. Ultimately, of course, the situation Santos seeks is as nonexistent in Europe as in the New World, but he tries, nevertheless, to impose just this "bookish" ideal on the realities of the *llanura*. It is also relevant that this entire image of Europe, like Santos's image of woman, is based on secondhand knowledge, knowledge he has gained from books and from what others have told him—he personally does not "know" Europe at all and has no experience of it.

Thus Santos's goal, his idealistic notion of civilizing the "backward" plain (again much like Cova), was inducement that came later both chronologically and textually. And his objective is altered and motivated primarily by his perception of the female, coupled with his sense of property. Santos decides to fight against "barbarity" only after he hears the legend of doña Bárbara (again, secondhand information): "había emprendido aquel viaje con un propósito y ya estaba abrazándose a otro, *completamente opuesto*" (p. 15, emphasis added) ("he had begun the voyage with one plan, and now he was embracing another *totally different* from the first," p. 17, emphasis added). His project is changed, apparently in large part because of his unfounded and irrational hatred of her—an antagonism based on his perception of her as a threat to his financial security. Again, without that financial security, that income, the motivation of his journey to the wilds, he cannot continue his voyage to Europe and the perceived true culture and refinement.

Also, it is important to our discussion of women to recognize the rhetorical subversion and twisting of purpose as Santos decides,

> meterse en el hato a luchar contra los enemigos, a defender sus propios derechos y también los ajenos, atropellados por los caciques de la llanura . . . a luchar contra la naturaleza: contra la insalubridad, que estaba aniquilando la raza llanera, contra la inundación y la sequía que se disputan la tierra todo el año, contra el desierto, que no deja penetrar la civilización. (P. 21)

> (many things: settling on the ranch to struggle against the enemy; defending his own property and his neighbours', outraged by the chiefs of the country. . . ; struggling against nature herself, against the unhealthful conditions which were wiping out the race of Plainsmen, against the alternate floods and droughts which fought over the land during the year, against the desert which [doesn't let civilization penetrate]. [P. 28])

Evidently, the first idea is to fight for his rights and property ("defender sus propios derechos"); then, the thought develops rhetorically, and he decides to defend the rights of others too ("y también los ajenos"), but that is clearly an afterthought. From here the goal expands to include a fight against nature which "estaba aniquilando la raza llanera," and one moves away from and quickly loses sight of his central purpose: "defender sus propios derechos." In addition, the very metaphor used here reinforces the association of the male with civilization and betrays the pejorative as well as sexual perception of woman and nature: "el desierto, que no deja *penetrar* la civilización" (emphasis added).

Similarly, Santos's veritable objective is again wrapped in layers of distracting language when the text notes, "lo apasionante ahora es la lucha . . . que él . . . subordinaba a un *ideal:* luchar contra doña Bárbara . . . *no sería solamente salvar Altamira,* sino contribuir a la destrucción de las fuerzas retardatarias de la *prosperidad* del Llano" (pp. 21–22, emphasis added) ("the words . . . had roused his impulse to struggle . . . but here it was subordinated to an *ideal. To struggle against Doña Barbara . . . was not only to free Altamira,* but to destroy the forces which were holding back the [*prosperity* of the] Plain," pp. 28–29, emphasis added). Thus, as the thought is presented, the ideal is prosperity—indeed, not an altruistic ideal. Again, Santos's personal financial gain is clearly one of his main purposes, hidden though it may be.

At the same time, one finds an identical eclipsing of the preoccupation with property and thus true incentive in the final page of the novel. The text concludes by noting that as a result of Santos's efforts, the property (El Miedo) has been returned to its rightful owner: Marisela. Nevertheless, by virtue of the laws of the land, the property will now become Santos's, as even the text suggests: "desaparece del Arauca el nombre de El Miedo y todo vuelve a ser Altamira [read, de Santos]" (p. 254) ("the name of El Miedo disappeared from the Arauca, and all the lands once more became known as Altamira" [read, Santos's property], p. 440). From here the text goes on to add still another layer of distraction and terminates with a glorious apostrophe (not unlike *La vorágine's* "¡En nombre de Dios!" ["In the name of God!"]): "¡Llanura venezolana! Propicia para el esfuerzo como lo fue para la hazaña, tierra de horizontes abiertos donde una raza buena, ama, sufre y espera!..." ("Venezuelan Plain! As favorable to the effort as it was to its achievement, land of endless horizons where a good line of people loves, suffers, and waits [hopes]!..." [omitted in English]). By concluding the novel in such a fashion, the narrator has made the ideal of civilizing the final thought with which the reader leaves the novel—one now awaits this wonderful, glorious moment—and the question of property, which I insist is the central issue, is once again pushed into the background and forgotten.

Significantly, this tendency to subvert and cover true motivation and idealize what is European not only predominates in the texts we are studying but is the same process upon which the very notions of civilization and barbarism are based. As José Antonio Fidalgo has very astutely noted, the concept of civilization in novels like *Doña Bárbara* is "una idealización desmedida de los valores europeos" ("Criollismo," p. 463), while the local "reality" is associated with the barbaric. Santos Luzardo, an advocate of civilization, is deeply influenced by the European mores and sees the European way of life as infinitely superior to the American. Obviously, doña Bárbara, by virtue of her distance from Europe and European standards, must be seen as barbaric. Thus, she is enveloped in an entire negative connotation which is imposed from the outside and entirely supplemental to her. At the same time, to civilize appears to be an honorable purpose mainly because its economic basis and motivation have been covered, hidden from view, supplemented. It cannot be irrelevant that much of the civilizing project of imperialism is a masked economic endeavor.

In fact, in many ways *Doña Bárbara* is the paradigm of the conquest, or perhaps better labeled, a portrayal of a second conquest. Santos, although American by birth, nonetheless embraces the European ideals. Doña Bárbara, on the other hand, is patently a reflection of what we consider the American, the mestizo: "Fruto engendrado por la violencia del blanco aventurero en la sombría sensualidad de la india" (p. 22) ("Fruit of the sowings of white adventurers in the dark passion of the Indian," p. 30). And, all that I am to say about civilizing might be said about the conquest itself, which was economically motivated and which perceived the European mores as good and civilized, the American as bad and barbaric.

Indeed, there is a close relationship between the oppositions of internal/external, male/female, civilization/barbarism, as is apparent in the very definition of civilization. In *Doña Bárbara* civilization is epitomized by the fencing in, closing in, limitation, and demarcation of boundaries. Clearly, the purpose of this activity in the text is to define and emphasize Santos (the imperialistic, economically motivated male) as center—that is, to define the self, separate it from the other. Thus Santos wishes to fence in Altamira so that it is set apart and patently differentiated from El Miedo, so all will recognize where one begins and the other ends.[17] Furthermore, he aspires to keep Altamira cattle and horses in and others out. Thus, underlying the superficially innocent and reputable desire to civilize (a desire in this case less than noble or innocent since it is economically motivated) is a whole philosophy of restriction, property, and limitation as necessary to the identification of the center and thus the self. Civilization, then, is a process by means of which I mark (or write, create, as was the case with Cova) what is mine, what pertains to my being, and separate that from what is yours, other, not self. And, of course, this has also been true historically. My "civilizing" efforts as epitomized by religious crusades, the conquest, or offers of cultural and economic development are necessarily a glorification of my culture, my religion, my economy, and a debasement of yours. Thus any civilizing gesture must inevitably produce a dichotomy, a split between what is mine and what is yours, and set up a series of hierarchical value judgments. In this sense, then, to civilize is to define, highlight, and glorify the self. This gesture is best dramatized in *Doña Bárbara* in the character of Marisela. Santos has found her, dirty and in rags; in an effort *to civilize* her, he has her wash herself. As a result of this civilizing gesture the text states, "¡Y ella no se había dado cuenta de que todo existía, *creado para que lo contemplaran sus ojos!*" (p. 82, emphasis added) "And she hadn't realized that all this existed, created so that her eyes might observe it!" omitted in English translation). Such a statement unequivocally underlines that the civilizing activity is one of placing the self at the center of the universe. All else becomes a function of the self and exists in relation to the self.

Thus, in *Doña Bárbara* culture is embodied in the fencing in of the plain, in barriers which define land and cattle, and to civilize is to impose a certain degree of conformity and homogeneity. One of the means of exacting this uniformity and one of the other foremost manifestations of civilizing is the labeling with one's own name all that is one's property (cf. the branding of cattle). Of names I shall have more to say, but let me note at this point that the irony in this entire process is that the demarcation itself, which is economic as well as egocentric, is inevitably closely followed by, and again must necessarily elicit, a series of value judgments. It necessarily follows that what is internal soon comes to be seen as inherently positive and good, and all that is external is understood as necessarily negative and bad insofar as it threatens (by its very definition) what is indigenous. What is mine is by definition good, and what is yours inevitably menaces mine and thus must be bad. And, it is precisely these value judgments which produce the pejorative perception of both nature and the female, both of which are necessarily external to the male protagonist, narrator, or writer.

Before continuing perhaps it is pertinent to point out that to speak of the two novels in question as simple conflicts between civilization and barbarism (as has often been done) is simplistic and underestimates the novels. The texts themselves, as already suggested, are not as antonymous as their readers and critics have often implied. Gallegos, especially, repeatedly insinuates the possibility of apparently antithetical connotations resident in the same noun, and once one understands the duplicity of the very notions of civilization and barbarism, it is difficult to envision the texts in such neat terms. In fact, what is perhaps most interesting in the two texts is the simultaneous double projection. The works seem to move toward simple oppositions: black/white, civilization/barbarism, victim/victimized, but at the same time they underscore, to the attentive reader, the naïveté of such simplistic divisions and emphasize the combination, within any one entity or signifier, of superficially contradictory characteristics. For example, in *Doña Bárbara* the peon was once a *caballero*, she is both victimizer and victim, Santos's character is composed of both civilizing and barbaric aspects.

Ultimately, even the two words (*civilización* and *barbarie*) become terms with more connotation and supplementation than meaning—connotations and supplementations added in turn by the characters, the readers, and the authors. During this historical period of pragmatic progress in which the two texts were written, civilization had come to mean all that was positive and of benefit to the "hero" (traditionally male) whereas barbarism was all that was negative and in opposition to that "hero." This contrast and connotation are especially evident in the very use of the terms "barbarism," *devoradora*, and the like. In *María* and many of the other Romantic works it was not named barbarism, but rather nature *(naturaleza)*; the change in terminology unequivocally reflects a transposition of attitude among mankind toward nature and in turn woman. While mankind has certainly always struggled with nature (although it may not have always viewed it as a struggle), it is in this period that the cosmos becomes most dialectically opposed to mankind and mankind seems either to see itself as already divorced from nature or to be trying to separate itself from it. In other words, the "natural" universe has now been placed in a position alienated from mankind, and barbarism with all its negative overtones is used to describe it. Because one no longer views oneself as a component of that "natural" universe, bestiality is the quality which pertains to the other. Santos is not savage, doña Bárbara and the *llanura* are; the barbaric or evil is always the other. Nevertheless, what is implicit within the texts is the irony of this credence, for the barbarism is within oneself as much as outside. One may try to expel the barbarism as Santos does, or impose the *vorágine* on the *selva* as Cova does, but it is ultimately inseparable from the self. In fact, Lorenzo Barquero, in one of his rhetorical discourses, refers to the *centauro* (later defined as *barbarie*) inside us all.[18]

The other irony generated by the notions of civilization and barbarism as presented in these texts is that the barbarism is presumed to be a primitive or "original" state, correctable or at least improvable by civilization and thus contingent upon time.[19] As already noted, time is one of the principal leitmotifs of the two novels, and the imperativeness of time is intricately woven into Cova's Romantic vision of the world; he, like other Romantic poets and not unlike Efraín, glorifies the past and remembers it as superior to what it was. In addition, the very focus of his *énonciation* as memoir or diary underlines the theme of time, for what are diaries or memoirs but overt attempts to capture and fix, by means of language, the fleeting (or already past) moment? Thus, Cova's very language is (as it must always be) an effort to make present that which is already past, already absent, although as already shown, even that was principally imaginary. In effect, the tension between romanticism and naturalism might be another means of underlining the passage of time insofar as time is an indispensable factor to progress. According to our Western beliefs in progress, what is more recent is an improvement over what is older; today we are more civilized than yesterday and more primitive than tomorrow.[20] Thus, advancement, civilization, and barbarism are inexorably predicated on the passage of time. (Note that even those more "primitive" tribes encountered in various parts of the world are said to be living in a different age.)

The theme of time may be less overt in *Doña Bárbara* than in *La vorágine*, but it is not absent. Unmistakably, the opening of the novel alludes to a temporal movement which is to be repeated years later in *Los pasos perdidos*. The text opens with a boat reclimbing (a term often used in a temporal sense) the river, and the ensuing description of the work of the *bogas* continually advancing only to return to the starting point underlines one of the recurrent themes of the text. Later in the text, Santos at age eighteen, described as "Vuelto en sí del embrujamiento de las nostalgías" (p. 19) ("Coming to himself after the sorceress nostalgia had lost her power," p. 25), decides to make up for lost time. As such it would appear that both women and time have the power to bewitch, and doña Bárbara is portrayed specifically in relation to this movement of time: "criatura y personificación de los tiempos que corrían" (p. 22) ("symbol of the times," p. 29). Now, the fact that Santos has left the city to *remontar* the river (of time?) implies that doña Bárbara, like our "primitive contemporaries," is living in an earlier time period.

In both texts there is an ironic twist to the notion of time which underscores the dependency of the concept of time on language. In *La vorágine* one encounters a continual dichotomy between what is and what might have been, much as one does in *Doña Bárbara*: a polarity which, explained in other words and simplified, is the opposition between what is present in actuality and what the past had foreseen for the future. Again our discussion points to the female, for Cova's problem centers on what he thought he would find in Alicia (Romantic or literary prefiguration) and the *selva*, and what he did find. However, I insist that what the past projected on the future was necessarily a linguistic fantasy, a purely linguistic creation which ought not to be, indeed cannot be, a basis for judgmental conclusions.

Actually, however, what is labeled barbarism in the two novels and thus presumed to be more primitive (the exploitation on the part of the *caucheros*, doña Bárbara and her local government) is not primigenial (in the sense of being more closely related to nature or a "natural" state) at all. In effect, the barbarism bemoaned in the two novels is but another form of what one would normally call civilization. It is man and his concept of civilization which have brought the *caucheros* to the jungle; the *caucheros* are ultimately as distant from nature or any supposedly natural state as is Cova himself. In a sense, within the fiction, they are all chasing a Romantic fantasy not terribly different from Cova's. Doña Bárbara, too, is able to function as she does because of the assistance she received from the local government—a direct product of the forces of civilization—and is what she is as a result of those same manifestations of "civilization." One must

understand the absurdity of Gallegos's narrator's statement about Mujiquita, "quien no podía concebir la autoridad sino a la manera despótica
como la entiende el bárbaro" (p. 199) ("[who couldn't conceive] authority
otherwise than the barbarian understood it," p. 337), and recognize that
this authority *is the product* of civilization.

In both novels, then, to understand the basic conflict as that between
civilization and nature or barbarism is not only to misread the texts but also
to suggest a primordial or natural quality in something which is already
unquestionably supplement, perverted, and added to by man. The only
true primitivism or "original" state must be that which is never beheld by
the eyes of man and thus by definition cannot be barbaric, inasmuch as
barbaric implies a value judgment, and good and bad are not inherent
qualities but rather adjectives which define proximity to the ideal of the
group in power (usually male). Nature, like the female, only becomes
barbaric with the supplementation afforded it by man, in either the direct
form of despoliation (e.g., doña Bárbara's rape by the boatmen) or in the
indirect form of reiteration in an attempt to understand it—that is, by
converting nature or women to words or other symbolic systems which can
never fully embrace the totality.

But even more important to our topic is the fact that the dichotomies
between civilization and barbarism, romanticism and naturalism, interior
and exterior are all directly pertinent to and paralleled by the male/female
duality. In many of the novels of the early twentieth century, but
specifically in these two novels, the woman and what psychologists like to
call the "female principle" have been implicitly linked with barbarism
while the male and the "masculine principle" have been linked with civilization.[21] Both Santos and Arturo are comprehended by the reader and
envision themselves as civilizers, city dwellers come to the wilds to right
the wrongs of barbarism. Their foes seem to be of three varieties: nature,
women, and other men affiliated with that nature or those women (for
example, Mujiquita, whose name even evokes woman). Each hero fights
against the forces of nature, and each personalizes them as women. There
is little doubt, however, that during the historical period in which the
novels were written this vision of the female united with nature against the
male was not unique to these two authors. The relationship is implied not
only in other novels but also in the nonfiction of the period. In fact, just
one year after the publication of *Doña Bárbara*, Freud published one of his
last works in which he explicitly stated what had only been intimated in
these two novels: "Women soon come into opposition to civilization and
display their retarding and restraining influence."[22]

Thus it would appear that civilizing is a male activity hindered by the
female (doña Bárbara or *la madona*). Such an image, of course, is the product of several factors—one of which is the conflict between identity and
separation, internal and external, as I have been discussing them. Women,

like nature (and perhaps because they are unfailingly psychologically linked with nature) are defined as separate from and external to the male, that is, other. Since, as already noted, anything external by definition threatens the self, then women too become a menace to the male self and the presumably male desire for civilization, limiting, closing in. In fact, the males of both texts consider the women as challenges to their very masculinity. Cova repeatedly demonstrates his need to remain totally dominant, a compulsion based on a fear of losing his virility or self-identity. Following what appears to be a period of depression resulting from the loss of Alicia he even states, "¿Y yo por qué me lamentaba como un eunuco?" (p. 103) ["and, I, why do I grieve as if I were a eunuch?," my translation], indirectly hinting that she may have (in his twisted mind at any rate) some powers over his masculine identity. Similarly, doña Bárbara, according to those who repeat her legend to Santos, "ha fustaneado a muchos hombres y al que no trambuca con sus carantoñas, lo compone un bebedizo o se lo amarra a las pretinas y *hace con él lo que se le antoje*" (p. 11, emphasis added) ("has pocketed heaps of men, and she never misses when she begins sweet-talking. She gives a man a love potion and ties him to her apron-strings, and then *does what she likes with him*," p. 11, emphasis added), a statement which again manifests a basic anxiety about the loss of self-determination, freedom, self-identification, and thus perhaps the very essences of manliness and "humanliness"as they are defined in the Western world. Similarly, after doña Bárbara has taken Lorenzo's land, he is referred to as "el ex-hombre" (p. 29) ["the ex-man"], and he refers to himself by saying that he is no longer a man,[23] suggesting that masculine identity is contingent upon property and possession. Interestingly, however, the text very subtly intimates that Lorenzo's downfall was his own sensuality (which, of course, is blamed on doña Bárbara as male sensuality is almost always attributed to the irresistible allure of the female). But what the reader forgets all too easily is the irrational nature of these fears. Let us consider their source.

Significantly, Santos's perception of doña Bárbara as well as all that he knows about her is legend, myth, a linguistic creation presented as such even within the confines of the fiction. As one of the myth's perpetuators points out, "eso es lo que cuenta la gente, pero no hay que fiarse mucho porque el llanero es mentiroso de nación, aunque me esté mal el decirlo, y hasta cuando cuenta algo que es verdad lo desagera tanto que es como si juera mentira" (p. 12) ("All this is what people say, but you don't need to put much faith in it, because the Plainsmen are a born race of liars, I'm sorry to say, and even when they are telling the truth they exaggerate it so much that it might as well be a lie," p. 11). Yet Santos (paradigm of the civilizing male) never seems to transcend this fiction. He accepts as fact statements such as "*Dicen que* es una mujer terrible, capitana de una pandilla de bandoleros, encargados de asesinar a mansalva a cuantos intenten

oponerse a sus designios" (p. 10, emphasis added) ("*They say* she's a des-
perate woman, and leader of a troop of bandits she orders to assassinate
anyone who shows any signs of opposing her," p. 8, emphasis added).
While it is germane that doña Bárbara is accused here of doing exactly what
Santos tries to do, the point is that the very lack of a subject for the verb
dicen ought to suggest to an educated man like Santos the dubious reliability of such a statement. In fact, the text itself often subtly highlights the
unreliability of such statements. While apparently asserting a pejorative
view of doña Bárbara, the text (narrator) simultaneously uses a variety of
rhetorical devices to undermine this negative portrayal—such as the *dicen*.
Indeed, one of the least studied aspects of this novel is its use of paradox
and self-contradiction, and these are precisely the techniques used most
frequently in the characterization of doña Bárbara. For example, after several pages of description of La Barquereña, the text notes, "Dice el cuento
que . . ." ("The story says that . . . ," omitted), and then a few paragraphs
later it continues, "Esto contaban. Tal vez habría mucho de leyenda en
cuanto se decía a propósito de su fortuna" (p. 31) ("This is what they say.
Perhaps there is a lot of legend in what they say about her fortune,"
omitted in English translation). Again, the lack of a definite, personal
subject for *se decía* and *contaban* combined with three terms which emphasize supposition or doubt *(tal vez, habría, leyenda)* undermines the authenticity of the statements. Thus, although readers have generally overlooked
this aspect of the novel, the text itself is stressing that much of what is
accepted as reality or truth in regard to doña Bárbara is invention, linguistic
creation,[24] and that as in *La vorágine* one ought not to, indeed cannot, accept
quite so literally all that one hears or reads, all that words promise.

Once again, the salient detail is that what the protagonists know about
the women in both cases is secondhand, repetition of a repetition. Luzardo
gets his information from the boatman, and Cova presumably learns most
of what he knows about women from literature. Nevertheless, the anxiety
that the males seem to experience is a fear of a collapse of limits or demar-
cations—an apprehension that surges from within but is imposed on the
outside world. In fact, at one point Cova himself posits a valid interpretation of his fear—"vamos huyendo de un fantasma cuyo poder se lo at-
ribuimos nosotros mismos" (p. 14) ("we are fleeing from a phantom born in
our own imaginations," p. 20). Obviously, the myths, the legends, and
other perceptions of woman in these texts are ultimately linguistic in basis.
They are formed of stories told, retold, invented, and changed. What may
perhaps be most pertinent and most reflective of the prototype of woman
as perceived by the male is very subtly exposed in *Doña Bárbara*. The *doma*
is the feat which proves Santos a true man according to the stereotypes of
the *llano,* and it is doña Bárbara's skill at the *doma* which makes her most
suspect. In a similar manner, she is condemned for trying to destroy what
has destroyed her, the male. In the form of Lorenzo she sees the earlier

men in her life who had harmed her and states, "Pero yo los destruiré a todos en ti" (p. 28) ("But I'll ruin them all, in you," p. 39)—which is precisely what Santos tries to do, destroy all bad caciques via doña Bárbara. Also, although she is labeled *devoradora de hombres* (devourer of men), she unquestionably represents what has been accepted as valid and positive in Darwin's theory of the survival of the fittest—eat or be eaten. Thus, throughout the text, the very adjectives which, when applied to him, are complimentary and laudatory are intended as offensive when applied to her. Obviously, then, the power of the word rests not in the term itself but rather in the supplementation which inevitably accompanies it.

What Santos has done, then, apparently is to accept at face value and without question the negative tales he hears because it is convenient to do so; it is easier to destroy a strong, hateful enemy than an insignificant being. As Antonio, the ranch hand, notes, "las cosas son verdad de dos maneras: cuando de veras lo son y cuando a uno le conviene creerlas o aparentar que las cree" (p. 52) ("things can be true in two different ways: when they really are true or when it is convenient to believe them or pretend you believe them," omitted in English translation). There can be no doubt that the legend of doña Bárbara is true for Santos for the second reason, but why does the reader also accept it so facilely? This is less clear, but the possibility exists that one accepts it because the implied author does. In spite of his occasional polysemous gestures, Gallegos basically picks up where *La vorágine* leaves off, premising his novel on the inimical character of woman and nature as posited by the demented poet, Arturo Cova.

Thus, in many ways *Doña Bárbara* might be understood as an analysis and perhaps repetition of the myth of doña Bárbara (or the myth of the female and nature as inherently antagonistic to man and society) and the facile acceptance of these inventions. The fabrications, like the one in José Donoso's *El obsceno pájaro de la noche*, are subject to so many transformations and supplementations that it is no longer possible either to totally accept or reject them. In reference to the legends of doña Bárbara, the narrator even notes, "inventando cada cual lo que se le antojara" (p. 245) ("as each invented whatever he took a notion to make up," p. 424).

But why does Santos hate doña Bárbara? Even he does not know— "pero, en seguida, lo asaltó un subitáneo sentimiento de repulsión por la compañía de aquella mujer, no porque fuera su enemiga, sino por algo mucho más íntimo y profundo, que por el momento *no pudo discernir*" (p. 128, emphasis added). ("but a sudden feeling of aversion for the woman immediately overcame him, not because she was his enemy, but because of something much more intimate and profound which *he could not distinguish* at the moment," p. 210, emphasis added). Thus, it becomes evident that it is the male's opinion and the fantasies he weaves which to a greater or lesser extent create the female in this case. That which is internal is imposed on what is external, and the supplement is miscomprehended and seen as the essence. The process is complete in this novel, for even doña Bárbara herself believes some of the myth and finds credence in the powers of *el Socio*. Although he is just another figment of the myth,[25] she believes in him and in her supernatural powers.

In many ways it is the delimitation, demarcation, and supplementation afforded by the word or language itself which ostensibly create the ambivalent position of the female. As Miller and Swift have observed in *Words and Women*, females are generally defined by their relationships to males.[26] That is, a woman has a surname and a certain function within society (she is wife, daughter, mother, etc.) because of her relationship to a father or husband—a relationship reflected linguistically in her name.[27] Now, doña Bárbara not only lacks such a kinship but consequently is estranged from the definition and limitation which are the essentials of "civilization." She has no surname, thus reflecting not only her lack of parentage or "origins," but also a lack of a current relationship to a male. By the same token, it is probably not fortuitous that Arturo Cova has a surname, but Alicia does not; although he presumably knows her intimately, she lacks the family name which even his most casual male acquaintances possess. In this sense both doña Bárbara and Alicia defy the concepts of property (which is basic to our Western society) and manliness, as I have demonstrated. Their lack of a surname reflects the lack of a possessor, and one of doña Bárbara's main problems, or one of her principal offenses to the male society, is that "Su privanza lo daba todo, incluso la incertidumbre perenne de poseerla realmente" (p. 67, emphasis added) ("Her favour gave such a one everything, including the eternal uncertainty of *really possessing her*," p. 105, emphasis added). Here apparently lies the crux of the issue. She not only opposes the fence which will allow for defining and naming, but, what is even worse, she does not "belong" to anyone; she is a maverick. She has taken on the functions and role (mask) reserved for only men within Santos's society. She defies female sexuality as traditionally defined in Western culture, for as the text notes, not only has her sensuality been erased by her greed, but also in the act itself "más era hombruno tomar que femenino entregarse" (p. 32) ("she was so more as a man who takes than as a woman who gives," p. 45). And, here, of course, is the main problem—her refusal to surrender herself, to hand herself over, to become property. Thus, in the very most basic manner she spurns what is defined as culture and must therefore be personified as the enemy to that civilization.

On the other hand, Marisela is limited and defined. She has a last name, a rapport with her father, and eventually an association with Santos. The fact that she consents to the socially acceptable female functions as nurse to her father and mistress to Santos's home further emphasizes her progress towards "civilization." In addition, Santos can apparently condone and even sanction her presence, her existence, to the extent that he feels he has created her, and thus she is no longer the other: "su verdadera obra . . . que le devolvía el bien recibido" (p. 240) ("It was his work, his real accomplishment . . . which was returning good for good," p. 413). The text goes on to state that the words spoken by Marisela came from her confidence in him which was "algo suyo [de Santos], lo mejor de sí mismo, puesto en otro corazón" ("part of him, the best part, sown in another heart," p. 414). Obviously, this is the same process by which nature is "tamed," civilized.

Thus man's desire to exteriorize what is interior, to label, and to possess has besmudged and imposed a negative valuation on both nature and woman. As has already been noted, this process is a direct result of language, and it is significant that in the texts under consideration language is controlled by men. Cova, the Romantic poet, regardless of his dubious reliability, nonetheless has a tight grasp on language and uses it to his benefit. Alicia rarely says anything. The Luzardo cousins, too, are both portrayed in full control of language (Lorenzo even won a series of rhetorical contests), while doña Bárbara is depicted as basically silent. And, it appears that the power of the language of the men is a form of wealth which eventually is used to violate or distort the images of women and nature. It is Cova, the Romantic poet, who demonstrates that he is an insensitive brute and thus quite the opposite from what is implied in the label "Romantic poet." As such, one is forced to recognize that language is not to be relied upon and that to say is not to be. Thus, Rivera criticizes the language of romanticism and demonstrates the basic mistrust of language reflected in the picaresque novels of the fifteenth and sixteenth centuries as Cova employs the language of romanticism in reverse: "Aquel ambiente de pesadilla [the plain] me enflaquecía el corazón, y era preciso volver a las tierras civilizadas, *al remanso de la molicie, al ensueño y a la quietud*" (p. 91) ("A nightmare seemed pressing my heart, weakening it. It was necessary to return to civilized lands, *to the backwaters of comfort, to dreaming and to peace*," p. 117, emphasis added). Note that not only is he incorrectly remembering the past but also he is using the emphasized words, commonly used in romanticism, to describe the city rather than nature. As Lorenzo states, "las palabras, puras palabras, lo hicieron todo" (p. 76) ("the words, pure words, did it all," p. 119), allowing him to be lauded when in fact it was all invention, all sham. Through the language he so cleverly controls, it appears that man can justify almost any act, including his negative portrayal of the female and nature. The danger again is that this justification, this supplementation, loses its appearance of a rationalization, of something added later, and comes to be understood as the inherent essence (cf. the rib story). Perhaps, then, the barbarity is language itself in the hands of the unscrupulous. And this is precisely what Santos, unlike Lorenzo, never fully understands: what the language, the words, produce is merely "aquella mixtificación de mí mismo" (p. 76) ("that mythification of myself," omitted).

Thus it appears that *Doña Bárbara* and *La vorágine* might be seen as twen-tieth-century adventure novels. As in the classical and renaissance adven-ture tales, they are structured around a journey whose purpose is (or becomes) the imposition of what the "hero's" society considers civilization. In this sense, although there is a dose of irony in the twentieth-century novels, we have not moved very far from the Arthurian cycle, *Amadís de Gaula*, *Chanson de Roland*, and so forth. And, in many ways, the portrayal of the female in the twentieth-century novels is even more closely tied to these tales of adventure. In both instances, the female is a peripheral being, distanced from the center of the story, imagined, and fantasized even more than the hero himself. Perhaps it is the satirical *Don Quijote* which most clearly evinces the attitude toward, and the position of, the female in the adventure tale.[28] Don Quijote, of course, is deeply enamored of Dulcinea and devotes all his deeds and exploits to her. But, she does not exist; *even within the fiction*, she is but a figment of his imagination and thus but a projection of himself. In many ways, the same has occurred in *Doña Bárbara* and *La vorágine* where women are just imagined fantasies, projec-tions of the male (the same characteristics in many cases which he also projects on nature). The ultimate irony and perhaps absurdity lies in man's inability to see either nature or the female except in relation to himself. Man repeatedly insists that nature exists as either friend or foe (depending on the period) and refuses to accept that nature may simply be there, as neither friend nor foe—just there (as woman is neither necessarily ally nor enemy). Thus the boatman in *Doña Bárbara* teaches Santos that nature is always lying in wait, Santos takes the credit for all the good that surfaces in Marisela, and Cova projects his own mental vortex on the jungle.

Inevitably, in the final analysis, the problem is linguistic and lies in the very attempt to place a label, a simplifying name, on either woman or nature. Thus we circle back to the notion of language which disguises an absence, and it must be concluded that the real *devoradora* is language itself as it is projected on the world, swallowing it, and transposing our "realities" into what language seems to tell us we perceive.

3

Women and the Not-So-Golden Silence (The Adulthood of Snow White): *Todo verdor perecerá* by Eduardo Mallea

ALTHOUGH Agata Cruz, protagonist of *Todo verdor perecerá*, published in 1941 by Eduardo Mallea (Argentina, 1903–82), is the first female character among the group of novels we are studying who is truly a protagonist, both she and the text which focuses on her are a series of contradictions and paradoxes in which nature is simultaneously accepted and rejected as an overwhelming influence on the characters' lives. Many critics have seen Mallea's work in terms of a movement away from the preoccupation with nature and the physical environment which was explicit in *Doña Bárbara* and *La vorágine*. Myron Lichtblau succinctly expresses what has come to be the general belief of the critics: "Aunque no hay claras líneas divisorias, la novela posterior a 1940 representa una reacción a los excesos del criollismo, considerando primero la totalidad psíquica del hombre sin la estrecha asociación con su ambiente. En primer plano está el hombre en su escueta esencia fundamental; en segundo término el ámbito exterior que éste habita y que puede influir sobre él, pero que no domina la novela."[1] While it is certainly true, as Lichtblau notes, that nature has been relegated to the background, many of the metaphors and tropes used in the novel are still based on various aspects of nature, and these elements are still very pertinent to the development of the plot and the characters' "psyches." Lichtblau also notes, in fact, speaking of *Todo verdor*, "la identificación del medio físico con el destino de los personajes asume un papel indispensable" (p. 144). Thus, as I shall demonstrate, although Agata's problems are not totally or directly created by nature, they are described by means of it; the overt presence and importance of nature have merely been covered.

At the same time, the contradictions of the text do not end here. As presented, Agata's objective is the formulation of the right word or phrase which will fill the blank space in her life and bring her happiness, but the text paradoxically negates the possibility of encountering this word and underscores the impotence of that word even if it could be found. In a similar paradoxical fashion, the novel affirms the universality (that is, the nonsexist aspect) of Agata's plight while demonstrating that it is a uniquely feminine problem. That is, on one level Agata's situation of incommunication seems to be the predicament of modern mankind in general, as Anderson Imbert notes: "la soledad de Agata . . . no es una soledad determinada por las circunstancias, sino la soledad de la existencia humana."[2] But on another level, one never suspects for a moment that the psychological agony portrayed could possibly be experienced by a male, for the emotional presentation of the female character (and all the presumedly feminine connotations underlined by that "emotion") suggests that the problem is uniquely feminine. Indeed, the text states, "¿Por qué *una mujer* de veinte años es inferior a una loba, a una garza, a una hembra de animal andariego, las cuales deciden a solas . . . su libre elección del camino?" (p. 39, emphasis added) ("Why is a *woman* of twenty inferior to a she-wolf, a heron, the roaming animals, who freely chose their way for themselves. . . ?" p. 141, emphasis added),[3] a statement which again implies a specifically feminine problem. Obviously, then, in spite of its pluralistic view and the sympathetic good intentions,[4] Mallea's text wavers between two dialectical positions, as it both creates and is created by the fairy tale, that vast body of mythology which surrounds the female sex. Thus, the focus of my study will be the integral, if sometimes contradictory, employment of images drawn from nature and fairy tales.

As in the other novels we have studied, one of the salient features of the text (as well as the above-quoted statement), is the use of various aspects of nature as metaphors for women. This lingering, although more subtle (or perhaps less visible),[5] preoccupation with nature is already accentuated in the title of the novel, taken from a verse of Isaiah and used as an epigraph on the first page: " 'Las aguas de Nimrim serán consumidas, y secaráse la hierba, marchitaránse los retoños, todo verdor perecerá.' ISAÍAS—XV, 6" (p. 9) (" 'For the waters of Nimrim shall be desolate; for the hay is withered away, the grass faileth, there is no green thing.' Isaiah XV, 6," p. 111).

Like *Todo verdor* itself, the theme of the biblical book is not necessarily nature, but the author depends upon metaphors of nature to explain himself. In fact, the particular verses used in the epigraph, from both Isaiah and Ecclesiastes, underscore the supremacy of nature, which has the power to destroy mankind and control his happiness and worldly success. Thus, applying the implications of Isaiah and Ecclesiastics to Mallea's text, one deduces that while nature may no longer be presented as having complete and total mastery over man's destiny, it still maintains a significant dominance, and its power surges at unexpected moments.

In many ways the relationship between the characters and nature in *Todo verdor* resembles what we have observed in *Doña Bárbara* and *La vorágine;*

that is, the supposedly internal problems of the character are projected outward and blamed on the external world. Thus, Agata, at moments, tends to see her unhappy marriage and the disappointing position she holds in Part I of the novel as closely related to, if in fact not caused by, the barrenness of the land and of herself. At several points the narrator indicates that Agata believes that either a good crop or a child would save the marriage and reverse their hatred for each other. "Agata odiaba cada vez más ese clima, al que miraba ya como un *protagonista influyente* en su vida" (p. 33, emphasis added) ("Agata came to hate the climate more and more. She already regarded it as an *influential protagonist* in her life," p. 135, emphasis added); "Agata habría necesitado un elemento sólido, una sola cosa resistente y concreta; . . . pensó en producirlo de su entraña" (p. 50) ("Agata needed a solid element, just one resistant and concrete thing; . . . she thought of producing it from her womb," p. 150).

In spite of this exteriorization of internal fears and preoccupations, *Todo verdor* differs from *La vorágine* and *Doña Bárbara* in that one is never allowed to fully believe (nor do the characters, within the fiction, seem to presume) that nature is solely responsible for their problems. Again, although nature is used to describe the problems, it is not the sole creator of them. The text, instead, takes a much less simplistic view, affirming that (as presumably one already knows) any situation is the product of a composite of factors and that it may well be this multiplicity of factors which makes the situation so difficult to change and the problems so hard to solve. Unlike the male characters studied here, Agata seems to recognize that much of the predicament in which she finds herself comes from within: "Esta desolación, ¿soy yo quien la comparto?" (p. 52) ("Am I the one who imparts this desolation?" p. 153). Although she ultimately answers these questions negatively, their very formulation (her willingness to accept the responsibility for factors over which she clearly and obviously can have no control—the air, etc.) at least presents the possibility that the culpability is inherent. In addition, one is often reminded by the narrator that the problems faced are to a large extent sociological (that is, external to the individual but internal to the society).

There are, in fact, several sociological questions implied by the narrator. First, the text implies that the woman's lack of freedom within this society directly contributes to the despondency and sense of isolation she experiences. While throughout Mallea's works most of the characters (male and female) are isolated and alone, the females seem to suffer more acutely; as in the other novels we have examined, the latter remain at home, alone, while the men go off to local clubs, etc, where they try, with limited success, to encounter a sense of brotherhood or community.[6] It is this same awareness of confinement, as experienced by the females of the texts, which appears to produce the second sociological problem implied here: that is, because the female is reduced to living with either a blood relative or a husband, marriage necessarily becomes an escape from the home of the family and is thus doomed from the beginning. Agata marries Cruz to escape from her father's house, to taste of the rest of the world, and because marriage is an ineluctable fact of life: "Ella sabía que alguna vez tendría que ofrecer a alguien su alma . . . por amor" (p. 31) ("she knew that sometime or other she would have to offer her soul to somebody . . . for love," p. 133); "¿Hasta cuándo iba a esperar y con qué suerte?" (p. 39) ("[Until when] would she have to wait . . . and with what luck?" (p. 140); "¡Ah, si hubiera sabido incorporar a su vida un germen de diversidad!" (p. 38) ("If only she had been able to incorporate a germ of variety into her life," p. 140). Agata marries Cruz to evade the boredom and monotony of her father's house—a boredom and monotony imposed upon her, in part, but only in part, by the society portrayed in the novel. Nevertheless, once again, Mallea comprehends the depth of the issue, and at no point does he attribute the problems and the boredom merely to society's demands nor simply to Agata herself. Instead, one is continually reminded that sociological, biological, and psychological factors all play a part in the ultimate destruction of the protagonist whose major problem may be her uncomprehending acceptance of the passive role which others have created for her. Having spent her childhood alone and dreaming, and never having been encouraged by the patriarchate which surrounds her to do anything else, she is truly impotent to forge her own future.

In fact, it would not be impertinent to consider the novel in terms of a traditional fairy tale which has been extended beyond its normal conclusion. Obviously, the difference between *Todo verdor perecerá* and a fairy tale is the time span involved. The fairy tale inevitably focuses on adolescence—from puberty to the marriage ceremony. *Todo verdor perecerá*, however, concentrates on adulthood, that is, the time span which postdates the marriage ceremony (opening after Nicanor and Agata have been married fifteen years), and relegates Agata's adolescence to a type of prehistory, which is nevertheless posited as the root of her adult problems. Thus, if one compares what one knows about Agata's adolescence with what one knows about Cinderella's and Snow White's, one finds some impressive similarities, for Mallea specifically begins where the fairy tale ends ("and they lived happily ever after") and demonstrates that this "ever after" is not so happy if Agata is the typical fairy-tale protagonist.

The narrative technique of the novel highlights certain qualities of the fairy tale. For example, the novel opens with forty-four successive days of drought and fire. Such an unobtrusive opening might be passed over unnoticed until one realizes that a fairy tale, too, always begins with a time reference: "Once upon a time . . . ," "A long time ago . . . ," or the equivalent. My reader will no doubt protest that the two time references are not at all related; "forty-four days" is very specific and concrete whereas "once upon a time" is vague and mythic. But, of course, such is precisely the irony of *Todo verdor perecerá.* "Forty-four days" does, indeed, appear to imply a very specific time period, but, to what forty-four days does the narrator refer? As one discovers that one cannot answer this question (at least not in the novel's first paragraph), one must simultaneously recognize that forty-four consecutive days is no more specific than "Once upon a time." They both point backward as the verb in the first sentence of *Todo verdor* indicates, but one cannot be quite sure how far backward. One is reminded, in fact, of the technique that García Márquez will use some twenty years later in *Cien años de soledad* where he, too, offers a series of what superficially appear to be concrete time markers ("Many years later," "One hundred years," etc.) but which prove to be meaningless on a more objective level since the larger time indicators (the temporal framework, if you prefer) are imaginary or mythic.[7] The subjective propensity of the time reference is further accentuated in the same paragraph when the narrator refers to "las horas del día, tan largo y tan alejado del cielo" ("the daylight hours, boundless and distant from the sky, stretching as far as the eye could see"). The second paragraph similarly begins, "Años antes" ("Years earlier"), but once again we are not told how many years earlier.

This temporal oscillation is also particularly typical of the fairy tale, which normally begins in the following format: "A long time ago, there lived a lovely princess called Snow White. Her mother, a good and beautiful queen, had died when Snow White was a baby."[8] Obviously, the structure begins by taking us back many years, sets the scene briefly, and then takes us back even further to an earlier time which was better: in the case of the fairy tale, when Snow White's mother lived; in *Todo verdor*, when the region had been fertile. From this point, we return to the recent past: in *Todo verdor*, the narrative reiterates the problems of the drought; in "Snow White," "After some years, Snow White's father married . . ." and things became very bad. But, of course, in the fairy-tale world, things have a way of arranging themselves—the prince finally finds the princess, and they live happily ever after. Structurally, *Todo verdor* again follows this model. Agata marries her prince, Nicanor. Although she does not live happily ever after, the conclusion of Part I, with the death of the husband, suggests the possibility for a Part II in which Agata indeed will find happiness now that the problem in her life, Nicanor, has been eliminated. But, I shall discuss this later.

It is apropos of the topic, too, that fairy-tale princesses are often described in terms of nature. Snow White, for example, "was as white as snow, and as red as blood, and her hair was as black as ebony; and she was therefore called Little Snow White."

Thus *Todo verdor* follows the general structural outlines of the fairy tale, but there are even more specific aspects which lead me to draw the analogy. Let us examine the characteristics which Agata has in common with

Snow White and Cinderella. To say that she lives in a fairy-tale world, while true, is too general and too glib. Specifically, Cinderella and Snow White (like Rapunzel and the Miller's daughter in "Rumpelstiltskin")[9] were both motherless from early childhood, as was Agata. Although, unlike Cinderella, Rapunzel, and Snow White, Agata was spared the torment of a stepmother (which in the fairy-tale world is worse than no mother at all), she did suffer in childhood much the same as the others. To have no "real" mother during one's fairy-tale childhood seems to generate two significant and related encumbrances: first, the child grows up without ever learning how to successfully interact with other people; and, secondly, and as a consequence of this, the adolescent is doomed to solitude, loneliness, and a lack of both human companionship and communicativeness.[10] Thus, Cinderella and Snow White, like Agata, spend their childhood and adolescence surrounded by people, but isolated from them, detached, and alone. Agata need not be physically locked in a tower like Rapunzel to lead as cloistered a life as the latter. Mallea's narrator, in fact, comments specifically on Agata's "infancia solitaria" (p. 27). And Agata's father is much like the fairy-tale male parents—generally well-intentioned if somewhat nebulous figures who are either impotent to aid and educate the child or oblivious to her emotional (or even physical) needs.

Furthermore, Cinderella and Snow White are unable to make friends with other females of their age group because of their beauty, which evokes jealousy in the other young women. It would appear, if one is to believe in fairy tales, that female beauty is an asset in terms of finding a husband but a liability in terms of other human relationships. Although *Todo verdor perecerá* never implies that Agata's isolation from other young women her age is directly related to her beauty, it does comment on her attractiveness: "la frecuentación de otras jóvenes y la idea—la primera idea grata—de su verdadera belleza abrieron una brecha en su encierro" (p. 23) ("She met other girls and learned for the first time—her first welcome thought—that she was beautiful. A gap opened in her confinement," p. 126). The text continues, "Tímida, dejaba que aquel montón de hombres giraron en torno a ella, cambiando entre sí las sonrisas pretenciosas y suspicaces de los que disputan galantes primacías" ("Shyly, she let the men crowd around her, as they exchange conceited and distrustful smiles of those who fight for gallant preferences"). This, of course, reminds one of Cinderella at the ball, and one must presume that if Agata is surrounded by this proliferation of male admirers, she will not be developing female relationship at the same time—another young woman would be unable to approach her since she is surrounded by males.

The other characteristic which Agata Cruz has in common with the fairy-tale protagonists is her complete passivity. Agata does nothing; like the others, she keeps house, nothing more, nothing less: "Sin religión, sin vocación de lectura, esta muchacha nacida al lado del Atlántico consumía largas tardes mirando el agua sin respuestas" (p. 28) ("With no religion, no vocation for reading, this young girl born by the Atlantic, spent long afternoons questioning the unanswering waters," p. 130). Agata remains quiescent, waiting for things to get better. The statement, "En quince años las cosas no se habían compuesto" (p. 13) ("But in fifteen years, things had not straightened out," p. 117) epitomizes Agata's attitude. Things, of course, cannot arrange themselves; someone must be active and take command, but, as the text later states, presumably in a direct quotation of Agata's thoughts, "Hacer las cosas es tan difícil" (p. 80) ("It is so hard to act," p. 177). The one potentially active gesture which Agata makes is still fraught with passivity. At the end of Part I, she decides "por fin entregarse a la vida" (p. 81) ("to give herself up to life at last," p. 178). While at first glance this sounds dynamic and forceful, the irony is implicit. This "life" to which she will hand herself over is not life at all but death, and she will "hand herself over" (implying a decisive action) by sitting on a chair ("se dejó caer"—"she collapsed") and allowing the wind to chill her. Again, all is laden with more lethargy than activity.

Andrea Dworkin has astutely pointed out that in fairy tales women are either very good or wicked, evil mothers (or stepmothers), but "When she is good, she is soon dead. In fact, when she is good, she is so passive in life that death must be only more of the same."[11] Her passivity creates for her a death in life and prevents her from making any effort to change her "lot" in life. Like Cinderella, Rapunzel, and Snow White—who never even protest out loud, never rebel against their circumstances—Agata merely sits passively and waits for the prince charming (or death) who had been implicitly promised her: "Ella sabía que en cada ser, el matrimonio desdobla la vida. . . . Incubó una atroz impaciencia" (p. 28) ("She knew that in each being, marriage releases and evokes life. . . . She developed within her a fearful impatience," p. 130). Similarly, Rapunzel agrees to marry the prince who happened to gain entrance to her tower because "she thought, 'He will love me more than old Dame Gothel does.'" Later, of course, Agata will complain (silently to herself) that the prince is not so charming; he does not meet her fantasy ideal. Since one never learns what happens to Cinderella, Rapunzel, or Snow White after their wedding days ("and they lived happily ever after" glibly encompasses a good many years), one is never allowed to question whether or not their prince charmings live up to the model. That Agata's ideal would have to be a total fantasy, removed from all realistic expectations, is underlined by the fact that she had never witnessed any type of human interaction (cf. Rapunzel particularly), much less interaction with erotic overtones; her knowledge of relationships between men and women is limited to the cinema, where she saw "entremezclarse en pasiones ficticias los corazones humanos" (p. 23) ("human hearts were joined in fictitious passions," p. 125).

Now, what is especially blatant and particularly significant in the Mallea

text, and what inclines me to view the novel as a more realistic version of
the "ever after" of the fairy tale, is that Agata repeats this pattern. As I have
noted, Part I concludes with Nicanor's death, and thus at the beginning of
Part II Agata is free to begin again, to reshape a life for herself. Presumably
she has been able to see the errors of her ways via her introspection during
so many years of life with Nicanor, and now she has been offered a second
chance, a rebirth. (That we are indeed meant to see Part II as a rebirth is
patent in that when the workers found Nicanor's body they found her livid
and unconscious, a description which one can easily comprehend as a
metaphoric death). But, the "old" Agata has unequivocally not died. She
has escaped from Cruz (her cross), but she cannot escape from herself, and
her problems lie within, for she continues to believe those childhood fairy
tales and continues to wait for a new prince charming. This time he takes
the form of Sotero, but he still falls short of the ideal. Apparently, the
image of the prince charming, the prince who will right all the wrongs,
make her happy, provide her with everything she will ever need, both
emotionally and physically, is too deeply ingrained, too readily accepted,
and Agata is predictably destined to a life of repeated failure in finding the
ideal who will accomplish all. It is apropos that blindness is so frequently a
punishment in the fairy tale if we understand blindness as a metaphoric
inability or unwillingness to see and understand the source of the problem
as in Agata's case. In many ways, *Todo verdor perecerá* is a dramatization of
the point made by Dworkin—that by filling the female child's mind with
fairy-tale patterns, we are creating roles and role models which cannot be
realized in life and thus condemning the child to adult failure.

While it is ultimately not of major importance with which fairy-tale
character I identify Agata, since I am focusing on the general stereotype of
the fairy-tale figures, there are nonetheless many small clues throughout
the novel which invite us to associate Agata expressly with Snow White. It
would be difficult to ignore the recurrence of the color white in *Todo verdor
perecerá*. The name, Snow White, of course, is a redundancy, a pleonasm,
which doubly accentuates whiteness and all its associative attributes. Similarly, Mallea repeatedly highlights the whiteness which surrounds Agata.
For example, the first page of the text contains the following: "una
superficie *calcinada, blanca* y enorme; *blanca* era la tierra seca; *blancos* los
pastos; *blancas* las cortaderas y el olmo esquelético; *blancos* el algarrobo y el
tala" (p. 9, emphasis added) ("*ashen* surface, vast and *white. White* was the
dry earth; *white* the pastures; *white* the pampas grass and the skeleton elm.
White the *carob* and the *tala*," p. 113). Thus there are no less than six
references to the color. Furthermore, Agata lived in Ingeniero White and
Bahia Blanca. I shall later discuss the contrast between white and green,
but for now one cannot help but wonder if all the whiteness, all this
barrenness of life and purity might not characterize what the future necessarily holds in store for a Snow White. Are we meant to see Agata as the

grown up Snow White, ready to be transformed, passively by the first interested male, into the Mother—the pure and perfect virgin surrounded by elves (eunuchs?), who is supposed to suddenly and magically metamorphose into what Donoso will later call "la suntuosidad del medallón siguiente" (p. 179) ("the sumptuousness of the next [medallion]," p. 145). Mallea seems to be implying, via his characterization of Agata, the simplistic nature and innocence of such an unrealistic expectation.

In addition, it cannot be completely fortuitous that the fairy-tale structure to which I have referred in *Todo verdor perecerá* centers around the eating of a piece of fruit, specifically an apple, which was, as we all know, the downfall of Snow White as well as Eve. In the middle of Agata's reminiscence about her adolescence, she is brought back to the present of the *énoncé* and the image of "este hombre todavía joven, que mastica ahora ante ella la fruta" (p. 27) ("this man still young, now chewing his fruit in front of her," p. 129). Later in the same paragraph one learns that *la fruta* is an apple. The significance of the fruit and its relationship to the fairy tale is patent. The apple is tied to the concept of eternal youth; Eve's eating of the apple resulted in the couple's expulsion from the Garden of Eden and the subsequent aging process. Snow White ate of the apple (sent by her wicked stepmother, who envied Snow White's beauty and youth) and fell into a deep sleep. Once again one is reminded that Snow White's predicament here is the indirect consequence of a motherless childhood; had her mother lived, she would never have been subjected to an evil stepmother's jealousy. Similarly, Agata is recalling her youth and remembering it as a form of golden age past as Nicanor eats the apple. It is pertinent too that after eating the apple Snow White falls into a deep sleep from which she is awakened by the prince. In many ways then, Snow White's sleep is a type of metaphoric death (the apple was supposed to kill her), and her awakening is a rebirth. The rebirth might be seen as a return to the prior golden age insofar as Snow White now rightfully recovers her original position in society (princess) of which the stepmother had deprived her. Similarly, the death of Nicanor and the pseudo death of Agata at the end of Part I are preceded by sleep; Nicanor, who earlier ate the apple, will never awaken from his sleep, but Agata, like Snow White, will. And, as she sits, half conscious, waiting for death to take her, her hallucinations return her to the premarriage days of her youth, days now seen as something of a golden age lost. When she awakens, Nicanor is gone, and she too is returned to the preproblem days (presumably). Again, like Snow White, Agata has ostensibly reached this drastic state as a result of her motherless childhood. The difference, of course, is that in *Todo verdor perecerá* Agata structually plays the role of both the evil queen and Snow White. It is she who, like the evil queen, has offered Nicanor the apple and she who ultimately induces his death by leaving the doors and windows open, while at the same time it is she who falls asleep to be later awakened. The strength and significance of Mallea's novel lies precisely in this elimination of the fairy-tale opposite extremes. The evil queen can coexist within the good and innocent princess (as obviously she must, since the evil queen presumably was once an innocent princess.) Thus, while Part I begins with intense heat and ends with intense cold, it is nature which encompasses such extremes, not people. The Mallea characters are depicted as neither terribly good nor awfully bad—merely human and fallible.

But perhaps the most significant characteristic of these fairy-tale heroines, like Agata, is their silence. If one examines fairy tales carefully, one discovers that the heroines (which is no doubt too strong, too active a word) rarely say anything at all within the context of their stories; like the "perfect" child, they are seen but seldom heard. The wicked stepmothers talk as do the other characters, but the apprentice princesses rarely verbalize anything. And this, of course, is the most serious problem facing the female in *Todo verdor perecerá*: language itself, or its absence. Critics have repeatedly noted the significance of the silence which is the leitmotif of so many of Mallea's works, and *Todo verdor* is no exception. The word or its absence creates much of the tension within the text; according to the narrator, the right word, shared between Agata and Nicanor, is the only thing, other than a good crop or a child, which would have saved their marriage, but even these products (crops and children) are directly paralleled by, if in fact not a metaphor for, the word. All are shown to be outgrowths of the commerce and communication that are essential to humanity. As Agata queries, "¿cuándo encontraré quien hable mi lenguaje?" (p. 138) ("when will I find someone who speaks my language?" p. 229). The entire novel might be explained as Agata's search (passive as it is) or expectant waiting (not unlike Snow White) for someone who speaks her language, for someone with whom she can trade words. Obviously, much of her search or quest is mental, but she nonetheless explores her past and scrutinizes her future for this partner in communication, while in the present she resorts to nature for this partner: "¡Con esos diferentes cuerpos [cumbres, árboles, etc.] . . . cuántas preguntas, quejas, desalientos, no había, aterida, murmurado!" (p. 16) ("Here [to the stardust sky, the hilltops, the forbidden trees, the very darkness] she had taken her questions, complaints, and disappointments," p. 119). Interestingly, nature can only be the present partner and, in this sense, can have no past or future—the past or future partner apparently must be human.

It is significant that, while any text is in fact a monologue which pretends to be or represent a dialogue, *Todo verdor* is more obviously and unequivocally monologue. There is never any meaningful two-way communication; there is just monologue after monologue as even the narrator himself continually lapses into a monologue, paradoxically based on the illusory *we*. As I have discussed in another place, the use of the first-person plural pronoun subsumes a conformity, a homogeneity among the *I* and the others implicitly included in that group of *we*.[12] By repeatedly utilizing the *we*, the narrator here negates even the fiction of the possibility of communication, for his use of the *we* implies that everyone in the group is identical (in some way at least), has the same opinion, and would express synonymous thoughts;[13] since he has just spoken for everyone—characters and readers alike—any dialogue or response (two-way communication) would be superfluous and repetitious. So the narrator (male) rattles on with his monologue which presumes to speak for everyone, controls language, and imposes a silence on the reader, which is not different from the one experienced by the characters. Although the narrator specifically describes Agata as "hermética" (p. 23) ("hermetic," p. 126), the fact is that every aspect of the text is closed upon itself, encircled by the monologue.

Nevertheless, Agata continues her quest for someone with whom she can communicate. When she temporarily finds that someone in Sotero, the text is quick to underline the linguistic attraction (in fact, the reader knows about him principally in this regard): "¡Qué voz tan extraña! Ella pensó que podría descansar oyéndola" (p. 102) ("What an unusual voice! She thought she could rest while hearing it," p. 196); "¿Por qué utilizaba él su mismo lenguaje, el de ella?" (p. 112) ("Why did he use her own language, her very own?" p. 205). Still, the right words are difficult to find, and (to use a metaphor borrowed from nature) silence continues to grow. In this sense, what is not verbalized is more important than what is said. In *La vorágine* Rivera used the metaphor of the jungle and declared "Los devoró la selva" ("The jungle devoured them"). In *Todo verdor*, although nature is affiliated with the silence which seems to grow between Nicanor and Agata, it is the silence itself, portrayed as a material substance, which is said to devour them: "Fué el monstruo de tan incalculable silencio lo que al fin debía devorarlos" (p. 49) ("It was the monster of incalculable silence which was to devour them in the end," p. 149). Notice, however, that although the destruction is now the silence rather than the jungle,[14] it is still presented as something corporeal, something external, and an entity at least indirectly related to nature, insofar as the silence itself is described as a monster, an animal or a wave (p. 48 [p. 149]). Again, the interconnection with *La vorágine* surges when the text (or Nicanor) says of Agata (in a manner not too distant from the way in which Cova articulated his wishes for a different Alicia): "Si hubiera sido menos orgullosa de alma, menos fría, imaginativa y presuntuosa" (p. 64) ("If only her soul had been less proud, not so cold, imaginative and presumptuous," pp. 163–64). What is significant, however, is that this if/then, contrary-to-fact sentence is never completed. That is, we are never told *how* Nicanor or the narrator thinks things would have been *if* Agata had been different, for the sentence concludes with a mere cliché: "otro gallo les cantara" ("everything could have been different"), suggesting, of course, that Nicanor does not concretely know what he wants or expects either. He only "knows" that "everything could have been different." Thus Nicanor like Agata is enmeshed in that fairy-tale, mythological world which would make the other the perfect complement to the self. And that perhaps is precisely the error of our protagonists—the thought that a perfect complement may exist in the other.

Finally, it appears that Nicanor's preconceptions and later resentment of Agata are based on two common beliefs. First, he clearly presumes (as does much of Western society) that the male of the species must always be strong, secure, "closed," and superior to the female (all just words, but words taken very seriously by both males and females). When he miscalculates the quantity of seed to sow and Agata tries to forewarn him of his error, this tenet is badly shaken as he is forced to doubt his own superiority and adequacy; and it is clear that the very foundations of the marriage are dependent upon this canon of supremacy. But what is most significant for this study is the second myth, which evolves ostensibly to counteract the destruction and toppling of the first myth. Agata had calculated well, Nicanor poorly, but neither the narrator nor Nicanor seems willing to give her credit for it. In spite of his empathy for the role of the woman in society, the narrator still seems reluctant to grant Agata even intellectual superiority, for her ascertainment is described as inexplicable. As the narrator states (presumably indirectly echoing Nicanor's thoughts), "*Emparentadas como están con la luna, ¿cómo pueden desconfiar de las mujeres, en su faz premonitoria y profética, los que no están emparentados más que con la realidad más inmediata?*" (pp. 49–50, emphasis added) ("How can those who are only related to the most immediate reality distrust women, *related as they are to the moon* in their premonitory and prophetic aspect?" p. 150, emphasis added).[15] Apparently, if one myth fails, the vacuum can simply be filled with new words and myths.

That woman is somehow mysteriously affiliated with the moon is a myth that has persisted through the ages (perhaps often perpetuated by woman herself).[16] While it is easy to understand how a primitive people might have developed and maintained such an illusion, it is enigmatical that it continues today. Its effect, however, whether intentional or not, is to deny Agata (and perhaps any other woman who falls victim to it) the credit for whatever wisdom and astuteness she may have displayed and in turn to help Nicanor (or the narrator) maintain, at least in part, his primacy over her. If Agata predicted accurately because of her obscure, dark, secret affiliation with the moon and nature, then that does not make her more sagacious than Nicanor, who, as the text affirms, is related only to the most immediate reality. But, the irony of this statement is not to be ignored— what is implicit is that Nicanor is tied to reality, while (on the contrary) Agata is akin to nature. But what is more "real," more a part of that "reality," than nature itself (or this abstract entity we call nature)? Thus, one must conclude that the second theory here (that of affiliation with the moon) is perpetuated in order to help support and substantiate the first hypothesis of male supremacy, since another very important aspect of that moon myth is ignored. According to the myth, the moon also grants fertility to her devotees, and thus Agata's infertility (if one is to accept the myth as literally as the narrator seems to) would negate her "moon connection."[17] In this respect, then, although her implicit affiliation with nature makes her in some ways more threatening to that precept of primacy, it also mitigates that menace, since the power is attributed to the supernatural and thus not ultimately controllable by either man or woman. The male cannot be held responsible for the omnipotence of nature, so if the female has some magical power with which nature (as if it were a conscious, intelligent being) has endowed her in some dark, obscure, and mysterious way, he cannot be expected to overcome it, for it is granted by the "gods." Nor can she be considered in any way superior, for she has not "earned" these powers nor are they truly hers but merely lent her until such time as the "gods" see fit to take them away. And so the myth goes and grows. Ultimately, then, as I have already suggested, what one finds is the same process observed in *Doña Bárbara* and *La vorágine* where the threats of "nature" (which, of course, were ultimately human and supplemental) were attributed to and imposed upon the woman.[18] Once again, the female becomes the scapegoat for the weaknesses within man.

It is imperative to recognize that, as already suggested, the source, if you will, of the use of nature as the principal and dominant metaphor in this particular novel stems from the book of Isaiah as does the title of the novel.[19] Even more important, perhaps, is the repeated attention Isaiah bestows upon the word or language, a leitmotif which is echoed in *Todo verdor* and linked to the presentation of both nature and the female. In fact, the main theme of both texts is language and/or its absence. In Isaiah there is an insistence on obedience, that is, on complying with the *words* of the father. But, already, the very expression, the "words of the father," underscores a recurrent metaphor of both texts, and before one continues this analysis of *Todo verdor* in relation to Isaiah, one must pause a moment to consider this metaphor, encountered so frequently in both works, which describes language or the word in terms of the family.

Obviously, the metaphor of the family is borrowed from the earlier books of the Bible where the word is God, the Father. Now, this traditional association between the word and God not only lends a particular strength to the power of the word to create (or destroy, as the case may be), but by uniting the word with the father, a certain masculine affinity is implied, and it is this underlying insinuation which the text develops.[20] It appears that in many of Mallea's novels the power of the word belongs specifically to the males. Certainly Mallea doubts the validity of this word and its ability to say anything meaningful, but he does seem to grant it primarily to the males; for example, both Agata's father and Mario Guillén *(Enemigos del alma)* can chatter on for hours without saying anything. And, while

Nicanor is described as taciturn, perhaps even more so than Agata, the latter is even more powerless and silent (wordless) than he.

The male's possession of the word is further emphasized (although perhaps unintentionally) in the narrative technique. Although the story is the tale of Agata, the narrator, like fairy-tale narrators, seldom confers the use of the word upon her; that is, she rarely "says" anything—the narrator expresses all for her. In fact, even at those moments when a fictionalized monologue (interior or not) might seem the most expedient and appropriate way to communicate to us what Agata is supposedly feeling, the narrator instead embarks on a monologue of his own, thus creating the problem to which I have already referred (note 15) of never allowing us to feel sure whether the words are to be attributed to him or to his character. Nevertheless, for the most part one must logically attribute the words to him (even on the fictional level) since if Agata were capable of understanding her emotions in such an articulate manner or of expressing herself thus, her problems with society and the people around her would be considerably ameliorated. Thus, in the most overt manner, the male controls the word within the text, and Agata is left to "talk" only to nature (p. 16).

Ultimately, however, it is not exclusively the father who is used as a metaphor for language, for at several points the words are also described as sons: "A los dos [a Nicanor y Agata] les costaban las palabras: madres tiránicas, sus entrañas no largaban fácilmente esos hijos" (p. 69; note that, again, it is the female, *madre*, who cannot issue the word) ("Words were difficult for both of them. The wombs of these words, like tyrannical mothers, did not give up their offspring easily," p. 168). Curiously, this son, like the crops, is not only the product of some type of commerce but at the same time ostensibly provides the commerce necessary for continued communication (that is, he is both the cause and the result): "Todo en la vida es comercio" (p. 49) ("Everything in life is commerce," p. 149); "todo es comercio" (p. 83) ("all is commerce," p. 180). In this manner, within *Todo verdor* both language and the production of offspring seem to be related to the notions of commerce and economy as found in "primitive" tribes and described by the structural anthropologists. In this sense, the twentieth-century values of production and marketing dominate.[21]

Now, if the word shares the characteristics of the son, then it too is a possession; that is, it belongs to the one who engenders it. Thus impersonal discourse, like the illegitimate son, belongs to no one and for that reason is either much more difficult to understand or meaningless inasmuch as one comprehends discourse (at least in part) in relationship to its producer, like Snow White who is reborn via the kiss of the prince and is his "dearest possession." Thus the son analogy on one level underlines the need for two interlocutors in order to produce meaningful discourse, while on another it points to the narrator's metaphorical self-sufficiency to produce the word, the son. There seems to be a similarity here between the primitive rites of passage as described by the anthropologists, the Adam and Eve story, and the Greek story of Athena. In each case, the gesture is a negation of the birth from woman and an affirmation of birth from man. The young primitives are "reborn" after their ritual period with the men, Eve was born from Adam's rib, Athena from Zeus's head, and Snow White is reborn via the kiss. But, once again, the entire employment of the family relationships as an analogy for linguistic relationships returns us to the text of Isaiah and the interconnection between nature and language.

Thus, returning to Isaiah, one also encounters there an expressed fear or credence that nature will punish mankind. While language and nature are separate (not one and the same), the biblical work states that the word can nevertheless control or destroy nature:

> A voice says, "Cry!"
>   And I said, "What shall I cry?"
> All flesh is grass,
>   and all its beauty is like the flower of the field.
> The grass withers, the flower fades,
>   when the breath of the Lord blows upon it;
>   surely the people is grass
> The grass withers, the flower fades;
>   but the word of our God will stand for ever.
>
> (Isa. 40.6–8)

Thus, all of nature is ephemeral, but the word is eternal and omnipotent. Throughout Isaiah in fact the message is that God, by means of nature, will punish mankind for its sins, for its refusal to comply with the word of God. If one accepts the text of *Todo verdor* as an extended metaphor based on the text of Isaiah, as suggested by Ghiano, then one must ask what sin has been committed in the novel.[22] In Isaiah the destruction of nature is a celestial retribution for the sins committed against God. But what sins have Agata and Nicanor committed? Perhaps we are meant to see their wrong-doing as purely linguistic, for the only apparent transgression they have committed is to change the name of the ranch from *Las flores* to *Agata*. Now, *Las flores* had been a very productive area before their arrival and before the name change. As Nicanor announced his intentions to change the name, a neighbor responded negatively: "No se cambia nunca de nombre a un establecimiento, a una nave. . . . 'Eso no se hace, compañero. . . . No se hace'" (p. 47) ("The name of an establishment or a ship should never be changed. . . . 'Those things are just not done, my friend. . . . They are not done,'" p. 148). Are we to believe then that the change of name from *Las flores*, with all its productive, cheery, vegetable connotations, to *Agata*, with all its cold, mineral connotations, was the instrument of the disaster?

Certainly, Nicanor had not shown the implied respect owed the venerability of the word, the logos.

The verses from Isaiah further bring to mind the repetitions of the descriptions of the wind in *Todo verdor* (and indeed in many of Mallea's novels). The wind (breath of God) continually whips the terrain until all the green is turned to white. The use of the color white here is particularly interesting since traditionally one thinks of green things dying to become brown, or perhaps yellow. That Mallea chooses the color white and is so insistent upon it is clearly significant. Perhaps no color (contrary to the suggestion of the title) dominates the novel more than white. I have already quoted the opening paragraph and noted that as a child Agata lived in Ingeniero White near Bahia Blanca. Now, traditionally, white is a color used in literature and art to represent what is pure, virginal, and untouched, but often underlying this virginal state is the promise of future fertility or productivity. (The prime example would be Snow White.) Thus the virginal maiden is dressed in white, but paradoxically the white not only symbolizes her purity of today but at the same time, her future motherhood, the promise of fertility. Similarly, the white part of the artist's canvas is that part upon which nothing has yet been painted, but upon which much could be painted. Thus white has generally suggested virginity, but a virginity fraught with imminent fecundity.

Nevertheless, in the novel by Mallea, the color white seems to take on quite the opposite connotations. White here is used to symbolize that which is already dead, that which has already produced whatever it is to produce and is now barren wasteland. Thus, white here implies death, drought, destruction—the white land was once productive but is no more. The comprehension of the implication of the color then becomes a function of time and directly related to the notion of language. As with the blank sheet of paper, before anything is written on it, we have the promise of words and worlds which can be created on that piece of paper; thus, with an eye to the future, the white symbolizes purity and absence in the present but fertility and production in the future. Later, however, once something has been produced and then erased (symbolically slain, destroyed), the whiteness then connotes quite the opposite; the white which remains after erasure signals death, destruction, absence. This white, of course, looks to the past and the paradise or production that was (or might have been), but, in both cases the blankness, the absence on the white page are not only related to language but are in fact metaphors for silence. In this sense, then, the silence is not only overtly a predominant theme in *Todo verdor*, but more subtly one might say that the entire novel is structured around this silence, this absence of the word, this present which simultaneously looks forward and backward.

It is the very concept of time which in fact maintains a curious position in *Todo verdor*. Part I of the novel encompasses roughly thirty-five years of

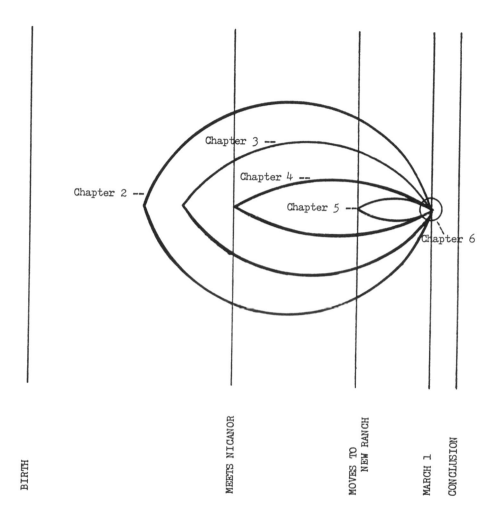

Agata's life, while Part II encompasses but a few months. Chapters 1 through 6 of Part I are all narrated on March 1; that is, all that happens in the novel during these chapters is a *mise en scène* which takes place only in Agata's mind as she remembers earlier periods (as presented to the reader by the omniscient narrator). Chapters 2 through 6, in fact, might be diagrammed as successively smaller circles, all returning to the same point of reference, March 1. Chapter 2 goes all the way back to her childhood before returning to March 1, while Chapter 6 goes back only a few months before returning to March 1.

Of course, the diagram is necessarily an oversimplification of the time structure of the novel. What one finds is an intricate intermingling of temporal reference points; in much of the novel, past, present, and future are interwoven in such a way as to continually demonstrate and emphasize their interdependence. In Part I Agata looks back to the past, remembers "earlier" times, and remembers herself looking ahead to a future which is now either present or already past. In Part II one encounters what might be considered the other side of the coin; that is, Agata looks ahead, imagines herself in the future, looking back on her life that was, on her past, but a past which is now only present. It is not irrelevant that Mallea has chosen March 1 as the focus date for Part I. March 1 psychologically connotes the beginning of autumn for those south of the equator, and becomes one more metaphor of nature, which applies nicely to Agata's life. Thus the principal action of Part I extends from the beginning of autumn through the worst of winter, ending in early August with Nicanor's death, and her metaphoric death. In a similar manner, Part II, while less carefully documented with dates, certainly implies that Agata arrived in Bahia Blanca in the spring and met Sotero in late summer. Her relationship with Sotero ends, predictably, in the fall, and the reader is left never knowing if her new symbolic death (insanity) will result in another rebirth (although there seems to be no indication that such will be the case).[23] Of course, ultimately, whether the movement in time is forward or backward, it is basically the same voyage, a voyage in search of the lost or future paradise (a utopia of language, communication, and "commerce") but a "voyage" which must necessarily fail and become "este viaje del hombre a su abismo, al yacimiento casi inhumano del ser, ese viaje de vuelta a la soledad original de la que todos venimos" (p. 54) ("this journey of Man toward his abyss, toward the almost inhuman source of his being, that return journey to the original solitude from which we all spring," p. 155). And one must wonder if Agata's problems do not stem from her inability to recognize the continuity of things.[24] Like Roquentin of *La nausée*, many of the characters I have been examining, and the typical fairy-tale character, she demonstrates a definite propensity to see life as a series of beginnings and endings rather than as a continuum. When she does recognize the continuum, she can see it only as tedium and must resort to complete alienation from it.

The color white, then, of which I have spoken, perhaps attains its greatest significance in the blank page (*página en blanco*). While all texts necessarily begin and end with a blank page, *Todo verdor*, in addition, is centered around a blank page—and in many ways, this blank page is the most meaningful of the text. In the Espasa-Calpe edition, Parts I and II are separated by a blank page, without a number, but which would be page 82. In the Sudamericana edition of 1969 (1st edition, 1947), that blank page is 106. In neither edition is the blank page the exact, physical center of the text although since it separates the two parts, it might be considered a structural, temporal center. Paradoxically, the blank page is meaningful to the extent that it reflects the meaninglessness of Agata's life. Within the fiction, the blank page represents a passage in time: that period between August 6 when Nicanor dies and the beginning of Agata's new life in Part II. This blank, this whiteness, represents a temporal period which includes both a death and a rebirth as well as the space in between them (that space of presumable nothingness). This structuring around a blank space brings to mind one of Juan Ramón Jiménez's poems on adolescence. Entitled "El adolescente," the poem, too, is structured around a blank space, the accentuated space between two stanzas. In the first stanza the young boy is preparing for his first journey away from the maternal hearth; in the second (not unlike Efraín as already discussed) he is already a young man, looking back on what he has lost. Thus, by means of the blank space, Jiménez, too, signals a metaphoric death (of the boy) and his subsequent rebirth (as the young man). What is particularly pertinent is that in both the poem and *Todo verdor,* the death and ensuing rebirth are the most significant aspects of the texts and the most fertile moments, and yet they are the moments left unexpressed, unverbalized, only insinuated. Their meaning is totally dependent upon the reader, upon the reader's ability to supplement. In a sense, it is the reader who "writes" this part of the text, filling it with his own words and interpretations, just as he "writes" Snow White's "ever after." In many ways, then, the silence is not only the main theme of *Todo verdor,* but the text itself is structured around this silence, this blank space, and lack of words—words which must be added by the reader.

One might carry the metaphor of the blank page one step further and note that Agata's life is indeed a blank page; that is, the structural center of the text reflects her essence. Her fictional life is an emptiness which needs to be filled with meaningful words, and the trajectory of the text is perhaps the journey in search of the words (again, the utopia) to fill this page. Like the blank page, Agata is full of potential but ultimately empty because those words never issue forth. But the metaphor is limited, for while the words cannot come from the blank page itself (they must come from outside the page, be added to or supplemented upon the page), the words might come from Agata, although she definitely does not recognize this and seems to insist they come from a male. (Obviously, it is only within the fiction that Agata can fill the blank pages. In fact, because of her status as a fictional entity, in truth those words must come from the outside—the author; in a very real sense any fictional character is necessarily a blank page with words imposed from the outside. Nevertheless, for the moment I shall consider the text from within the fiction.) And, within that fiction, Agata expects the words and her happiness which should result from them to be delivered to her from the outside (preferably from a male); she expects her blank page to be filled with someone else's words, to be written by someone else, and accepts the notion that the words are necessarily masculine. Thus, Agata herself accepts the social myth that her lines, and consequently the role she will play, will be written by the resident male. The result is that Agata is portrayed as the not uncommon, but all too tragic, figure of the female who expects her happiness, in effect her very existence and *raison d'être*, to come from the outside rather than from within, who expects a male to enter her life and produce those words, those circumstances, which will give her cause to exist. (And, on another level that is precisely what has occurred inasmuch as she is the product of a male author.) In this sense she is again in every way the fairy-tale princess. The true problem, within the fiction, is that she accepts herself as a tabula rasa and forgets that the blank page is only a metaphor.

It is only toward the conclusion of the novel that Agata finally seems to recognize the futility of these words she has esteemed so highly and accept that they are as meaningless and empty as the blank page itself. In fact, one might understand the movement of the text as a movement from a type of blind faith in the ability of the word to communicate, to fill in blank spaces and create relationships, toward the recognition of the futility of the word and its inability to create anything but surfaces, pretenses, fictions, and partial truths. As the text notes, "¿Para qué sirven las palabras? Con ellas en el orden humano, uno no explica nada, todo se confunde y se empeora. ¡Pobre del que no traiga en su silencio un idioma!" (p. 156) ("What were words for? With them, by human laws, one could explain nothing, everything became more and more confused. Poor creature, the one who couldn't bring a language into her silence!" p. 245).

The complex and curious function (or paradoxical nonfunction) of the word is epitomized in the mythology which surges up around Agata during her life in the city. It appears that the myths and rumors which surround her grow as a result of her silence, her nonverbal presence. That is, because she is silent, others proffer words to try to fill the gap left by her silence, but since those words are founded on nothing (they are without referent), they must create only partial truths and, subsequently, myths. The words pour forth to fill in the lack of knowledge but can do so only imperfectly and only falsely. The words themselves, then, become empty repositories, as empty as the spaces they attempt to fill. Thus, at the beginning of the novel Agata had demonstrated an innocent belief in the powers of language, a belief which is not unlike that of the children with whom she felt such an affinity, but the conclusion of the novel underscores the discovery that neither language nor the children were as perfect, pure, and innocent as she had previously believed. In fact, the children, whom she had earlier viewed as her salvation, prove themselves her enemy.

Thus the blank page around which *Todo verdor* is centered depends, like any blank page, upon the temporal stance for its connotation. Looking ahead, it promises new life, rebirth, the imposition of words on the page; looking back, it reflects death, erasure, absence. In effect, the antithetic allusions to both pregnant potential and preterit death are characteristic of many other aspects of the text in addition to the blank page. These two apparently oppositional concepts are already implicit in the very title: *Todo verdor perecerá*. The juxtaposition of the words *verdor* and *perecerá* already suggests this antithesis, inasmuch as one traditionally views the color green as the color of fertility and hope or potential, while the word *perecerá* negates this potential, hope, or fertility. Similarly, the very word *perecerá* implies both qualities: the quality of death, destruction, is latent in the signification of the verb, while the quality of future expectation is implied by the use of the future tense of the verb.

But, most important to my topic, the very concept of women, within the mythology in which they are presented, also carries both of these dialectical opposites. In this particular text, everything holds both potential and destruction for Agata: marriage, a new life, the word. In general, the very concept of female holds these same qualities too: fertile potential and death, for the female is traditionally perceived as both the mother and the destroyer, the good (virgin) and the evil (Eve) (see Diner's discussion of black and white egg mothers, in *Mothers and Amazons*). But these myths, like everything else in *Todo verdor* are based on words imposed from the outside, and the creation of the myth is the result of supplementation by the other. Once again, the true dilemma arises when the woman, herself, believes and accepts these myths and thus is left mute.

Thus the entire ironic position of any discourse is underlined in the conclusion of the novel, and one discovers throughout the novel that, contrary to the popular saying, silence is not golden; it is cold, hard, blank, and white, but the word offers little improvement. As the text openly destroys one folk saying, it forces the reader perhaps to reconsider the validity of other "folk truths" (and many of our "truths" about women come from folk "wisdom" and old sayings). Like *María*, *Todo verdor* ends with a monument with the printed message: "Ego sum via, veritas et vita"—I am the way, the truth, and the life. But the *I* is without a referent, and one is never quite sure if the narrator means it to refer to God (the father), the church, or the word. In any case, the text concludes with silence, darkness, and a blank page, a setting which makes one think ahead several decades to the publication of José Donoso's *Tres novelitas burguesas*.[25] But, the white of the page absorbs nothing; it reflects all, and in and of itself is sterile. Nevertheless, it is this tabula rasa on which the reader can become writer, write his own conclusion, and make the page fertile (veracious or fairy-tale) by means of his supplementation. But, Agata will die apparently without having understood where the words came from, without having been able to produce her own linguistic world, and thus without having broken out of the fairy-tale realm.[26]

4

Voices from Beyond: Women, Death, and Sacrifice in the Works of Carlos Fuentes and Juan Rulfo

WITH the 1955 publication of *Pedro Páramo* by Juan Rulfo (Mexico, b. 1918) and the 1962 publication of *La muerte de Artemio Cruz* by Carlos Fuentes (Mexico, b. 1929), many of the topics already discussed can be found juxtaposed in the same novels.[1] *Pedro Páramo* and *Artemio Cruz* combine *María*'s preoccupation with language and the quest to return to origins via that language with *Doña Bárbara*'s treatment of rural life lorded over by the cacique. Similarly, in both one finds *La vorágine*'s labyrinth of prose and unreliable narrators coupled with a presentation of the solitude of nonconformity and the leitmotifs of drought, death, and rain, not unlike that of *Todo verdor perecerá*.

Both novels are dominated by voices that create an aura of mystery and death and reflect a thematic fascination on the part of the narrators. Artemio Cruz is dying while Pedro Páramo enters the world of the dead. The protagonists' preoccupation with death motivates their attempts to return to origins and repeat or relive that which was, much as it inspires the discourse itself. Significantly, in both, these mysterious voices, the preoccupation with death, and the desire to return to origins are intricately tied to the female characters as they were in the Eve story.

As popularly presented, Eve caused the expulsion of mankind from the Garden, and our efforts ever since have been directed at compensating for this loss and/or endeavoring to find a means of returning to that paradise lost. Furthermore, as the Fall is presented to us in Book 3 of Genesis, and as we have popularly come to understand it, Eve is directly responsible for the existence of death in the world. God had said, " 'You shall not eat of the fruit of the tree which is in the midst of the garden, neither shall you touch it, *lest you die*' " (Gen. 3.3, emphasis added). According to the story, both she and Adam did eat of the tree, with the result that she was condemned to pain in childbirth and both were destined to return to dust, that is, die. In our mythic structure, then, death was not a possibility before the female's treachery. Thus, by inference the female is intricately related to both death and the language used to describe it, as I shall demonstrate in these two novels.

If one thinks of literature as a reflection of reality (a dubious premise at best), then one accepts as an implicit accord between the reader and the author that the former will believe what the latter posits as long as it resembles reality as the former knows it. In accordance with this pact, then, the story must be presented in the first or third person, as the biblical story is, and it must be narrated in the past tense, since if the authenticity of the referent is a given, obviously the tale cannot be told unless the event has already occurred. On the other hand, the use of the second-person pronoun in the present or future tense, as proposed by both these Mexican authors, repudiates the mythology of verity and authenticity which surrounds literature and the printed word.[2] It negates the implicit pact to which I have referred and disallows the possibility or necessity of a literal, verifiable referent. From the moment that one seriously acknowledges the loss of the referent or concedes the nonexistence of that referent, one writes in the present or future tense and in the second person in order to avoid the old traps into which we so easily fall, as well as to underscore the fact that reality, if one can even talk about reality, exists only within the work; that is, the text is its own reality, its own referent. At the same time, since the *tú* cannot exist without the *yo*, the latter creates the former while creating itself, causing the narrator to subtly reaffirm his own fictionality. Paradoxically, because the use of the future tense in conjunction with the *tú* (particularly in the case of *Artemio Cruz* and *Aura*) seems to function as a mandate, as if a god or a king were speaking to a subject and commanding him, the *tú* in each of the novels, underlines a certain authority on the part of the *yo* (even though the reader may not know who or what this *yo* is) while it undermines that same authority insofar as it is a self-appointed sovereignty.[3] Again, this question of authority will lead to the female.[4]

Critics have differed greatly in their interpretations of *Pedro Páramo*. What all do agree upon is that the text is composed of a series of first-person narrations and that while the identity of the narrators is not always apparent on the first reading, the narrator is never anonymous; there are always sufficient markers and details for the reader to be able to name him on the second or third reading. As in *Artemio Cruz*, the sections in *Pedro Páramo* are not ordered chronologically, and the reader is left to fit the pieces together. Contrary to much of the criticism and scholarship which has been dedicated to this novel, I would suggest that perhaps the identification of places, characters, dates, and the chronological ordering of events is not vitally important for an analysis of the text. This zeal for classification and ordering has led critics to attempt to see the novel as a history of Mexico and the Mexican people or to affix an extratextual date to each of the events of the novel.[5] Had the author himself found these "facts" of significance, clearly he would have written or structured the text in such a way as to be sure that such extratextual events and places were patent and/or more accessible to the reader. I propose, then, that pinpointing these "facts" is not essential to our comprehension of the message of the text; indeed, the implication of the text as reflected in the narrative structure itself is precisely that such "facts" are not readily accessible nor determinable, inside or outside of the novel. Bell, in fact, validly notes that Juan Preciado went to Comala essentially to test his preconceived notions about his father and that in doing so he descends from the land of reality to the land of illusion.[6] I would add only that the latter is populated, significantly, by women.

What one does find, on the other hand, is a text that is obsessed with voices, with rumors, with second-hand discourse, none of which, as I shall show, is particularly reliable. If one examines the text carefully, one finds that there are basically four varieties of discourse within the novel. There is direct discourse; that is, discourse without quotation marks directed toward a *you* who is often implicit rather than explicit and who is presumably the reader. Such discourse implies a quality of the present since, although the *énoncé* is necessarily past, the *énonciation* seems to be occurring in the present. The novel opens with just this type of discourse: "Vine a Comala" (p. 7) ("I came to Comala," p. 1). As one later discovers, this section of the novel is narrated by Juan Preciado, as are many of the segments of the first half of the novel, but it is never quite clear who is narrating the second half of the novel and telling all that Juan could not know about Pedro Páramo.

The second type of discourse is also direct, set off by dashes, but the *you* is not the reader.[7] This discourse is first found when Juan quotes his mother: "—No vayas a pedirle nada" (p. 7) ("—Don't ask him for anything," p. 1), and implies greater temporal distance than does the first type. It is overtly presented as repetition, as something which happened previously; in fact, the quotaton cited is introduced by "Todavía antes me había dicho" (p. 7) ("Before that she told me," p. 1), a statement which, because of the pluperfect tense in the original Spanish, situates the *énonciation* in the somewhat remote past.

The other two structures of discourse have less clear functions and significance. At times one finds quotations which use quotation marks rather than dashes, a structure which obviously implies discourse of a different status: "Hubiera querido decirle: 'Te equivocaste de domicilio' " (p. 12) ("I wanted to tell her, 'You made a mistake,' " p. 6), while at other times one finds italicized discourse enclosed in quotation marks: "El camino subía y bajaba; *'sube o baja según se va o se viene'* " (p. 8) ("the road went up and down, up and down. They say 'a road goes up or down depending,' " pp. 1–2). If one judges by the two bits quoted here, the first type of discourse would appear to be imagined conversation which never took place (what he would have liked to have told her, but, as the past subjunctive implies, did not tell her) and the second, the italicized quotations, would appear to represent the unverbalized memories of Juan— memories of what his mother said to him, memories that he "hears" in his mind, but which he chooses not to articulate to the *you*. Nevertheless, the intermingling of these four varieties of discourse results in a lack of differentiation to any but the most careful reader. Rulfo has clearly intended that his reader should perceive the differences in these enunciations (otherwise he would not have been so careful about providing visual markers), but I suspect that very few of his readers have noted them, probably because all ultimately exist on the level of printed text. The result, then, is a lack of discrimination on the part of the reader/listener (which I suspect is also one of the messages of the text), and the remaining composite of enunciations parallels our "real world" insofar as we receive discourse where all levels of "Truth," reliability, and authority mingle and are accepted as analogous, and where discourse functions in a quasi-religious manner, as I shall discuss later.

Thus, one finds that the question of authority, as underlined by the very form of the discourse, enters the texts early. In *Pedro Páramo*, Juan states, "Vine a Comala porque me *dijeron* que acá vivía mi padre, un tal Pedro Páramo" (p. 7, emphasis added) ("I came to Comala because [*they told me*] that my father, a certain Pedro Páramo, was living here," p. 1, emphasis added). *They* told him that his father lived here: *they*—that vague pronoun which seems to include everyone as a referent (since the specific referents are not stipulated) and which, at first glance, inevitably lends a tone of credibility (if everyone says so, it must be so). Implied is a certain Truth. But, the next sentence derogates this authority while reinforcing it from a different source: "Mi madre me lo *dijo*" (again emphasis added) ("My mother told me so"). *They* has suddenly been converted into *my mother*. The potential authority of the mother, who has functioned as both mother and father for Juan, is patent. The possibility exists that Juan, in fact, uses the plural pronoun to imply just this double function of his mother. Now that his mother is dead, he seeks the father, the other form of sovereignty.

At the same time, however, the use of the plural third-person pronoun reflects a gesture we have seen already in *Doña Bárbara*, as well as the propensity of this entire novel. It is a gesture which is often repeated in our everyday life, a mythic gesture, for, as Elizabeth Janeway has observed, myth is an expression of desire—it substitutes for action a will to believe that what one desires does exist (pp. 27–28). In *Doña Bárbara* we watched rumors grow as "they" said; we saw entire mythologies which had grown up around doña Bárbara—folklore (as I demonstrated) with little basis in fact but which protected (psychologically at least) the mythmakers, the male ruling class. In *Pedro Páramo* one witnesses the very creation of those

rumors (myths). Juan's mother has told him a single fact—that Pedro
Páramo lives in Comala. What begins as a simple statement of one being's
experience or perception of that experience is elaborated, adorned, supplemented, and converted into a universal Truth.

Significantly, the authority of this parental discourse is emphasized by
the circumstances of the mother's discourse. The mother's words are always presented in quotation marks, and the addressee is always Juan
himself. The quotation marks signal the authority of the mother (one generally does not bother to quote those whose ideas are valueless).
Significantly, however, the discourse of the mother, as demonstrated particularly in the first segment, is strangely abstract—a vagueness which,
when carefully considered, negates the very authority the discourse seems
to affirm. Her speech is full of indeterminateness, obscure references: "un
tal Pedro Páramo" (p. 7); "Se llama de este modo y de este otro" (p. 7);
"Exígele lo nuestro" (p. 7; she does not specify what *lo nuestro* is); "*sube o
baja según se va o se viene*" (p. 8) ("a certain Pedro Páramo," p. 1; ["He calls
himself this or that"], p. 7, Spanish; "[Ask] for what he should have given
me," p. 1, she does not specify what; "a road goes up or down depending
on whether you're coming or going," pp. 1–2). What one notes, then, is an
overt contrast between the specific, which lends authority, veracity, or
trustworthiness to the discourse, and the vague, which evokes fallibility
and a dreamlike quality in the text. In fact, Juan himself notes, "comencé a
llenarme de sueños, a darle vuelo a las ilusiones. Y de este modo se me fue
formando un mundo alrededor de la esperanza" (p. 7) ("I couldn't stop
thinking and even dreaming about it, and building a whole world around
that Pedro Páramo," p. 1).

Thus the language functions on a quasi-religious or quasi-mythic level.[8]
Any religion is based on a hierarchal structure. At the top of that structure
is the god, who is never seen but whose "voice" is heard by a select few—
the prophets. The prophets link this world with that world. But prophets
are mortal and must eventually leave this world to go on to the other. After
their passing, however, their words (which are often repetitions of the
words of the god) remain and are brought to us by their disciples and
priests,[9] whose major functions include quoting to us, repeating the
"words of God." The result, then, is a series of men and their subsequent
discourses which are placed at varying degrees of distance from the de-
votee. The god and the prophet are already absent or dead, passed on into
that "other world." The disciple or priest may be physically present, but
he, too, is at a distance from the populace; he may perform the rites before
the eyes of the devotees, but he always does so at a significant physical
distance, which usually includes some means of elevation. What remain
finally are memories or symbols (if the discourse is written), repetitions of
words, quotations of quotations, echoes, rumors, which take on increasingly greater authority.

Clearly, the hierarchy of discourse in *Pedro Páramo* is parallel. Dolores, the absent one, is not present in the text but her "voice" is heard by Juan and by the other characters who relate her words to us. Her "distance" from us and, indeed, from Juan himself, is as undeniable as the distance of all the characters from Pedro Páramo (another god?) in one direction and us in the other. As Juan implies in the passage cited above, his mother's voice created a whole world of dreams (heaven) and her voice, like that of any prophet or celestial messenger, was "secreta, casi apagada" (p. 8) ("soft and secret, almost a whisper," p. 2). It would appear then that mere words alone can resurrect almost anything.

Similarly, *La muerte de Artemio Cruz* is a conglomerate of voices that reflect, refract, and fragment the main character—refraction and fragmentation which are visually portrayed in the opening pages:[10] "abro el ojo derecho y lo veo reflejado en las incrustaciones de vidrio de una bolsa de mujer. . . . Soy este viejo con las facciones partidas por los cuadros desiguales del vidrio. Soy este ojo. . . . Soy esta nariz. . . . Soy estos pómulos. . . . Soy esta mueca." (p. 9) ("I . . . open my right eye and see it reflected in the squares of silvered glass that encrust a woman's purse. I am this . . . old man with his face reflected in pieces by different-sized squares of glass: I am this eye. . . . I am this nose. . . . I am these cheeks. . . . [I am this] grimace," p. 4). The "voices" are superficially divided into three formats, but each of the three is further subdivided to encompass several other forms. The first form one encounters is a first-person narration in the present tense. The narrator is the title character, Artemio Cruz, who is dying. In these sections we are presented the somewhat disjointed internal monologues of a dying man. These monologues are furnished without any identifying punctuation and are alternated with other forms of discourse: his statements directed to those who accompany him in his final hours and which center principally on a request to have a window opened and fragments from past conversations which had been recorded and are being played back. His comments to those who accompany him and their responses are indicated by dashes, while the recorded discourse is distinguished by means of quotation marks plus dashes—punctuation which by its own duplication draws attention to the status of the discourse as repetition. Furthermore, one finds in these first-person segments an interesting juxtaposition of forms of rhetoric. For example, the business conversations of the tape (with all the rhetoric appropriate to this form of language) are juxtaposed with the religious rhetoric of the priest who is trying to persuade Artemio to confess so that his soul will be saved.

The second format employed in the novel is the second-person familiar in the future tense. Artemio is the *tú* being spoken to, but the identity of the *yo* addressing him is never completely clear; presumably it is one of Artemio's alter egos. In these segments there are no quotation marks, and the rules of punctuation and capitalization are often ignored. The voice is omniscient and authoritative. So authoritative, in fact, that the future tense again seems to function as a command rather than as a temporal marker.

The third format in this novel is the more traditional third-person discourse in the past tense; these segments are flashbacks to significant moments in Artemio's life and are presented with descriptions of the situation and his or other characters' reactions (both overt and covert) as well as past dialogues (marked by dashes) and past internal monologues (marked by quotation marks). Significantly, the past, internal monologues are marked by only one set of quotation marks even when they are memories of prior quotations, that is, citations of quotations. Each of these segments is carefully marked as to its date, and analysis of the dates reveals significantly that the only month not included is March, and the only day of the week omitted is Monday. The missing Monday, of course, would imply the beginning of a new week, while March would evoke the beginning of spring, rebirth, a new cycle. In total, there are thirteen first-person narrations, thirteen second-person narrations, and twelve third-person narrations. Since in each of the third-person narrations Artemio regresses, while in the second-person he moves toward his death, we are no doubt meant to understand the missing, final third-person narration, which should have followed the thirteenth second-person narration, as his birth; the circle is "complete," and he returns to origins, the womb, at the same time as he moves ahead to death—death and birth are now one. Thus the narrative structure implicates the female in the issue of death. If the missing third-person narration is indeed Artemio's return to the womb, then the book is framed between women. The first segment is marked by the presence of Catalina and Teresa, Artemio's wife and daughter, who according to him are anxiously awaiting his death. Similarly, the missing segment would be marked by the presence of his mother, to whose womb he metaphorically returns in death.

This tie between the women and death is dramatized perhaps even more startlingly in *Pedro Páramo.* In the opening discourse, the *you* appears to be the reader, and the narrator, as mentioned, is Juan Preciado. One later discovers surprisingly that the *you* is not the reader at all, as one had believed, but rather Dorotea, a dead woman who shares a grave with Juan, as if at last she had found the son she never had. Needless to say, the effect of this discovery is as disconcerting as it is significant. If his audience, Dorotea, is dead, then, of course, as we are to learn, he is too. Furthermore, how can we, as readers, "hear" words from beyond the grave. Are we also dead? And how are we, as readers, to react to the discourse of already dead characters?

Obviously, the relevance of death here is multiple and female-oriented insofar as the females to whom he speaks and who speak to him are all dead.[11] One might think of the text as a series of "memories" which are necessarily always already dead even within the fiction. As "alive" as they might seem, memories belong to the past, and although while narrating them one may *seem* to relive them, one never truly can. As in *María*, the actual events or people are always absent; it is merely language which appears to revive them. (Such, of course, is quite precisely the case in *Aura* where Consuelo, with the help of Felipe, has the power to conjure up the past. The direct and immediate link between this necromancy and language is underscored by the fact that Felipe is by profession a historian, an editor, a translator—that is, one who works with language and words [much like Adam, whose task in the world was also linguistic since he was charged with naming all creatures], creates, and re-creates by means of those words, vitalizes the already extinct. In fact, Felipe's specific duty within the text is to "complete" the memories of General Llorente. Consuelo says of Llorente, "Murió hace sesenta años, señor. Son sus memorias *inconclusas*. Deben ser completadas" [pp. 15–16, my emphasis] ["He died seventy years ago, sir. They are his *unfinished* memoirs. They must be completed."] And, is this not what each of the protagonists attempts to do—complete the memories?)

But one must not lose sight of the metaphor so casually employed here: life/death. One might go so far as to say that memories, in effect, because they belong to language, always necessarily maintain an intermediary position, as do these literary characters (especially as presented in these texts), between the metaphoric extremes, life and death, for they are never truly alive or truly dead. Life and death are simply convenient, conventional metaphors we have borrowed from nature and have imposed on these memories, forgetting that they are metaphoric classifications. Such is precisely the case in both *Pedro Páramo* and *Artemio Cruz*. Each of the narrators via the narrative process attempts to relive the past, to make what is past present. Their endeavors can only be partially successful, for, although Pedro Páramo can finally make Susana San Juan physically present again (at least the first time), he cannot revive her feelings toward him (if, indeed, they ever existed and are not mere mental chimeras) nor those happy, youthful moments they spent together. In effect, the ultimate irony which is underscored by the narrative structure is that the narration itself rather than resuscitating anything merely effectuates or reflects a movement which metaphorically advances further and further into "death." That is, the narrative structures themselves take us from "life" to "death" insofar as Artemio's discourse ends with his death, as does Juan Preciado's. At the same time the novelistic discourse of *Pedro Páramo* ends very specifically with the death of Pedro Páramo himself. On both a figurative and a literal level, then, it is language which "kills" these protagonists for as Juan insists, "Me mataron los murmullos" (p. 62) (" 'It was the voices that killed me,' " p. 56), voices which all issued, significantly, from women, a fact which unfortunately suggests that the demise of the narrators is due precisely to these voices, this dream world created by the enunciations of the females.

It is, of course, only logical that narrations such as these, specifically concerned with the contestation of the mimetic principle, should all offer narrators who are dead. Julia Kristeva has very ably shown that, linguistically, any narrative structures itself around the act of addressing the other and that at the origin of narration, that is, at the moment the author appears, we encounter death (p. 82). I would suggest that Kristeva's theory is equally viable when we speak of fictitious authors (or narrators) as I do here.[12] Again, it would appear that this "death" may well be the demise of authority, since the "word" in each case has been turned over to the other, whose authority can never be validated or judged within the context of the fiction, and since the level of discourse—that is, the status of the author (authority) of the various presentations—is nearly impossible to ascertain.

Furthermore, the stance of the characters of *Pedro Páramo* reminds one of the position of all characters (again halfway between "life" and "death," if one must insist on imposing this metaphor). Because we willingly suspend our disbelief as we enter the novel, we tend to think of characters as living beings, or at the very least, as verbal representations whose referents are living beings. Rulfo's narrators like Fuentes's (particularly in *Aura*) remind us that they are neither. Even Artemio Cruz maintains an intermediary position within his fiction since he is neither "here" nor "there." Obviously, one of the main purposes of each novel is to underline this "unreality," to place in doubt the process whereby we receive our "knowledge," and to cause us to mistrust our perceptions of that "reality."[13]

Significantly, authority in Western tradition and literature has tended to be male. As I pointed out in the introduction, males have generally written both the sacred and the secular books and laws. Similarly, much of the division in these novels between life and death, reality and fantasy, are male/female–oriented divisions. The epigraph of *Aura* quite accurately reflects the popular beliefs of society and the initial stance of the novels:

> El hombre caza y lucha. La mujer intriga y sueña; es la madre de la fantasía, de los dioses. Posee la segunda visión, las alas que le permiten volar hacia el infinito del deseo y de la imaginación.... Los dioses son como los hombres: nacen y mueren sobre el pecho de una mujer...

> (The man hunts and fights. The woman plots and dreams: she is the mother of fantasy, of the gods. She possesses a second vision, the wings which permit her to fly toward the extreme limits of desire and imagination.... The gods are like men: they are born and die on a woman's breast...)

One is, then, led to consider the possibility that the whole "female" problem in literature is ultimately a problem of authority, as these male narrators seem to want to divide the world neatly into bipolar concepts—Life/

Death, Reality/Dream, Male/Female, Authority/Impotence—and, within these novels at any rate, the females seem to oppose these divisions and cause them to merge.[14]

The question of female authority and the lack thereof is poignantly dramatized in both novels. Juan Preciado's mother had commanded, "No dejes de ir a visitarlo" (p. 7) and "Exígele lo nuestro" ("Be sure you go and visit him", p. 1, and ["Demand what is ours"], p. 7, Spanish), and Juan attempted to do both, but everything that his mother, potential source of authority, had told him proved to be unreliable. Thus, her authority is simultaneously affirmed (Juan did as he was told) and undermined. Her world seems to be a dream world of the dead since she had created a world, which as I pointed out earlier, existed only linguistically, even within the fiction. Similarly, another early scene in *Pedro Páramo*, in which the protagonist is Pedro as a boy, shows the female as the object of desire as well as the authority which will thwart that desire.[15] In this scene (reminiscent of Joyce's *Ulysses*), Pedro is in the *excusado* thinking of Susana when his mother brings him sharply back to what one might erroneously label "reality" by growling, "Si sigues allí va a salir una culebra y te va a morder" (p. 16) ("If you stay there, a snake'll come and bite you", p. 9). Clearly, this statement, like everything else in *Pedro Páramo*, has been very carefully phrased for the symbolical and mythical powers of the word.[16] Thus, as presented in the two texts, the mother figure has the power to mandate the actions of the male child and coerce him into doing what he does not wish to do. Pedro clearly does not want to come out and does not until the order is repeated—"Te he dicho que te salgas del excusado" (p. 16) ("I told you to come out of the toilet," p. 10)—and Juan, it appears, had no particular desire to go to Comala for he promised only because "ella estaba por morirse y yo en un plan de prometerlo todo. . . . Entonces no pude hacer otra cosa sino decirle que así lo haría" (p. 7) ("she was dying and I was in the mood to promise her anything. . . . So all I could do was to keep telling her I would do it," p. 1), but ultimately she evidences no, or only minimal, validity. I have discussed the unreliability of all Juan's mother had told him—an unreliability which created this world of dreams and fantasy—and it is clear that the words of Pedro's mother function on a similar pseudofactual level. The threat of the snake bite is surely more evocative than prognostic. It cannot be irrelevant either that the threat is very specifically tied to a snake, an animal which has been metaphorically associated with the female and human sexuality. (Presumably, Adam did not "know" Eve in the biblical sense until after they had eaten of the apple proffered by the snake.)[17] Thus, the adolescent Pedro, thinking of Susana and her "manos suaves," her "labios . . . mojados como si los hubiera besado el roció" (p. 16) ("gentle hands," her "lips . . . moist, as if they had been kissing the dew," p. 10), immersed as he is in a nascent, adolescent eroticism, is threatened with the eternal snake which exists only as a figment of someone else's mythology and dream world. In other words, in this case, the female authority figure is substituting one *pleasant* dream world (the boy's, in which the female is a necessary ingredient) with another *less pleasant* but equally fantastic one which promises punishment and danger if one should continue to persist in the former. Both fantasies, however, rest at the same distance from reality, and both, significantly, are stimulated by females, who are both the promised fruit and the instrument of punishment. Paradoxically, however, it is ultimately the males who continue and multiply these dream worlds and who, in these novels at least, are shown to be as enmeshed in the chimeras as the female herself.

In many ways, then, the novels undermine the presumed authority and break down the barriers between the polar opposites—Life/Death, Reality/Dream, Authority/Lack of Authority—as Juan and Artemio ultimately discover that these antitheses do, indeed must, *co*exist, much as life and death do not negate each other. Thus, as in the story of the Fall, life and death are female related; Eve caused death to be brought to man, yet she was also "the mother of all living" (Gen. 3.20). Similarly, Dolores, mother of Juan and giver of life to Juan, is also the character who entices him into Comala and death.[18]

A significant irony emerges, however, as one examines the associations between women and death in these novels, as well as in the Bible. On a superficial level, it would appear that each of the male protagonists (Artemio, Juan, and Adam) is a victim, that he has died or been "sacrificed" within the text as the result of a whim, weakness, or capriciousness of a female. Dolores Preciado's desire for revenge would seem to have sent Juan to his death; Adam surely was tricked and his future happiness sacrificed by Eve, while Artemio might appear to have been victimized by the present indifference of the female members of his family (and the other women who surrounded him throughout his life); and was he not, as a child, abandoned by his mother and victim of the foolish pride of a crazy old woman? Perhaps, but let us examine the facts, beginning with a brief, second look at the story of the Fall in the Bible.

Our folklore and the Church have agreed that Eve caused the loss of paradise, but, if one accepts the story exactly as the male scribes have presented it in the Bible and examines it carefully, some doubts begin to form. Genesis states:

> But the serpent said to the woman, "You will not die. For God knows that when you eat of it your eyes will be opened, and you will be like God, knowing good and evil." So when the woman saw that the tree was good for food, and that it was a delight to the eyes, and that the tree was to be desired to make one wise, she took of its fruit and ate; she also gave some to her husband, and he ate. (Gen. 3.4–6)

A few verses later God asks of Adam:

"Have you eaten of the tree of which I commanded you not to eat?" The man said, "The woman whom thou gavest to be with me, she gave me fruit of the tree, and I ate." Then the Lord God said to the woman, "What is this that you have done?" The woman said, "The serpent beguiled me, and I ate". (Gen. 3.11–13)

What one tends to overlook or forget, however, is that in the narrative portion of the cited text, no mention is made of Eve's forcing Adam to eat, or duping him in any way.[19] Only when confronted by God does Adam, like the child who has been caught in an act of mischief, defend himself by saying that *she* gave it to him. Notice, he does not even go so far as to retort that she *made* him do it, as our subsequent understanding of the text has led us to believe. She in turn, equally childishly, casts the blame on the serpent. The Bible, then, in and of itself, does not cast the aspersions on Eve that its commentators have been wont to claim. Eve has been maligned for merely having shared with man that which was nourishing, aesthetically pleasing, and wisdom-inspiring.[20] Phrased in this manner her sin seems less odious, and one wonders why she has received so much vilification for so many centuries. Were Adam so righteous and virtuous, not to mention wise, why did he not simply resist the woman and let her eat alone? Is he not equally to blame, if there is any blame to be placed? It would appear that Eve has been censured for a crime they shared. Furthermore, Eve received double punishment (as well as a bad reputation) for not only would she know pain in childbirth, but she, like Adam, would also die.

A similar ideological stance regarding the culpability of the female is patent in *La muerte de Artemio Cruz* in the excursus on the term *chingada*, a treatment which no doubt reflects the common attitude of the Mexican people (males at least): "la chingada que envenena el amor, disuelve la amistad, aplasta la ternura, la chingada que divide, la chingada que separa, la chingada que destruye, la chingada que emponzoña" (p. 146) ("[la chingada] the word that poisons love, breaks friendships, hardens tenderness, . . . that divides, destroys, envenoms," p. 139). Thus, to the *chingada* are imputed all the evils of contemporary life. But, what is overlooked, buried in the rhetoric, is a very simple fact: the word *chingada* itself means she who has been brutally, forcefully, violated. The wrong, the evil, has been done *to* her not *by* her. She is not the ravisher, the despoiler as Artemio's tirade would suggest, but rather the ravished, the despoiled as even the term itself conveys.

What becomes clear, then, as one seriously analyzes the Mexican texts is a similar stance in regard to the females' position in these novels. Although it might appear that the male protagonists have been victimized, at least psychologically within the framework of the fiction, by the whims and capriciousness of the female characters who surround them, in fact, it is

the female characters who, while ostensibly peripheral to the message of
the text and the action of the story, are actually victims of the males.[21]
Indeed, the female characters precisely fit the role of sacrificial victims as
studied by René Girard *(Violence)* in spite of the fact that none of them is
sacrificed in the sense of being brutally murdered.

In his comprehensive study, *Violence and the Sacred*, René Girard has
shown that sacrifice, particularly religious sacrifice, is merely a socially
acceptable outlet or diversion for the basic violence inherent to mankind.
Thus, the sacrificial victim is necessarily desired and despised as he/she
represents both the violence inherent to the sacrificer and the potential for
surmounting that violence. In *Pedro Páramo* and *Artemio Cruz*, one finds no
apparent sacrifice, religious or otherwise, and the violence which does
exist within the novels might appear more overt than covert and thus in
need of no further study. Nevertheless, let me carry Girard's theory of
sacrifice and violence one step further and examine it in connection with
the portrayal of the female characters in the novels.

As Girard points out, sacrifice is the product or final phase of ritual,
while the purpose of the sacrificial rite is to channel mankind's violence,
violence which might otherwise run rampant and destroy the society and/
or the culture. In other words, the sacrificial rite serves to unite the society
and keep it united, while the true meaning of the rite and its veritable
purpose are necessarily hidden from its participants—the celebrants *believe*
its function to be *other* than what it is. They see another meaning in the
ritual and necessarily fail to comprehend it as an outlet for their own
violence. In addition, the sacrificial ritual is always dependent upon a
substitution; we sacrifice X in order not to do violence to Y. At the same
time, Girard's repeated insistence on the link between violence and desire
(in this study as well as in *Deceit, Desire and the Novel*) leads me to posit that
both the object of the violence and the object of desire are substituted. That
is, not only do we sacrifice X in order not to harm Y, but we perform this
sacrifice because our desire for Z has been thwarted (probably by Y). Additionally, it appears that there is an entire set of criteria by which the
sacrificial victim is selected. He (She) must be a part of the society or the
group to some degree, but simultaneously must be marginal to that group.
In other words, there must be some semblance of identity between victim
X and the substituted being Y, but not so much similarity as to confuse the
issue.

Of course, throughout his study Girard is discussing sacrifice as killing
(or exile, which he considers a form of death) and violence in its most overt
form (death, mutilation, etc.). What he overlooks and what becomes pertinent to the discussion which follows is that sacrifice, ritual sacrifice, is
covert in more ways than one. I suggest that if the ultimate meaning of the
sacrifice is metaphoric and hidden from the participants, then the sacrifice
itself, that is, the death, may also be figurative and hidden from its partici-

pants. Girard, in fact, indirectly alludes to this possibility at several points, as for example when he sees exile as a form of death—if it is a form of death then surely it is a metaphoric form; he suggests, too, that some rites conclude with only a symbolic death. I suggest, then, that sacrifice as defined by Girard is directly related to the portrayal of the female in these two novels insofar as she is related to death, metaphoric or otherwise.

But, let me ask what there is in these texts that might be construed as sacrifice. Or better yet, let me pursue the question from the other direction. What acts are performed to prevent greater violence and/or to create or maintain social order and unity? Considering the question in its relationship to the female characters which most specifically interest us here, one discovers that the social order is maintained in both *Artemio Cruz* and *Pedro Páramo* via the *ritual* of marriage. Here, my reader will surely respond that marriage certainly cannot be viewed as sacrifice of the female. On the contrary, the popular view of marriage in Western civilization portrays it as the ultimate goal of the female, the fulfillment of all her dreams. Paradoxically, such a popular concept is not contradictory to sacrifice as studied by Girard for, as he demonstrates so convincingly, the sacrificial victim is often a *willing* victim, for reasons I shall discuss later. But let me first examine the marriages in the texts.

Pedro Páramo marries twice. First, he weds Juan Preciado's mother, Dolores Preciado, significantly, because he wants her land and because he owes her family a great deal of money:

> — . . . Mañana comenzaremos a arreglar nuestros asuntos. Empezaremos por las Preciados. ¿Dices que a ellas les debemos más?
> —Sí. Y a las que les hemos pagado menos. . . . Y la Lola, quiero decir, doña Dolores, ha quedado como dueña de todo. Usted sabe: el rancho de Enmedio. Y es a ella a la que le tenemos que pagar.
> —Mañana vas a pedir la mano de la Lola. (P. 40)

> (". . . Tomorrow we'll start to work. The Preciados first. Didn't you say we owe them the most?"
> "Yes. And we've paid them the least. . . . And, Lola... I mean Doña Dolores... is the owner of everything. You know, the Enmedio farm. And she's the one we have to pay."
> "Tomorrow you're going to propose to Lola." [P. 34])

Later, Pedro marries Susana San Juan whom he has loved since adolescence. The violence which surrounds this marriage is far more overt than that of his first marriage, for in order to marry Susana, Pedro has her father killed, and one wonders if she is not being kept in that room in Pedro's house by force. Similarly, Artemio Cruz marries Catalina in order to have access to her family's wealth, land, and position. Her father, knowing this full well, nonetheless hands her over to the stranger, Artemio, saying to her as she meekly protests: "Este hombre puede salvarnos. Cualquier otra consideración sale sobrando. . . . Piensa en los últimos años de tu padre. ¿Crees que no merezco un poco de...?" (p. 52) ("This man can save us. Every other consideration must be put aside. . . . Think about your father's last years. Don't you think he deserves a little..." p. 47). What both texts suggest (whether consciously or not on the part of the authors) is that the ritual of marriage forestalls a more overt, more dangerous form of violence.[22] Had the two protagonists been unable to marry the landed daughters, they would have had to kill the father or brother and/or take the land by force, by physical violence. But, can violence ever truly be forestalled? Or do we simply (as Girard suggests) redirect it in a more suitable (read, socially acceptable) form so that it becomes more covert and *appears* less violent? Are we not dealing with different forms, different manifestations, of the same violent gesture as portrayed in the novels?

As mentioned, substitution is also considered a basic tenet of sacrifice, and, clearly, both *La muerte de Artemio Cruz* and *Pedro Páramo* are overtly concerned with substitution. But these substitutions must be examined with more rigor if they are to fit the structure of the sacrificial ritual, for the so-called victim must not only be a substitute but must also be marginal to the society which he or she is "saving" via the sacrifice. Since I have already suggested that the women are the sacrificial victims and that the marriage is the sacrificial rite, let us look specifically at the women who are married in these texts. Do they fit the criteria for sacrificial victims?

It seems clear that in each case, the female's position as female makes her marginal to that society. As Consuelo complained, "Es que nos amurallaron, señor Montero. . . . nos han quitado la luz" (p. 27) ("It's that they walled us in, Mr. Montero. . . . They have taken the light from us"). Similarly, her family ties make her a suitable representative for the family (thus, she has some identity with the "society" involved), but her femaleness makes her peripheral to that family and society. In fact, the females' marginality to the societies portrayed in the novels may be best evinced by the female victims' patent impotence, lack of power, and lack of authority. They have no say in their own destinies; all is decided for them by familial males. Catalina yields relatively facilely to the demand of her father ("Los ojos de ella sólo le devolvían este extraño mensaje de dura fatalidad, como si se mostrara dispuesta a aceptarlo todo", p. 41 ["Her eyes returned only that strange message of hard fatality, as if she would show herself disposed to accept everything," p. 37]), and Susana is eventually overpowered by the will of Pedro. Perhaps the point is manifested most blatantly in the character of Dolores, who, although not under the tutelage of a male, nonetheless conducts herself as if she were, for she willingly hands herself over to Pedro. But of this I shall have more to say later.

Clearly, the females' lack of power and authority is closely tied to the act of substitution. Unquestionably, the bent of their rapport with the males of their families is repeated when those familial males are replaced (via the *ritual* of marriage) by extrafamilial males. Interestingly, the female characters are not completely oblivious to the substitutory nature of the ritual; they recognize that nothing is truly changing—the rite only marks the presence of a different male to control their lives. The underlying implications of unusual relationships—I am tempted here to use the word incestuous but that may be too strong an expression[23]—between Catalina and her brother and between Susana and her father further emphasize the fact that the family rapport is merely a mirror reflection of the marital. The similarity of the position and attitude of the female in each of the two relationships is manifest quite patently in the novels. In *Pedro Páramo*, Susana remembers the scene with her father when she is lowered into a "pequeño agujero abierto entre las tablas" (p. 94) where she "estaba colgada de aquella soga que le lastimaba la cintura, que le sangraba sus manos; pero que no quería soltar: era como el único hilo que la sostenía al mundo de afuera" (p. 94) and "ella bajó en columpio, meciéndose en la profundidad, con sus pies bamboleando 'en el no encuentro dónde poner los pies'" (p. 94) ("a little hole among the slabs," p. 89, where she "was hanging from a rope. It hurt her waist and made her hands bleed, but she didn't want to get loose because it was the only thread that joined her with the world outside," pp. 88–89, and "she went down and down, swaying and rocking in the darkness, with her feet searching for a hold," p. 89). This scene is clearly not distant from those scenes in the bedroom at Pedro's house: "Y se volvió a hundir entre la sepultura de sus sábanas" (p. 115) ("And she buried herself again in the tomb of her bedclothes," p. 109). In both cases we might see Susana metaphorically buried alive and connected to reality by a mere thread as a result of the greed and desire of, first, her father and, then, Pedro. Catalina's life before and after her marriage to Artemio is also portrayed as nearly identical. Describing her life before the ritual, the text notes, "Gonzalo había muerto. Desde entonces, padre e hija se habían ido acercando hasta convertir este lento discurrir de las tardes, sentados sobre las sillas de mimbre del patio, en algo más que una consolación: en una costumbre que, según el viejo, habría de prolongarse hasta su muerte" (p. 48), and after her marriage, "Ella se meció lentamente. Recordaba, contaba días y a menudo meses durante los cuales sus labios no se abrieron" (p. 96), "'Inmóvil y muda'" (p. 99); "Largas horas pasó frente a la ventana abierta sobre el campo, perdida en la contemplación del valle sombreado de pirules, meciendo a veces la cuna del niño" (p. 104) ("Three years ago they had received the news of Gonzalo's death. Since that time father and daughter had drawn together to make the slow passing of their afternoons seated on the wicker patio chairs into something more than a consolation—into a custom that, according to the old man, would be maintained until he himself died," p. 43, and after her marriage, "She rocked slowly back and forth, remembering the days and even months during which her lips had not opened", p. 89, *"Motionless and mute,"* p. 92; "She spent long hours at the window looking out over the valley shaded with wild-pear trees, rocking the child's cradle from time to time," p. 98). Thus, one sees that the substitution of one male for another is patent insofar as the females' lives are essentially unvaried. They are at the whim of a different male, but nothing is truly altered. At the same time each of the females herself replaces either another female (Catalina replaces Regina, Dolores replaces Susana) or perhaps even a male (Catalina on some level replaces Gonzalo).

Girard's study, of course, seems to directly contradict my premise here to the extent that he begins his study by insisting that women are rarely sacrificial victims (p. 12). Within the context in which he states this, he is no doubt correct, for he is specifically speaking of a much more grandiose, large-scale sacrifice—a sacrifice in which a majority of the society actively and simultaneously participates and which results in the death or mutilation of the victim. On the other hand, he seems to overlook the fact that the female (particularly as dramatized in these novels) is regularly "sacrificed," handed over by her family. It is revealing that in a study of violence and the sacred, he includes a chapter on marriage and, indeed, studies sexuality as a form of violence which is "cleansed" to some degree by marriage although "Even within the *ritualistic* framework of marriage . . . sexuality is accompanied by violence" (p. 35, emphasis added), and "Like violence, sexual desire tends to fasten upon surrogate objects if the object to which it was originally attracted remains inaccessible." He later continues, now seeming to support my position, and asks "whether this process of symbolization does not respond to some half-suppressed desire to place the blame for all forms of violence on women" (p. 36), noting that "the function of ritual is to 'purify' violence" by eliminating one member of society associated with that violence (i.e., the female?).[24] Similarly in these novels in each case the female is blamed for the continued violence. I earlier pointed out Artemio's facile condemnation of the *chingada* for all that is amiss in the world. Similarly, in *Pedro Páramo*, it is pertinent that Donis's sister (who apparently has no name) is blamed for their incestuous relationship and censured by all. It would appear, if one is to judge by the reactions of the other characters, that Donis, her partner in this transgression, is somehow less reprehensible. And does one not presume that Artemio and Pedro might have been less cruel-hearted and more humane in their dealings with others had they received the love and affection they "deserved" from Catalina and Susana (or Regina and Dolores)?

Further contradicting his stance on women, Girard finally states:

Like the animal and the infant, but to a lesser degree, the woman qualifies for sacrificial status by reason of her weakness and relatively marginal social status. That is why she can be viewed as a quasi-sacred figure, both desired and disdained, alternately elevated and abused. (Pp. 141–42)

Thus, the sacrificial victim always lacks power and authority (a situation which, as already pointed out, is not rare in the female, particularly in these novels). Consider, for example, Catalina, whose lack of authority is reflected in the fact that she essentially has no voice and is rarely allowed to say anything in the novel. But the rite of sacrifice confers certain powers, although ultimately no authority, on the victim herself. In a paradoxical manner, the victim, like the prostituted female characters of pornography as discussed by Andrea Dworkin and Elizabeth Janeway, takes on the powers of a goddess who is simultaneously an object of scorn *and* venerated and who must accept her "noble" position of victim and submit willingly in order to sanctify, ennoble, and justify the actions of her sacrificer. Later, when she has been converted into a quasi-goddess figure, she can now absolve the guilt of her sacrificer(s). As Floyd Merrell has noted, "Her [Catalina's] secret aim is to sacrifice herself for her father and her brother, to lose herself in 'godliness' so that others (the Other) might vicariously receive retribution" (p. 345). Like the pharmakos studied by Girard, "the victim draws to itself all the violence infecting the original victim [in this case, the male protagonist] and through its own death [or perhaps the rite itself] transforms this baneful violence into beneficial violence, into harmony and abundance" (p. 95).

The catch is, of course, that the sacrificers must somehow "partake," so to speak, of the death. In the case of the sacrificed animal, they eat of the meat; in the case of a sacrificed person, who is only metaphorically rather than actually killed, the victim must absolve the sacrificers so that the latter will be "cleansed" of their own violence.

Thus, we see that to both Artemio and Pedro the forgiveness of the victims, Catalina and Susana, is essential but not forthcoming.[25] In fact, one of the narrative sections of *Artemio Cruz*, June 3, 1924, is dedicated to Artemio's attempts to secure this very forgiveness and acceptance by Catalina: "El deseaba borrar el recuerdo del origen y hacerse querer sin memorias del acto que la obligó a tomarlo por esposo" (p. 101) ("He wanted to erase the memory of how their life together had begun; he wanted her to love, without thinking of the act that had forced her to take him as her husband," p. 95). He, in fact, tells her, "No sé si te haya ofendido en algo. Si lo he hecho, te ruego que me perdones" (p. 105), because "todos necesitamos testigos de nuestra vida para poder vivirla" (p. 110) ("Have I done something to offend you? If I have, please forgive me," p. 98, because "we all need someone to see and know our life, so we can live our life," p. 103). Nonetheless, she astutely recognizes that she must "dejarse victimar para poder desquitarse" (p. 113) ("let herself be sacrificed now, in order to avenge the sacrifice later," p. 106). In fact, the difference between his relationship with Catalina and that with Regina is marked by the latter's ready forgiveness (and willing lapse of memory) regarding the violence of their first encounter. Both Artemio and Regina *pretend* that they met on a beautiful beach: "esa playa mítica, que nunca existió . . . esa mentira de la niña adorada . . . esa ficción de un encuentro junto al mar, inventado por ella *para que él se sintiera limpio, inocente*, seguro del amor. . . . Era una hermosa mentira" (p. 82, emphasis added) ("that make-believe beach that never existed anywhere . . . her child's lie . . . their sea fiction that she had conjured up *that [he] might feel clean and innocent* and sure of love . . . pretty lies," p. 76, emphasis added), but the ugly truth of the violent encounter is that "aquella muchacha de dieciocho años había sido montada *a la fuerza* en un caballo y *violada* en silencio en el dormitorio común de los oficiales" (pp. 82–83, emphasis added) ("a girl of eighteen had been thrown helplessly across his horse and carried back to the officers' dormitory to be *violated* in silence," p. 76, emphasis added). It was this play-acting, this pretense, this lie which would result in the forgiveness which Catalina refuses to grant him in response to his "Olvídate de este día" (p. 112) ("let's forget this day," p. 105). Significantly, as Roberto González Echevarría has underlined, "el poder y la voluntad de Artemio no logran dominar dos aspectos cruciales en su vida: el amor, que sólo puede comprar, y la muerte, contra la cual lucha en vano," and, as I have shown, these two, love and death, are distinctly feminine related.[26]

Thus, one must note that in these novels, when the female is seen as powerful, it is because of the covert power she holds by refusing to forgive the violence done her and thereby inspiring both love and hatred. Apparently, she, like Oedipus as studied by Girard, goes willingly to the sacrifice, knowing that it will make of her a goddess and confer on her otherwise inaccessible powers. As Catalina recognizes, "Sólo podía vengarse esa muerte [her brother's] . . . abrazando a este hombre, abrazándolo pero negando la ternura que él quisiera encontrar en ella. Matándolo en vida, destilando la amargura hasta envenenarlo" (p. 53) ("She could avenge her brother's death . . . only by embracing this stranger, embracing him but denying him the tenderness he would like to find in her. She would murder him living, distilling bitterness until he would be poisoned," p. 48), because she must "dejarse victimar para poder desquitarse," and ultimately "el sacrificio exigido sería pequeño y, en cierta manera, no muy repulsivo" (p. 50) ("let herself be sacrificed now, in order to avenge the sacrifice later," and ultimately, "the sacrifice demanded would be slight and, in a certain sense, by no means repulsive," p. 45).

Similarly, Pedro's view of Susana as a goddess figure is apparent in his reaction to her death. He describes her death, "Pasaste rozando con tu cuerpo las ramas del paraíso" (p. 122) ("you passed among the boughs of the paradise tree," p. 117), and, of course, the town's failure to suitably mourn the passing of the goddess caused him in turn to cross his arms and allow the town to die. "Me cruzaré de brazos y Comala se morirá de hambre" (p. 121) ("'I'll fold my arms and Comala will starve to death,'" p. 115). There is almost a pagan implication here that only proper adoration of the goddess figure might result in her forgiveness and, thus, in the possibility of the town's salvation. Like Catalina, however, Susana also refuses to pardon the violence done her.

In fact, the repetition of the leitmotif of the cross in the novels surely intentionally, if indeed paradoxically, evokes the image of Christ and the notion of Christian sacrifice. The cross symbol itself becomes relevant in *La muerte de Artemio Cruz* where the image is already present in the protagonist's name, and one is led to wonder if one is meant to see Catalina as Artemio's metaphoric cross or vice versa. Or, does the image point back to Artemio's mother and the issue of sacrifice? Indeed, the most blatant form of violence and sacrifice is to be found in the final pages of *Artemio Cruz*, when we learn of Artemio's mother, Isabel Cruz or Cruz Isabel, as the case may be. Symbolic of the history of Mexico, Artemio is depicted as the product of violence, sacrifice, or, to quote Octavio Paz, as the "hijo de la chingada," the son of the violation of a mulata or Indian by a European.[27] There can be little doubt that what occurred historically parallels the marriage rites in these novels: the female (the conquered Mexico or the Indian) is given to the other group (the Europeans) to prevent greater violence.[28]

The implied reversibility of Isabel Cruz's name also suggests that perhaps one is intended to reverse Artemio's name; to do so produces *Cruzar temió*, and as we know, the common theme which links all sections of the novel is the protagonist's fear (and avoidance) of crossing over into the other sphere of death. Significantly, too, at the moment when Catalina refuses to absolve his earlier "sins," we are presented with a scene which directly mirrors the one in *Pedro Páramo* when the latter crosses his arms and allows Comala to die of hunger and drought. In *Artemio Cruz* it is also nighttime, and Artemio's reaction to Catalina is the following: "Cruzó los brazos y salió a la noche. . . . La lluvia había cesado" (p. 115) ("He crossed his arms and walked out into the country night. . . . The rain had stopped," p. 108). In both cases, the female-related "paradise" is lost; the rain (female symbol) has stopped, and all that will follow is drought and slow, relentless desiccation and death as dreams dissolve.

In the texts I have noted the conversion of the idealized young woman, often initially distanced from the youth by the barrier of his own mother, into the wife and mother, as negatively viewed and unexalted as his own. Only in the case of Juan Preciado does one find this process reversed, for in his presentation the mother maintains the status of beloved while the young woman (the incestuous female) embodies all the negative aspects of femininity.[29] Thus, although the young woman may be powerless and merely a sacrificial victim, the sacrifice (and/or motherhood) confers power on her so that in her maturity she too is viewed as the powerful authority (cf. Juan's and Pedro's mothers).

Much of Girard's study, then, points to the final step which he never takes but which seems clearly suggested by these novels: that marriage, particularly as presented in these novels, is indeed a form of ritual sacrifice to the extent that (1) sexuality and violence are interchangeable; (2) marriage is an approved ritual form of violence; (3) the woman is given to the other group or individual to prevent a greater form of violence. Significantly, too, the rite itself, the marriage ceremony, is glaringly absent in each of the texts. Not a word is mentioned about the ceremony itself as it maintains its "hidden" and secret position.

It is pertinent, too, that in these novels one watches the process of mythmaking, a process which no doubt is directly tied to the question of language, authority, and ritual sacrifice. According to Girard, at the basis of all myth is a terror of the absolute violence which would surge as a result of a lack of differentiation. Thus, one of the functions of myth (and in turn sacrifice) is to create differences and set up hierarchies if none exist already. Such, of course, is the goal of the myths (particularly those myths which envelop the female characters) in the novels—to establish differences, hierarchies of power and authority where these differences either do not exist or seem to be dissolving because all is interchangeable.

In summary, then, both *Pedro Páramo* and *La muerte de Artemio Cruz* might be described as the story of the death of the cacique, who, in spite of having destroyed the lives of all those who surrounded him, still never realized fulfillment because he never fully conquered or possessed that ideal woman who eternally escaped him.[30] In light of the Girard study, however, one must also view the novels as the dramatization of the ritual sacrifice designed to cover and redirect the basic violence inherent to mankind in much the same way as the Mexican vulgarity, *la chingada*, covers and refocuses that violence. Like the Malinche, the woman of these novels is simultaneously despised and adored because of her role within the sacrificial ritual, a role which makes of her a goddess as well as a symbol of death and a mediator of the same. Just as the Malinche is viewed as the Mother of the Mexican mestizo and as a traitor to her people (thus, instrument of the death of her race), the female characters in these two novels are intricately linked to the death the male protagonists cannot negate. Like the sacrificial victim she is, and like the pharmakos and Oedipus, the female character, *la chingada*, is blamed for all that is evil in man and stands as a reflection of that same evil. Because she refuses to forgive him that evil, he is denied the positive reflection of himself that he needs to survive.[31] Her sacrifice then has been necessary so that order, peace, and hierarchical differentiations can continue to reign, but like death, violence and chaos continue to exist merely hidden below the thin mask of order, for her failure to forgive makes of her, ironically, a symbol of his own negative aspects.

5

La ciudad y los perros: Women and Language

je n'étais que le produit d'une exigence collective

Sartre, *Les mots*

y nadie escapa a esta dialéctica feroz

Paz, *El laberinto de la soledad*

ALTHOUGH *La ciudad y los perros* (1962) by Mario Vargas Llosa (Peru, b. 1936) has already been studied from numerous vantage points, one significant aspect of the text remains virtually unexplored: the male/female opposition.[1] A careful scrutiny reveals that the male/female dichotomy is one of the novel's principal structural and thematic features.

Lest there be any doubt about the primacy of the female in this apparently male-dominated novel, let us note that each action within the story, if followed through to its fullest implications, is prompted by a female figure. For example, each of the novel's major characters is interned in the military academy, Leoncio Prado, as a direct result of the disintegration of his association with one or more females. In two different ways the text underlines the feminine influence in the boys' induction into the school (a moment which, of course, is basic to and necessarily precedes all the textual discourse). First, returning us to the origins of life in the academy, the narrative repeatedly reverts to the preschool era of each of the three protagonists and shows how a female influenced his decision to enter. Secondly, in each case, an allusion to the entrance examination subtly demonstrates the ambition and motivation on the part of each to do well on that test and leave the known, female-dominated world, filled with disintegrated and disintegrating relationships, in order to enter the unknown, male-oriented world of the military academy. Ricardo Arana, deprived of his utopian, almost oedipal relationship with his mother, transfers to the school because he wants to escape his father *and* because he has realized that his mother is his father's accomplice—"ella está de su lado, es su cómplice" ("She's on his side, she's his accomplice").[2] Similarly, Alberto, ostensibly sent to the school because of poor grades, willingly enters because he has been rejected by Helena, because his father (a don Juan) feels he is marring the family honor, and because his mother has become overly protective and solicitous owing to his father's recent life-style. The feminine influence on his volition to enter is apparent when Arana asks Alberto, "¿Por qué no te hiciste jalar en el examen de ingreso?" ("Why didn't you just flunk the entrance exams?") and the latter answers, "Por culpa de una chica. Por una decepción, ¿me entiendes?" (p. 116) ("On account of a girl. She was just stringing me along, you know what I mean?" p. 134). In the same manner, Jaguar's matriculation is the oblique consequence of Teresa's prior rebuff (her rejection of him produced the change in his life and thus the events immediately preceding his entrance) and the direct result of his desire to escape his *padrino*'s wife and his difficult life with the couple.

Once in the academy, the boys are still directly and indirectly stimulated by the force of the female figures, which not only supply the motivating force for the boys' actions but frequently inspire the males' discourse in whatever form it may take. In other words, the female influence is felt in both the *énoncé* and the *énonciation* as she directly produces the actions described as well as the narrative gesture itself.[3] Each voice of the novel concentrates on a woman, and somewhat less overtly, the name of the voice "producing" each segment of discourse is identified not only by its rhetoric but also through the repetition of the female figure on which that discourse centers. For example, we recognize the first-person narration of Jaguar because it concentrates on Teresa and his relationship with her.

The female's intricate dominance in the *énoncé* of the text is echoed in her relationship to a past golden age. Like *María*, the culmination of Spanish-American romanticism, this text fluctuates between present and past narration, but the female figure evoked by that articulation is always past and absent. For example, Richi's mother is already doubly absent when her image is elicited by the *énonciation*. She is absent insofar as Richi "ha olvidado" and insofar as the perfect, sheltering mother of his childhood has now joined forces with the threatening image of his father and has ceased to exist as that protecting agent. Her alliance with the male, in fact, is not very different from the manner in which the other females have also "sold out," exchanged integrity for security, as I shall discuss at a later point. Thus, not only has Richi forgotten this female figure, but she has ceased to exist in the same form. Similarly, Alberto's discourse continually alternates between the pitiful figure his mother now exhibits (in the present and recent past of the narrative) and the vivacious, social "proper" mother she was during his childhood. Likewise, the images that Jaguar evokes of both his mother and Tere are already past and absent; his mother has died, and Tere is no longer that innocent child with whom he studied (if, in fact, she was innocent even then).

This absence of the female is further reflected in the very narration of each of the male characters. Just as any discourse which pretends to be interior is necessarily directed to an already absent, already repetitious *you*, so most of the interior discourse of this novel is directed toward an already past, already absent, *female you*. Alberto, for example, aims his words at several absent women. He is portrayed as he subconsciously addresses his mother (or his mental impression of her, since she is not present at the moment of discourse): " 'Ir y decirle qué ganamos con no aceptar un medio, deja que nos mande un cheque cada mes hasta que se arrepienta de sus pecados y vuelva a casa' " (p. 17) [" 'I could go and tell her, what do we gain by not accepting a cent? Let him send us a check each month until he repents and returns home' "]. At other moments he verbalizes his thoughts to the imagined prostitute (imagined since he has never encountered her and has only second-hand information about her) or to the nonpresent Teresa. And, even before he had entered Leoncio Prado, his words were frequently already repetitious, directed toward an already absent female; he and his friends practiced what they would say before they "declared themselves": " 'Helena, tengo que decirte algo muy importante ' " (p. 147) (" 'Helena, I've got something very important to say to you,' " p. 172). Obviously, at the moment when the boys are rehearsing these words, the female is not present, but imagined, and the language is repetitious insofar as each male courts the female with approximately the same words as the other boys, repeats those words as he declares his love, and then again reiterates the terminology as he recounts the love scene to his companions. And, finally, the letters Alberto writes for the other cadets are also always directed to an absent, feminine *you*.

(Significantly, even at those moments when Alberto's discourse is not intended for females, it still reflects his attitude toward them. In those interior monologues directed toward his father, what is most interesting is the opposition between the words destined for his father and those aimed at his mother. The contradiction in the words reflects either his hypocrisy [or perhaps just moral confusion] and ability to adapt to the immediate situation or his understanding that one says different things to audiences of different sexes. Just before he admonishes his mother to accept his father's checks until the latter repents and returns home, he has mentally forgiven his father for his moral position as long as he keeps sending money. It is patent, then, that the money is more important than his father's sins or his mother's forgiveness of them.)

Another instance of discourse directed to an absent, repetitious, female *you* occurs in the epilogue when Jaguar retells his dialogue with Tere: " 'Le dije otra vez:—hola, Teresa. ¿No te acuerdas de mí?—' " (p. 337) (" 'I repeated, "Hello, Teresa. Don't you remember me?" ' " p. 401). Earlier in the story one encounters (although here the primary interlocutor is not identified), "Había pensado decirle: 'te he traído este regalo, Tere' y cuando entré a su casa todavía pensaba hacerlo, pero apenas la vi me arrepentí y sólo le dije: 'me han regalado esto en el colegio y las tizas no me sirven para nada. ¿Tú las quieres?' " (p. 141) ("I was thinking of telling her, 'I've brought you a present, Tere,' and when I went to her house I was still thinking of saying it. But as soon as I saw her I changed my mind and just said, 'They gave me this at school but I haven't got any use for it. Would you like it?' " pp. 163–64). In both cases the repetition is explicit, and Jaguar is portrayed telling one *you* what he said to another *you*, who is female and absent at the moment of *énonciation*. In effect, then, we are reading an *énonciation* of an *énonciation* of an *énonciation*, so that the female *you* figure is three times removed from the "present" *énonciation*.

In this manner, each *énonciation* as attributed to each of the various characters demonstrates the past, repetitive, and absent quality of the female *you*'s to which that narration is directed, as well as the past, repetitive, and absent nature of the very *énoncé* (which in many instances is but another *énonciation*). While the *énonciation* (one of them, at any rate) is always present (even though it may be repetitious), its object and the *énoncé* itself are always past and absent.

The question, then, is why the repeated insistence on the past, now absent female and the linguistic attempts to re-present her (linguistic attempts within the fiction). The boys at the military academy evoke this past life, this past female-oriented utopia in what would appear to be an effort to escape the unpleasant, masculine world in which they are living. Inasmuch as escape always implies a flight to the opposite direction, one might see the mental preoccupation with the women as an escape from the male-dominated and threatening world of the present of the *énonciation*. Another explanation might be that throughout Western history and tradition the female has been associated with the past golden age. Seen as the mother and thus the origin of life, the female, Eve, has become intricately related to the utopian, protected, unthreatened and unthreatening environment of the prelapsarian moment which is now past, never to be retrieved. To name her, to remember her, to speak of her (all linguistic endeavors) is an effort to make her and her world present again through the medium of the word. (Of course, paradoxically, it is this same act which merely emphasizes the absence of that world, as I hope to show.)

Thus, the evocation of the female figure becomes an overt manifestation of the desire to regress to the lost paradise and to origins, to return to the good life with "good" women, and simultaneously demonstrates the impossibility (and perhaps undesirability) of such a return. The insistence on returning to origins is underscored throughout the novel. I have already noted the repeated narrative regressions to the preacademy world, and one must also note that most of Boa's internal monologue is a re-creation, re-presentation of the origins of life within the academy and the birth of the *círculo*. To this extent the novel is not different from most myths which locate the golden age at that point when man was more closely and directly related to and in tune with *mother* nature and *mother* earth, before man entered the social (and masculine?) world which threatens him at every corner. However, the males of this novel contradictorily evoke and repudiate that feminine world. They yearn for that past life, but at the same time a total renunciation of that primitive, protected, feminine state would seem to be the only defense against the civilized, masculine, threatening world (as portrayed in the novel) in which the young men find themselves.

The insistence on, and repetition of, the past quality of the female figure also becomes another manner of emphasizing the masculinity of each boy and proving him nonfemale. The actions of every male character are affected by the notion of the female insofar as each action is designed to prove the character NOT FEMALE, that is, manly. The boys do everything possible to prove that they have none of the characteristics they have associated with women: weakness, emotionalism, passivity, reception of cruelty (as opposed to the perpetration of cruel acts). The text here seems to accept the theory expressed by Octavio Paz in *El laberinto de la soledad* and to apply it to the students. Paz sees the Mexicans as two distinct types: the conquerors and the conquered. The fact that he, too, uses a sexual metaphor—*los chingados* and *los chingones*—parallels the male/female division within *La ciudad y los perros.*

The most obvious example of this struggle to be NOT FEMALE might be seen in Jaguar, who performs all his actions to prove himself courageous, manly, and honorable according to his very personal code of honor. What is particularly interesting is that for Jaguar, women (as portrayed by the wife of his *padrino,* the Tere of his childhood, and the prostitutes) are incapable of honorable, noble actions. Even his mother fits this concept of the female, for one of his last recollections of her includes a degree of "dishonor"—the moment when she threatens to strike him but does not, only because he admonishes, " 'si me tocas, no vuelvo a darte un centavo' " (p. 258) (" 'If you touch me, I'll never give you another centavo,' " p. 304). In his final childhood encounter with Tere he calls her a *puta* (p. 274 [p. 324]), a label which underlines what he considers the dishonorable quality of her acts, and he notes that the wife of his *padrino* acted like a *puta* as she betrayed her husband (p. 300 [p. 356]). Thus, it appears that for Jaguar honor and honorable behavior are very specifically male-related traits; it is honorable to be the *chingón* and dishonorable to be the *chingado* or *puta*. Thus, his insistence upon acting within a very specific code of behavior merely emphasizes his striving to be NOT FEMALE.

By simultaneously evoking the woman and banishing her to a position in the past, to a form of nonexistence, the boys reaffirm their own separation from her and to this extent their own distance from any feminine characteristics. By relegating their positive relationships with women to the past the boys purge themselves of any and all potentially feminine participation.[4] However, inasmuch as rejection of anything contradictorily implies a concurrent recognition and re-presentation of that which is to be rejected or negated, the evocation of the female figure, as I have suggested, maintains an interesting position: to one extent, to remember, to re-present the past female is to make her present again, but in an unthreatening manner; however, at the same time, this re-presentation underscores the past quality of that female and the boys' current distance from her.

This entire myth of origins and the subsequent renunciation of those origins directly parallels language. The female figure here, like any referent, is paradoxically always corporally absent and always semiologically present. That is, she is always past, already repetition, but the word, the name, the memory (through the medium of language) consistently strive to re-present her and the prelapsarian world associated with her. The paradox is that even the very force to make her and the utopia present underlines the fact that she and her world are not and were not nearly as paradisiacal as the memory (formulated by language) would make them appear.

The problem, of course, is that in the novel, the female figure, like everything else, has already been converted into signs, into signifiers of signifiers. The semiotic position of the textual discourse is stressed from the very beginning as the novel opens with the word, " 'Four.' " Four is a sign for Cava, a sign that it is he who has been chosen to steal the chemistry examination for the group. The opening lines of the book, then, reveal the orientation of the discourse as it centers on repetition, language, and the written text. The dice (white surfaces with black dots or "lettering") unquestionably demonstrate an overt similarity to the written page—both function as graphic signifiers, more or less arbitrary, and fortuitous. The fact that four signifies Cava rather than one of the other boys is as totally arbitrary and fortuitous as the fact that the dice turned up four rather than some other number. The fortuity of the opening word makes one wonder if one is not meant to see all the textual signs as arbitrary, fortuitous, and supplemental.

In this fashion, then, *La ciudad y los perros* explicitly depicts itself as signs representing signs, signifiers pointing to other signifiers, *énonciations* whose *énoncés* are but other *énonciations*. The boys have converted the entire world into signs (often dichotomous), and the textual signs have become signs of these other signs. This semiotic removal and distance is perhaps most apparent in the discourse of Boa, whose narration is directed to a *tú* which is only a dog (but a female dog!). Significantly, Boa narrates to la Malpapeada, remembering what he said to her in the past and underlining the fact that the dog, like all the other boys and women, has changed, is no longer the same as she was before. On the linguistic level, he can address her only insofar as she repeats and represents (for him, at least) some degree of human female characteristics as he has experienced them. To this extent his discourse pretends to re-present a referent which signals still another more removed referent. As Derrida has noted in "Le vouloir-dire et la représentation" of *La voix et le phénomène* (Paris: Presses Universitaires, 1972), it is this type of construction which accentuates the repetitive nature of all discourse.

At the same time, however, there is the suggestion that the more removed these linguistic structures are from any tangible referent, the less threatening they become. Perhaps for this reason, Boa "talks" to the dog and Alberto writes his pornographic novels (novels which provide a neat, ordered, unthreatening world, filled with available women). In both cases the discourse is removed from and far less threatening than "real" discourses with tangible women or "real" sexual experience.

What strikes the reader about *La ciudad y los perros* is the fact that not only is the world reduced to signs recognized as such, even within the fiction, but that the fictitious world is founded (overtly so) on a system of dichotomy and difference. The boys' world is set up on an either/or basis. From the linguistic perspective of the characters, the world comes to be reduced to that inside the academy and that outside—the two ways of life demand different language and different behavior. Similarly, within the text, one is either masculine or feminine; there seems little possibility here of degrees or gradations. In the boys' perceptions, the female is further reduced to two oppositional possibilities: the Mother (good) or the Prostitute (bad). The text suggests that the boys' comprehension of the world (and perhaps in turn our own world perception) is not only dualistic, but that it is dualistic as a direct result of our language. Through the total reduction of everything to language and the subsequent simplification of the very complex world in which we live, the words become mutually exclusive. Conversely, since the world of the boys is formulated to a greater or lesser extent by language, their world vision or perception becomes as dualistic and oppositional as their language. Their language encompasses words for male and female but lacks words for the varying gradations in between, so the characters see the world in terms of totally male or totally female. Similarly, their language holds nouns like *madre* and *puta*, but lacks a term for anything that combines or mediates those two extremes.

The oppositional quality of their respective visions of male and female is reinforced by their concept of the parents. In Arana's case, the mother is viewed as kind, tender, and loving while the father is hard, cruel, and unkind. Alberto's father epitomizes the modern man whose primary occupations are divided between making money and enjoying illicit affairs, while his mother (at least in later years) superficially demonstrates the values of the old-fashioned, upright, and religious woman. By the same token, Jaguar perceived his *padrino* as kind, generous, and moral while he viewed the wife as cheap, immoral, and unkind. Thus, the novel attests that this tendency to view the world in dichotomous form is present from the child's earliest experiences with the parents. This oppositional vision is probably apparent as early as the child's first two utterances: *mamá* and *papá*.

Through its portrayal of an oppositional world vision, the text not only underlines the Western propensity to see the world on an either/or basis, but it also calls this tendency into question by dramatizing the possibility of coalescence of various signifiers within one signified (as it seems the Russians and other Eastern groups have long suggested). But, it is only in the final moments that this possibility emerges. Up to the last section, the text and its world have been mostly oppositional: inside the academy or outside, self or other, strong or weak, male or female, military or civilian, mother or prostitute. The final scene not only disputes this entire structure, but it simultaneously challenges the most basic tenets of mimesis by questioning the accuracy of our vision of that world insofar as our perceptions are formulated and regulated by language.

The influence of language on one's cognizance of the world is perhaps best demonstrated by the affiliation between the manner in which each of the characters perceives language itself and the way he apprehends women. I have noted in another place that each boy succeeds or fails in direct relation to his ability to manage and employ words and language,[5] and each character's notion of women directly reflects his concept of language and vice versa. For Arana, language is an extremely powerful commodity, something he feels uncomfortable using, and for that reason holds in awe. In the same manner, for him women are objects to be contemplated and held in awe but not fully understood; women "belong to" and are "possessed" by the men who best control that language.

But, for Alberto, both women and language are mediums of exchange, directly related to money and economic well-being. Women are "possessed" in exchange for money, and only the male with sufficient economic and linguistic resources has access to them; one exchanges either words or currency for women. From the very first moment the reader is introduced to Alberto, this intricate relationship between language, women, and money becomes apparent: he is thinking about how to get money from his father, about how it is his mother's fault that he does not have that money, and about how he will spend the money to affirm his masculinity by going to the bordello. Thus, he overtly links his (and his mother's) financial difficulties to the fact that his father has dedicated himself to *puterío* (which again connects women and money), at the same time as he affiliates money and sexual experience (sexual experience which in turn is tied to manliness). The connection between money and women is further exemplified by the fact that his writing, his source of income, is intricately feminine-oriented. He sells love letters to the other boys so that they may send them to their girlfriends (note again the repetitious quality of the *énonciations*), and he writes explicit, pornographic novels which he also markets. In each case he regards both the females and language as merchandise, something to sell, exploit, or profit by.[6]

The linguistic and mental parallel between women and language produces a life-style based on similarly dichotomous precepts, and we circularly return to the notion that to be masculine is to be NOT FEMALE. As noted, all the boys' actions are designed to prove them MALE and, therefore, NOT FEMALE; their acts endeavor to separate SELF from OTHER, but one soon discovers that there are two types of OTHER: the female and the other male. Thus, this separation from the OTHER becomes a double-edged, bidirectional endeavor. There must be total separation from and negation of the female OTHER in order to define masculinity, since the SELF is identifiable insofar as it recognizes, separates itself from, and stands in contrast to the OTHER.[7] At the same time, and in relationship to other males, the SELF must demarcate itself only partially from that OTHER. Each male seeks individuality and identification, but the uniqueness must not be total; the overall personality must evidence common traits, shared and approved by the other men. To the degree that each character feels himself at times *too* deviant from the other males (that is, he has a strong recognition of the disjunction between himself and the others), he overcompensates in his efforts to be NOT FEMALE—perhaps because such a dichotomous vision of the world automatically categorizes any deviation from the male norm as female, or perhaps because the cadets are victims of that same idealization of the OTHER that Derrida has criticized in Lévi-Strauss *(Grammatologie)*.

The self/other, male/female series of oppositions is dramatized through the act of naming, which is one of the primary concerns of the text. Our entire linguistic structure, as well as the principles of the proper name, are based on the canons of difference and divergence. Two objects or entities are linguistically accorded two distinct names because they are in some way different. This disparity or disjunction does not negate the possibility of some similarity between the two objects, similarities, often seen by poets, which take the form of analogies, metaphors, or similes, but the two entities have two names because, in some way or another, they are distinct, they are not identical.[8] This same principle has traditionally applied to fictitious proper nouns and to the literary character.[9] Within any given work of fiction, a character is created when an author groups a set of more or less concordant signifiers—linguistic components, nouns, adjectives, sometimes verbs—and assigns them a proper name, or perhaps just a pronoun. Once this system has been set up by the author, one can very comfortably recognize each character in one of two ways: one sees the name and associates the given set of traits which accompany it, or, inversely, one sees the distinctive features, attributes, and adjectives and applies the label one has come to identify with that set of characteristics. In either case, the conglomerate of signifiers, although of course ultimately arbitrary, is more or less congruent and harmonious. That is, for the most part the set does not include opposing signifiers. For example, the set of signifiers which defines the character X does not normally include both obesity and leanness, or tallness and shortness.[10] A distinct proper name is given to each set of linguistic signifiers because each set varies from the others to some degree. Therefore, traditionally, the linguistic or literary character has been based on the following formula:

$$\text{NAME X} = \text{SET X OF CHARACTERISTICS}$$

but

$$\text{SET X OF CHARACTERISTICS} \neq \text{SET Y}$$

and

$$\text{NAME X} \neq \text{NAME Y}$$

(although the sets may overlap, the sum is necessarily different). Clearly, this entire formulation in literature has embodied a simplification of extra literary linguistic processes, but it has proven a comfortable simplification.

The uniqueness of *La ciudad y los perros* perhaps resides in the final rejection of this formulation and principle. Mario Vargas Llosa, by means of the character of Jaguar, has directly defied this tenet. Until the concluding pages of the text we have understood the noun, *Jaguar*, as a signifier for the following group of characteristics: cruelty, agility, strength, brutality, heartlessness, mystery, unreceptiveness, manliness, self-sufficiency, dispassion, etc. And, at the same time, one of the unnamed *yo* narrators of the work embodied the following antipodal characteristics: openness, selflessness, kindness, discomfiture, susceptibility, etc. The discovery that the *yo* and Jaguar are one and the same leaves the reader in a very uncomfortable position since he is confronted with two opposing sets of signifiers, each given the same label, the same proper noun. Clearly, then, the textual movement questions the exclusiveness of language, calls into doubt the formulation of our perceptions which are based on the premise of opposition and demarcation, and challenges our perceptions of the world as a series of oppositions (intricately related to and effectuated by our language of difference).

Furthermore, one finds that in the text the portrayal of this process of naming is closely related to the theory of Derrida. That is, one finds that naming is linked to violence (actual or metaphorical). One obvious example of this violence bursts forth the moment the unidentified *yo* is recognized as Jaguar. The realization that the cruel, heartless Jaguar is the pathetic victim of circumstances who has been narrating in the first person is a jolt which cannot but violate the image perpetuated by that first person.[11] Our perception of that kind, unfortunate first person is inevitably radically altered as we try to coordinate it with the signifiers we couple with the word *Jaguar*. By the same token, our image of Jaguar is metamorphosed when we supplement it with the first person's characteristics. Ultimately, of course, both of these attitudes presuppose an originary character, the precedence or dominance of either Jaguar or the first person; since neither precedes nor exists on a prior level, the violence perhaps lies in assigning the characteristics to the name (and vice versa), since to do so is to violate, supplement, and assign human characteristics to what is but a six-letter signifier for a cat. (Nonetheless, by nature of the connotation of the word, at least some of these same animal characteristics have carried over to Jaguar.)

If, then, there is a violence or a violation in naming, it is certainly a result of the exclusiveness of the sign. Thus, the text suggests that to name is the first step in the ultimate debasement and effacement, just as the allocation of a linguistic sign (in more general terms), by virtue of its inherent simplicity, distortion, and opposition to other signs, might be seen as the first step away from the object and toward an eventual loss.

In a manner which is both more overt and more covert, the violence is dramatized through the naming of the mother. *Mentar la madre* is a common, euphemistic expression in Spanish which, superficially deceiving, translates "to name or mention the mother," in spite of the fact that it does not mean this at all. The accepted significance of the expression is to call one's mother a *puta*, and by inference to call one a bastard or the son of a *puta*—one of the greatest insults in the language and one of the most frequently used in this narration. What the expression implies, by reason of the metaphor, is that to mention or to name the mother is to label her a *puta*. The expression has force only because the mother represents the weak, vulnerable spot of each of the characters—as weak and as vulnerable as any of the potentially "feminine" character traits he may have retained from her. Silence, then (that is, not mentioning the mother at all, not naming her), confers purity on her, while naming her defiles that purity and perfection.

In addition, a violence is perpetuated in the expression in that it underscores the separation of the SELF from the rest of the community. I have indicated the struggle each of the boys endures to maintain a degree of similarity with the other males, but, as Octavio Paz has noted, the very act of calling one an *hijo de puta* (or *hijo de la chingada* in Mexico) is a gesture which stresses separation from the OTHER. Only the OTHER is an *hijo de puta*, never the SELF: "Los demás son los 'hijos de la chingada': los extranjeros, los malos mexicanos, nuestros enemigos, nuestros rivales. En todo caso, los 'otros.' Esto es, todos aquellos que no son lo que nosotros somos" (*Laberinto*, p. 68). Thus, *mentar la madre* is an act of differentiation rather than unification of the SELF and the OTHER. Paradoxically, at the same time the boys label each other *hijos de puta*, they also christen each other with nicknames, usually inhuman and frequently zoological. This imposition of non-Christian designations implies the lack of a human mother to be named. A jaguar or a boa cannot be the son of a prostitute, for he is just an animal. In this sense the violence is multiplied, for not only is the mother defiled, but the son and the mother are stripped of all human qualities, even the name. In terms of his nickname, then, each boy is the son of NO WOMAN, and once again we deny that man is born of woman.

The paradox of the whole process of calling another an *hijo de puta* (unlike the expression *hijo de la chingada*) is that to be a prostitute implies a willing sale or giving of the body, and to this extent the absence of violence rather than any violation (violation, of course, suggests unwilling participation). Thus, it would appear that in the final analysis *mentar la madre* implies a violation of the *image* of the mother as opposed to any violation of the tangible woman. And, of course, this image can be desecrated only to the extent that the mother and the prostitute are viewed as polarities, oppositions. Harm may be done only insofar as the referent for the word *mother* is understood to be totally positive, totally pure, and honorable, while that of the word *puta* is totally negative, impure, and dishonorable.

But, in this text the traditional *madre/puta* opposition, like most other oppositions, is ultimately suspected, undermined, and eventually dissolved. While la Pies Dorados may sell her body and favors to the highest bidder, it soon becomes apparent that each of the females (potential mothers) is portrayed in the text as doing quite the same. It is most possible to see the final reconciliation between Alberto's parents in conjunction with a commodity bought and sold. It is apparent that Alberto's mother reunites with his father in spite of the latter's continued extramarital activities in order to regain her social position and financial security. Similarly, Jaguar's mother ceases to conduct herself in a motherly manner and to discipline him accordingly in exchange for monetary remuneration. And Tere, portrayed in all the innocence (?) of the future mother, has two main preoccupations (concerns nurtured and encouraged by her aunt and by her mother as she remembers her): (1) to find a husband to support her and her aunt; (2) to find that husband from the highest possible economic class. To this extent, then, the interest of the mother figures in financial security, and their willingness to exchange their "honor" for that money is not different from that of the prostitute. In effect, as I have already suggested, there is a direct and immediate relationship in the narrative between women, money, and language; each implies the others.

The ultimate result, then, in the text is that the female, like language and money, is both despicable and desirable. She is desirable in two ways. First, she provides a negative counterbalance; that is, the male can prove his masculinity by demonstrating how different he is from her. Second, he can (and needs to) conquer her to prove his superiority. Inversely, however, the very process of conquest confers power on her, degrades him, and makes that very superiority vulnerable as I noted in Chapters 1 and 4. Thus, the female directly and indirectly confers manliness but at the same time is a threat to that manliness, just as language (in the world portrayed in the text at the very least) is both essential and threatening to that masculinity.

Thus the text dramatizes the basic, repeated contradiction one generally finds in the representation of both women and language. On the one hand each implies a creative ability, a means of production or reproduction (in terms of either the mother or creative language), but at the same time each insinuates contamination, perversion, distortion (in the form of the prostitute or translation—any semiological conversion). Nevertheless, each female, each unit of language, encompasses both aspects—the word is simultaneously and paradoxically creative and destructive, desirable and feared, necessary and superfluous, just as the woman is all these things.

Finally, the text suggests in a dramatic way that just as language is necessarily translation, the person in modern society is necessarily prostituted.[12] It is important to recognize that it is not only the women in this text who are *putas;* obviously, the gesture of calling one an *hijo de puta* confers on the son the qualities of the mother. Each of the male characters (with the possible exception of Gamboa) sells his integrity, exchanges his scruples for money. Thus, the whole notion of *puta* and *puterío* becomes synonomous with degradation, transgression, exchange, and translation, aspects of each textual personality and each written discourse. For this reason, then, the name *poeta* is necessarily ironic, for Alberto's "poetry" is not poetry at all but cheap, poorly written pornography—collections of prostituted words. While there is no doubt that his "literary" endeavors demonstrate imagination (since he has no first-hand experience of what he writes), his creations certainly lack the insight and eloquence one generally associates with poetry.

Ultimately, the complexity of the problem of naming and subsequently identifying the object or world is prefigured and reaffirmed by the manipulation of the terms of light and darkness. From the opening page almost every scene at the academy is characterized as foggy, misty, semidark, shadowy. Thus, the cadets' difficulties in identifying and naming the world around them are brought forth in a very pictorial way. They have trouble "seeing" this new, masculine world and are grappling with ways to identify, name, and thus cope with it. But, there are two notable exceptions to the shadowy portrayal of the world surrounding the boys; there are two brilliantly and painfully lit scenes which stand in sharp contrast.

The first of these scenes is in the administration building at the academy when Alberto is about to be "encouraged" to retract his accusation against Jaguar: "El vestíbulo . . . estaba iluminado por una luz *artificial* muy fuerte y Alberto cerró los ojos varias veces, *cegado*" (p. 281, emphasis added) ("in the vestibule . . . the artificial light was so strong that Alberto closed his eyes several times, half *blinded*," p. 332, emphasis added). The second scene is in the epilogue when Alberto has left the academy and returned to his upper-middle-class society. Throughout this section, as he meets his old friends, the strength and brillance of the light is continually stressed: "Había una luz blanca y penetrante que parecía brotar de los techos de las casas y elevarse verticalmente hacia el cielo sin nubes. Alberto tenía la sensación de que sus ojos estallarían al encontrar los reflejos, si miraba fijamente una de esas fachadas de ventanales amplios, que absorbían y despedían el sol como esponjas multicolores" (p. 327) ("There was a penetrating white light that seemed to burst from the roofs of the houses and ascend straight up into the cloudless sky. Alberto had the feeling that his eyes would explode from the reflections if he stared hard at those wide windows that caught and shot back the sun," p. 388).

If one understands the use of light here in its most conventional sense as illumination, knowledge, understanding, ability to "see," then it becomes clear that this scene must be ironic. The years that the boys have spent at the academy are years of initiation, years of learning to "see," learning to supply names and signs to the world around them. Thus, during the apprenticeship things are necessarily shrouded in semidarkness and mist and everything has "una apariencia irreal" (p. 12) ["an unreal appearance"]. But, as the cadets learn how to apply the sign and discover, subconsciously at least, that signs are not mutually exclusive, their lives begin metaphorically to fill with light. The pattern would suggest, then, that in the epilogue the brilliance of the light surrounding Alberto is a result of his ability to "see," and that the semidarkness in which we find Jaguar in the final scene suggests that he does not "see." Such is clearly not the case. If Alberto sees and understands anything at all it is how to take advantage of and how to profit from his newly acquired language skills and hypocrisy. And surely his eyes will explode if he looks steadily at the facades, for he will see that they are only facades, and he will see the contradictions behind them. This irony is supported by the fact that the other well-lighted scene was in the colonel's office—a scene which overtly shows language and the imposition of signifiers being used in its most powerful, dangerous, double-edged way. Thus, it seems that in the final analysis, the play between light and shadows again merely underscores the accessibility of ironic "enlightenment" and language to the upper middle classes; like the military, they stand ready to use their linguistic skills to maintain the status quo. Thus, while Alberto will always remain in the limelight of society, Jaguar will remain in the shadowy sidelines (shadows and semidarkness which are repeated in the final scene of the epilogue). It is not that Jaguar fails to understand the inevitable overlapping of what had appeared to be mutually exclusive commodities (e.g., *madre/puta*) or fails to comprehend the power of words, but he will resign himself to life with these facts, and without that power, and not profit from them as Alberto will.[13]

La ciudad y los perros portrays women as signifiers which are exchangeable and interchangeable. But, more importantly, as signifiers women are repetitive, supplemented, and supplemental. Like any referent, the tangible woman has very little to do with the male's image of her and vice versa. This is particularly apparent in the character of Teresa. Each of the three young men perceives her quite differently because he has supplemented the signifier with traces that remain of his earlier experience with his mother. Each sees Teresa as repetition, substitution, and supplementation of his own mother. In this manner, comprehension of the world and subsequently any potential for mimesis become suspect insofar as they are dependent upon this language which is inevitably and continually supplementation and distortion. Finally, each of the male characters becomes the very embodiment of writing insofar as each depicts the dialectic between the feminine and the masculine. Written discourse, like each character, strives to be open, encompassing, and receptive, while it simultaneously closes back on itself and is self-sufficient and self-protecting.

6

Manuel Puig's *La traición de Rita Hayworth:*
Betrayed by the Cross-Stitch

CROSS-STITCH. Embroidery. Voices, often anonymous. Hidden creator. These are the initial observations and reactions as one begins *La traición de Rita Hayworth* (1968) by Manuel Puig (Argentina, b. 1932). Not only are these the first impressions as one opens the novel, but they are also the crux of the entire text. Because Chapter 1, with its "voices" and idle prattle, presents itself as an insignificant introduction into the world from which Toto has sprung, it is all too easy to dismiss the chapter as trite and gossipy and to examine only the rest of the book which appears to be more meaningful—especially since this first chapter is the one least related to Toto, the seeming protagonist of the novel. Nevertheless, the beginning of this first chapter, that is, the very first sentence, sets the tone for the rest of the novel, functions as a metaphor for the entire text (and perhaps for the bulk of Puig's other works), and provides the vital link to the comprehension of Puig's portrayal of women.

The chapter opens with an anonymous conversation (an anonymity which already underlines the plurality of the text):[1] " 'El punto cruz hecho con hilo marrón sobre la tela de lino color crudo, por eso te quedó tan lindo el mantel.' 'Me dio más trabajo este mantel que el juego de carpetas, que son ocho pares...' " (" 'A brown cross-stitch over beige linen, that's why your tablecloth turned out so well.' 'This tablecloth alone gave me more trouble than the whole set of doilies, a full eight pairs...' ").[2] The importance of this opening conversation becomes patent via the repetition throughout the text of the embroidery motif, along with the multiple direct references to this same tablecloth. Of the many, many ways in which a novel might begin, surely a seemingly anonymous discussion of embroidery and tablecloths must be one of the least conventional. Such a beginning is particularly disconcerting to the reader because the novel's title suggests that one will be reading about the North American movie star.[3] What does embroidery have to do with Rita Hayworth and/or the movies? As I shall show, everything.

The *American College Dictionary* (New York: Random House, 1964) defines the verb "to embroider" in the following manner: "1. to *decorate* with ornamental needlework. 2. to produce or form in needlework. 3. to *adorn* or *embellish* rhetorically, esp. with *fictitious additions.*" What is patently manifest in such a definition is the additional, supplemental nature of the embroidery and its function as adornment. Such a beginning suggests that one is meant to see the entire text in terms of its metaphoric embroidery, that is, as adornment and "fictitious additions." Indeed, the novel is a conglomeration of narrations (some presumably oral), most of which function as rhetorical embellishments on several levels. Even within the framework of the fiction, most of what each character narrates about himself and his life is a fictitious adornment of that character and life—that is, it is an embellishment or fictionalization of what pretends to be or what we pretend is "reality," or the referent.

Unequivocally, the language of a novel creates a fictitious world and then refers to this world as if it were fact (i.e., nonfictional)—a "nonfiction" which patently depends upon the reader's willing suspension of disbelief.[4] Sometimes, however, within any given novel, we watch as characters "lie" about or refuse to accept the premises of this already fictitious world.[5] In other words, the world (W), presumably external to the text, is reduced, elaborated upon, and distorted to create the fictional world (FW) of the text. This, of course, is a strictly linguistic world, created by words and all they are capable of evoking. The latter is again reduced, distorted, and adorned to create the individual character's fictional world (CFW) according to the following progression (which is often erroneously seen as a hierarchy):

$$W \longrightarrow FW \longrightarrow CFW$$

The CFW is normally recognized by the careful reader as fictitious, as creation within creation, but the FW is not often overtly recognized as such since, as mentioned, it depends upon the reader's willing suspension of disbelief.

In *Rita Hayworth*, each of the characters further fictionalizes the already fictional world of the text by adding layers on top of layers, masking the mask, supplementing the supplement—emphasizing the vacuity of the "bottom layer." Each "voice" adamantly refuses to see his or her own life in terms of the absurdity and triteness which surround it. For example, in Chapter 2 Amparo's embellishment of her life and expression of her dreams, which cannot appear very idealistic to the middle-class reader, disintegrate into obscenities and aggression, reflections of her basic frustration and her underlying recognition (although perhaps even meant to be seen as subconscious) of the futility of such dreams: "Cuando tu mamá se decida a comprar los muebles me voy a quedar a dormir acá en tu casa. Si hubiera una cama para mí me quedaría a cuidarte toda la noche. ¿Cuesta más una cama o un novillo? Si tu papá tuviera mucha plata" (p. 26); "Si esta noche a ustedes les sobra una milanesa mañana a la mañana se la pido a tu mamá y me la va a dar. La Pelusa nunca comió milanesas. Vos todavía sos muy chico para pedir milanesas, pero tendrías que pedir una milanesa esta noche en la cena. Pero sos muy chico, si no la podrías esconder y yo se la llevo mañana a la Pelusa. Pero piojo de mierda todavía no sabés hablar" (pp. 29–30) (" 'And when your mommy decides to buy the furniture I'm going to sleep here in your house. If there was a bed for me I'd stay over to take care of you all night. What cost more, a bed or a steer? If your daddy had a lot of money,' " p. 20; " 'If you people have a leftover cutlet tonight, I'll ask your mommy and she'll give it to me tomorrow. Fuzzy [Pelusa] never ate one cutlet. You're still too young to ask for veal cutlets, but you ought to ask for one tonight at supper. But you're too young, if not you could hide it and I'd take it to Fuzzy tomorrow. But you shitty little bedbug, you don't even know how to talk yet,' " p. 22). Thus, language not only creates this imaginary world within an imaginary world but subsequently is viewed as a barrier to the realization of the former—Toto cannot talk, therefore la Pelusa will be deprived of her *milanesa.*

Later, Toto lives through a variety of fantasies and imaginative discursive meanderings, as do (among others) Hector (Chapter 9), Paquita (Chapter 10), Esther (Chapter 12), Herminia (Chapter 15). Each, whether on paper or mentally, fictionalizes and embellishes his life by focusing on the dreams, on that which "would be" or might be. It is not irrelevant that on the very first page of the novel, there are not less than five past-subjunctive constructions in contrary-to-fact clauses (one of the most repeated constructions in the novel): "si pagaran mejor"; "parece que no cansaran"; "si yo tuviera más tiempo"; "si yo viviera en esta casa"; "me parecía . . . que se fuera por un año" (p. 9) ("if they paid more"; ["it seems that they wouldn't tire one"]; "If I had more time"; "If I lived in this house"; ["it seemed like she went away for a year"], p. 5). Such, of course, is the basis of the book—what might be, but what is not (as the past-subjunctive construction demonstrates). The ideal in each case is the sum of the referent (the FW, which significantly is already fiction and supplement) plus the embellishment (supplement, embroidery) that each character adds to make that world more appealing, prettier, and more palatable. And such is the very function of embroidery—to make pretty what is not, to present what might be, what looks like something else but what is not.[6] The character's fictional world (CFW) is based on another fictional world (FW) which is already the linguistic adornment of the world (W) as we know it.

Within this notion of embroidery, it is particularly significant that Puig has selected precisely the cross-stitch rather than some other stitch. The cross-stitch is the most basic of all embroidery stitches; it is the first one learned by the would-be embroiderer and requires the least skill to execute well. It is a stitch produced by crossing two simple stitches, one over the other in the form of an X, and results in a figure which gives the impression of two threads meeting and merging, although the fusion or unification is only illusory. The cross-stitch, in this sense, functions as a metaphor for the interpersonal (intercharacter) communication which is repeatedly dramatized in the novel. Each of the characters continually attempts to communicate or relate with another (either verbally or physically), to unite or merge with another mind or body, and thus create a sense of being a part of something greater than the self. By means of a letter, Berto tries to communicate with his brother; similarly, Toto incessantly tries to relate to his mother (often identifying with her);[7] and Choli and Mita talk at length (without saying anything of import). Hector strives to merge physically with each female he encounters, whereas the piano teacher seeks a kindred soul. All the various forms of communication represented in the novel (dialogue, monologue, letters, diaries, compositions, etc.) point to the ultimate tragedy of the novel; in spite of all these attempts, no one has succeeded in communicating what he believed he wanted to convey.[8] In fact, the very formats chosen for the exchange often inevitably lead to and underline the lack of communication: letters not sent, dialogues which are really monologues since the interlocutors do not respond to each other, diaries, internal monologues, anonymous letters.

Thus, the text as a whole presents a series of discourses which fail to achieve what should be their primary goal: social intercourse. This failure of communication is apparent from the opening lines and the embroidery leitmotif. Embroidery, of course, depicts in a very stylized form certain objects or beings, but it rarely "says" anything, relays information. When it does reproduce words, the message is generally trite and repetitive, as in "Home Sweet Home." Its function is patently decorative, not utilitarian or enlightening. Similarly, the opening conversation in which this stitchery is discussed is equally lacking in communication and information. The language here appears to serve as mere decoration, mere "noise" to fill in the silence insofar as no one says anything of any import, anything which might need to be imparted. In fact, it often appears in this opening dialogue that the characters are talking to themselves and openly not listening to the others:

—Las labores parece que no cansaran pero después de unas horas se siente la espalda que está un poco dolorida.
—Pero Mita quiere que le haga un cubrecama para la camita del nene, con colores vivos porque tiene poca luz en los dormitorios. Son tres piezas seguidas que dan las tres a un jol con ventanales todos tapados con una tela de toldo que se puede correr.
—Si yo tuviera más tiempo, me haría un cubrecama. ¿Sabés qué es lo que

más cansa? Escribir a máquina sobre una mesa alta como la que tengo en la oficina.
—Si yo viviera en esta casa, me sentaría al lado de esta ventana el rato que pudiera dedicarle al cubrecama de Mita, por la luz. (P. 9)

(—Embroidery doesn't seem tiring, but after a few hours your back begins to ache.
—But Mita wants me to make her a bedspread for the baby's crib, with bright colors since the bedrooms get so little light. Three rooms one after the other leading into a hallway with big windows, all covered with canvas curtains that you can pull open.
—If I had more time, I'd make myself a bedspread. You know what's really tiring? Typewriting on a high desk like the one I have in the office.
—If I lived in this house, I'd sit next to the window whenever I had a minute to work on Mita's bedspread—for the light. [P. 5])

There is no logical or syntactical relationship between the discourse of the various characters. It is as if each were talking alone.

This sense of a lack of communication is further accentuated by the presentation of the dialogue without any reference to the interlocutors. In none of these articulations are we given the name of the *I*, the speaker, or the name of the *you*, the addressee. All we can discern are certain linguistic traits, idiosyncracies which will later help us to identify the speakers. Thus, as readers, our position is exactly that of Berto who listens to conversations behind closed doors, and what we are "hearing" are characters discoursing with themselves. In other sections of the book, this lack of communication is even more overt. Toto's recounting the plots of various movies (to himself) cannot relay anything new; he already knows the plot, he has already seen the movies. His renarrations are noise to fill up the silence and boredom of the siesta hour. And, just as unsent letters fail to communicate, so in fact does a diary insofar as the writer and the reader are precisely the same character. The similarity to be found in all the various forms of discourse presented in this novel is that in each case the narrator is directing his discourse toward a *you* who is only himself; that is, the character divides himself neatly into an *I* and a *you*, a self and an other. On the few occasions when the *you*, the other, seems to be a distinct entity, a different character, this distinction or separation is definitively negated by the physical absence of that other. In all these cases, then, the discourse serves as form of embroidery, adding to the base, or core. The narration is a pastime, a diversion which makes things prettier, which adds another layer (a partial mask), but which changes nothing. In this respect, the characters unanimously fail in all interpersonal relationships, in all attempts at bonding and unification. What appears to be the linguistic conjunction of two lives, two beings, is as illusory as the fusion in the cross-stitch—the two lines or threads touch superficially but do not merge in essence.

Of course, in the final analysis, and paradoxically, the text does communicate. While each of the forms of discourse fails to communicate to its intended fictional recipient, that is, it fails to communicate within the text, the text as a whole does impart a message to its intended recipient, the reader. In some sense, then, the presumable inside and outside of the text are reversed, turned inside out. Thus, we find ourselves in a bidirectional paradox as the text simultaneously does and does not communicate (the message, again paradoxically, is that a message is not communicated), while on another level the reader is allowed a self-congratulatory superiority as he recognizes that he comprehends what the characters do not. But again, the irony is that the reader, like the critic, because he believes himself outside the text (which ultimately has no inside or outside), always feels falsely superior, as does Toto in his "reading" of the movies.

Significantly, the cross-stitch, that is the X, is also the sign of anonymity. In mathematics, it generally represents an unknown quantity, which the problem seeks to identify. In our society, Mr. X is always the mysterious stranger whose identity we actively seek to uncover or discover. It is pertinent that the novel's discussion of the cross-stitch takes place precisely in the most anonymous section of the text, when the reader is most ignorant of the identities of the interlocutors. It is not until we have completed the novel that we are able to go back and identify the characters we encounter in this opening chapter. In the rest of the text, on the contrary, the interlocutors, the "voices," are more clearly identified, or at least more easily named.

At the same time, however, X is a negation, a crossing out, a sign of pseudo nonexistence. When one has written something and later wishes to retract the word or statement, one puts an X through what has been written and thus antithetically negates while simultaneously affirming whatever has been crossed out. For example, if I write RITA HAYWORTH

IS ~~CRUEL~~ BEAUTIFUL, the fact that I have crossed out *cruel* and replaced it

with *beautiful* allows the reader to read "RITA HAYWORTH IS BEAUTIFUL" and at the same time recognize that my first thought (or at least my first statement) was "RITA HAYWORTH IS CRUEL." Thus, the reader understands that Rita Hayworth is *both* cruel and beautiful, while I am somewhat alleviated of the responsibility for having said she is cruel. An X, then, is the most basic form of metanoia. In fact, the very purpose of the crossing out (as opposed to an erasure) may be simultaneous negation and affirmation.

Similarly, in the first sentence of the novel, the use of the cross-stitch (made with *hilo marrón*, the color of dried blood) does not cover up or obliterate the fact that the fabric itself is unbleached linen. The embroidery decorates but does not hide the fabric completely. Significantly, the fabric is not a fine linen but merely unbleached. Bleached linen is a "pure," white fabric, but unbleached linen is off-white, less "pure" looking. The latter is generally less expensive and thus more accessible to those not belonging to the upper classes. One wonders if Puig has not meant us to understand the fabric here as a metaphor for the lives of the characters. The local elite (the goal or model for most of the characters) will have fine linen tablecloths and percale sheets, but the families in *Rita Hayworth* are condemned to less: unbleached linen. The psychological connotations of the fabrics are unmistakable: "pure," white fabric vs. "impure," off-white fabric. To the characters, no doubt, the lives of their idols, be they the gentry or the movie heroes and heroines, are pure, ideal, and stand in sharp contrast to their own metaphorically impure and off-white lives, which do not meet the standards of the upper classes.

The validity of this metaphoric interpretation is underscored by the fact that the second statement of the novel. " 'Me dio más trabajo este mantel que el juego de carpetas, que son ocho pares ...' " (" 'This tablecloth alone gave me more trouble than the whole set of doilies, a full eight pairs ...' "), continues, " 'si pagaran mejor las labores me convendría tomar una sirvienta con cama' " (" 'if they paid more for needlework, I could hire a sleep-in maid' "). Such a statement accentuates the character's awareness of the next step up in the social hierarchy; as a seamstress she would be frequently exposed to this social group, since she works for them. The exposure would certainly have created a desire to partake of the luxuries of such a life.

These ideals are further reflected in the characterization and deification of Mita in this opening conversation. Mita is depicted here as something of a goddess—the absent daughter and sister who understands all the finer things of life and apparently possesses most of those same "luxury" items. Obviously, the "facts" of the economic situation of Berto and Mita (the FW), as one later discovers, stand in sharp contrast to this idealization, a mythicization which is underscored by the paradoxical word play in her name. Mita, diminuitive of *mamá, mamita,* closely resembles the Spanish word *mito,* myth, and Mita has been mythicized as surely as she has been depersonalized. She has no proper name per se, and in this respect is nearly as anonymous as the X. *Mita* merely denotes her function as she is apotheosized as a mother-goddess figure. Paradoxically, however, *mita* also means forced, paid labor, perhaps in reference to her job to support Berto and Toto while Berto takes complete credit for the support of his family, and, in Argentina, it means a lot of cattle to be transported by train (a far cry from the exalted goddess).

But returning to the notion of embroidery, one notes that the important aspect is not the fabric on which the embroidery is worked (although it is most significant that the embroidery, for all its beauty, cannot hide the nature of the fabric), but rather the presence of the embroidery itself. The needlework generates a double-layered object (embroidery is always superimposed on top of fabric). The stitchery, as I have insisted, simultaneously pretends to cover as it reveals the fabric (the bottom level), but it does not change the function of the object; it cannot change its nature. This paradoxical position of embroidery as simultaneous revelation and concealment is directly related to the rest of this text as well as to the movies which provide one of the principal referents of the novel. Most would agree on the metaphoric relationship between movies and embroidery. In fact, it seems likely that the films of the period encompassed by the text were intended as and served as an escape, a distancing, from the socioeconomic realities of the period (socioeconomic problems which are also reflected in *Rita Hayworth*), perhaps in much the same way as embroidery serves to underplay and mitigate the fact that the tablecloth is only unbleached linen.

No doubt such is precisely the relationship between Puig's novel and the movie from which the title proceeds, *Sangre y arena*. Toto's ability to identify with the protagonist of the movie is what allows him to see Rita's reaction to his hero as betrayal. In the movie, which is of course the reworking (embroidery) of the novel, Gallardo is a poor boy who rises from his social position via the bull ring. Once he is famous and successful, he begins to mingle with the higher social classes, dressing as they do and attending their social functions. But, under the elegant clothing and in spite of his apparent assimilation into the elite (apparent to others of his own class, although not to those of the upper class), he still remains socially plebeian. The upward movement is only illusory since he clearly lacks the skills to function suitably in this different social milieu. Thus, once again, the embroidery has made the object (in this case Gallardo) more attractive, but the substance has remained unaltered.

Like embroidery and like the novel itself, movies also demonstrate a dual function of revealment and concealment. In each movie, the actors are simultaneously themselves and their characters, and the audience is patently aware of this duality. One goes to see the movie star himself as much as to see the part he is playing. The paradox is that the audience is alternately conscious of the star's true personality (although probably even this personality is another fiction, another embroidery) and aware of the part he is playing. While surely the audience comprehends the differences between the two, sometimes these two roles (or rather the lines of division between the two) become blurred. Toto, for example, while certainly cognizant of the two distinct entities, frequently confuses them. When speaking of Norma Shearer, he notes, "*Romeo y Julieta* es de amor, termina mal que se mueren y es triste: una de las cintas que más me gustó. Norma Shearer es una artista que nunca es mala" (p. 37) ("*Romeo and Juliet* is about love, it has a sad ending when they die, one of the movies I liked best. Norma Shearer is an actress who's never [bad]," p. 29). In this case, it is not clear whether Toto is referring to Norma's acting ability or to the parts she plays as a heroine. Later, speaking of Rita Hayworth, Toto states, "no la cara traicionera de Rita Hayworth. . . . Pero en *Sangre y arena* traiciona al muchacho bueno" (p. 82) ("not the betrayer face Rita Hayworth has. . . . But in *Blood and Sand* she betrays the good boy," p. 70). Thus Toto has confused Rita with her role. He sees Rita, rather than doña Sol, as having betrayed Gallardo. Clearly, then, this is a situation not unlike the one described by Ortega y Gasset in which as one looks out a window, one might see either the scene beyond or the window itself, or, I suggest, if one squints just right, a little of both, but neither very distinctly.[9] In this respect one can view all the characters as both mask and masked.

This ability to see a little of both, that is, to conceal and reveal at the same time, is what was noted in the cross-out. Obviously, the most revealing cross-out in the novel is Berto's letter to his brother. We know from the concluding lines that Berto did not send the letter: "Esta carta va al tacho de la basura, para vos no pienso gastar un centavo en estampillas" (p. 294) ("This letter is going into the wastepaper basket, I wouldn't spend a cent on stamps for you," p. 254). A paradoxical form of discourse, then, the eight-page letter reflects some of Berto's innermost feelings and thoughts but negates itself as surely as it affirms itself. As I pointed out, there is no exchange between the sender and the receiver. Ironically, it is not worth one cent to communicate.

And finally, the X is a symbol of illiteracy, for the illiterate or agraphic person signs his name with an X. Although a signature is presumably the sign of the person, that is, a graphic symbol of the self, the individual, the X of the illiterate is anything but personal and unique. The X at the bottom of a document merely indicates that *some* (whoever he might be) person has signed the paper; it in no way indicates what person signed it (unless his name is added—written by another person). Thus, the X, the sign of the illiterate, unlike a signature, is not intended to be a sign of the individual. Rather, it is (again paradoxically) a sign of illiteracy, and more importantly a symbol for writing per se. When one cannot write, that is, sign his name, one "writes" an X, performs a stylized gesture, leaving a trace of what might be interpreted as writing (although like the cross-out, this X both affirms and negates writing). Thus, the X signals, "I cannot write, but I shall pretend to." Anyone who has watched a child pretending to write knows that a series of X's represents (is) writing in the child's mind.[10] Thus, seen in this manner, writing too, particularly the writing of the novel, is patently a form of simultaneous revelation and concealment, as are all the written documents contained within the text of *Rita Hayworth*. These documents, along with other forms of discourse, pretend to cover, but ultimately divulge, what we are meant to understand about the character's personalities, because ultimately it is the cover or the mask itself which proves informative, significant, apocalyptic.

Surely, our consideration of the cross-stitch, the *X*, leads us directly to the topic which most interests us here: the female. The *X* is, of course, the international genetic symbol for female.[11] As one ponders the representation of women in this work and the portrayal of *the males' reactions to those females*, the following terms come to mind: betrayed, devoured, absorbed, annihilated, effaced, obliterated, emasculated, castrated, swallowed up. In the works of Puig, man's underlying (and often hidden) terror of woman rises to the surface and becomes overt. In fact, in reading *La traición de Rita Hayworth* and *El beso de la mujer araña*, one fleetingly wonders if Puig is not intentionally dramatizing Wolfgang Lederer's *Fear of Women*. But, the questions I shall address here are why this particular anxiety; from where does it evolve? The essential fear and preoccupations which were well disguised and hidden in *La ciudad y los perros* are manifest to all in this novel.

But, let me begin by noting some of the ways in which females are characterized or described in *La traición de Rita Hayworth*. Perhaps the attitude of the male characters toward the female characters is typified in the unusual associations in the mind of the child, Toto. One initially "enters" Toto's mind at age six when he first discovers the differences between males and females, differences and delineations which, as we saw in *La ciudad y los perros*, are essential to our culture. One of his earliest (although certainly not "original") observations on the female gender results from and is indirectly related to his biological need to urinate. While attending a school play, his father sends him to the lavatory with a girl, and Toto is dreadfully worried that she or her dress might prick him. Such a concern is not unique to Toto; it is an apprehension already set forth in Carlos Solórzano's *Los fantoches*, among other places, where the puppet whose dress is full of *picos* is precisely *la mujer que ama*. In *Los fantoches*, as in *La traición de Rita Hayworth*, the pertinent fact which is overlooked by the male characters is that it is *not* the woman who is pricking him, causing his discomfort, but rather her dress. In both cases, the dress, the embroidery, the supplement, has become confused with the essence of woman, and it is she who seems threatening and dangerous rather than her dress. Although Toto does realize that it is the dress which pricks, he does not overtly understand that the dress is not her, that is, that the inside is not the outside, the surface is not the core. Such, of course, is Toto's principal problem throughout the text—understanding that while the two certainly overlap, they are not necessarily one and the same.

Returning specifically to the incident at the school play, the mission was apparently successfully completed, and Toto returned to his father's side without any serious damage to his masculinity (although also without having urinated). At this point he notes that his father, "le dio un beso [a la niña] en la frente sin que el vestido duro lo pinchara 'decile gracias a la nena' " (p. 34) ("gave her a kiss on the forehead without getting scratched by her stiff dress 'say thank you to the girl,' " omitted in English translation); somehow grown men, as opposed to boys, are able to escape the dangers of women. Toto's reaction, however, is still one of fear: "¡y yo estoy escondido! ¡escondo la cabeza entre los pantalones de papi!" ("I'm hidden! I hide my head in Daddy's pants!" omitted in English translation). From here he proceeds to comment on the male/female differences as he perceives them at this point: "pero mucho mejor para esconderse son tus [his mother's] polleras porque escondo la cabeza y si papá abre las piernas me ven" ("but your skirts [his mother's] are much better for hiding because I hide my head but if Daddy opens his legs, they'll see me," also omitted).

Two pages later, he further delineates the disparities he finds between a mother and a father: "Papá la llamó y mamá tuvo que irse a dormir la siesta" (p. 36) ("Daddy called her and Mommy had to go in to take a nap," p. 28), suggesting, of course, that mother is as powerless as he before the will of the father; and, "Mamá pega cachetadas que no duelen mucho y papá pega cachetadas que deshacen" (p. 37) ("Mommy slaps me but it doesn't hurt much but when Daddy slaps you he breaks you in two," p. 29). The latter statement, again an appraisal of the perceived power hierarchy, is particularly significant insofar as it is mythic and without basis in reality, since it is totally a linguistic creation. Toto has experienced his mother's slaps and knows that they do not hurt much. His father, on the other hand, has *never* slapped him; what he "knows" about his father's slaps are only what his father (certainly not a very reliable source) has told him: " 'nunca te he pegado pero el día que te ponga la mano encima te deshago' " (p. 37) (" 'I never slapped you but the day I put my hands on you I'll break you in two,' " p. 29).

It appears, too, that Toto is introduced to sex, sex roles, and sexual terminology by a gratuitous association between a movie he has seen and what a little girl (who in relation to Toto is definitely an "older woman"— she is twelve) teaches him (or insinuates to him).[12] In the movie that he watched with his mother, he saw "una planta que se mueve en el agua clarita del fondo del mar y tiene todos pelos que flotan como serpentinas" (p. 41) ("a plant that moves in the nice clear water at the bottom of the sea and it has hairs that look like streamers," pp. 32–33). Since his mother had commanded him not to look, he freely associated this incident with the term taught to him by Pocha, *cogía*. The link between the two moments emanates from the prohibition, the illicitness, the taboo: "Pocha decime qué quiere decir cogía 'no podemos jugar a eso, tiene que ser un muchacho con pelo' " (pp. 41–42). ("Pocha tells me what 'fucks' means 'We can't play that, you have to be a big boy with hairs,' " p. 33). Both situations, then, are marked by the cross-out, the negation (discussed a few pages ago), and which merely accentuates and reaffirms precisely what is being negated, as well as the repetition of the metaphor, *pelo* (hair). To Pocha's cross-out, Toto adds his own: "y no le dije a la Pocha que yo había visto una cinta del fondo del mar con la planta llena de pelos que se come a los pescaditos. . . . Los pelos son los que se comen a los pescaditos en la cinta del fondo del mar. Los pelos largos primero se mueven blanditos en el agua ¿y los pescaditos que se habían acercado?' 'Toto, ¡bajá la vista!' ¡ya! no se ven más porque la planta de pelos *se los tragó*" (p. 42, emphasis added) ("and I didn't tell Pocha I had seen a movie about the bottom of the sea with the plant full of hairs that eats the colored fishies. . . . The hairs are what eat the fishies in the movie about the bottom of the sea. First the long hairs move all soft and the water and the fishies came near, right? 'Toto, don't look!' now you don't see them any more! because the hairy plant *swallowed them*," pp. 33–34, emphasis added). It is clear that Toto's association between the movie with the fish-eating plant and coitus is effectuated by means of the taboo placed on each as well as by means of the purely linguistic relationship, for, as explained to him by Pocha, coitus is defined in the following manner: " 'es una cosa mala que no se puede hacer [again the cross-out, it is but it is not], se puede jugar nomás porque si una chica lo hace está perdida, está terminada para siempre [as is the fish]' " (p. 41) (" 'It's a bad thing that you can't do, you can only make believe, because if a girl does it she's lost, finished forever,' " p. 33). She continues, again underlining the linguistic similarities between the two incidents, " 'no podemos jugar a eso [another negation, first they could not do it, they could only play at it; now they cannot even play at it], tiene que ser un muchacho con pelo [like the plant]' " (p. 42) (" 'We can't play that, you have to be a big boy with hairs,' " p. 33), and in turn Toto notes, "Los pelos son los que se comen a los pescaditos" (p. 42) ("The hairs are what eat the fishies," p. 34). Thus, in the child's mind, since we use the same terminology and since we have the same reaction to the two incidents, the two must somehow be related. Logically then (or illogically, but linguistically) it is only a short step from this association to one in which Toto might conclude, again, through the simple use of everyday metaphoric terms (terms so commonly used that we forget their metaphoric value), something of this nature: "el hombre con pelo en el pecho podrá comer a las mujeres" ("The man with hair on his chest—i.e., suitably manly—can eat—destroy—women") or vice versa, "la mujer con pelos puede devorar al hombre" ("The woman with hair—i.e., suitably aggressive, castrating—can devour the man"). Thus, the myth is created, and its status as supplemental embroidery, invention is soon forgotten.

Unquestionably, there is a contradictory *vaivén* throughout this section of the text in regard to the male/female symbolism—a *vaivén* which is no doubt intended to correspond to Toto's confusion regarding coitus and the sex roles. On the one hand, the fish would appear to be a masculine symbol, destroyed by the hairy plant—female symbol. On the other hand, the girl who plays this game of coitus is apparently destroyed as is the fish. Perhaps the point is that in the adult semiological perception, the female "loses" or is destroyed in the game (la Poncha here being the older, wiser point of view) whereas in the male child's perception it is his masculinity which is threatened by the game. Obviously, the error inherent in both postures is the insistence on seeing analogies or symbolism in everything and particularly the twentieth-century insistence on the game metaphor, which automatically implies that all aspects of life embody winners and losers, the former capable of devouring the latter.

Before continuing this analysis of Toto's associations here, it is pertinent to consider the other linguistic imports of these passages. There are two significant linguistic principles at work here whose relevance in the text must not be ignored. First, I shall examine the status of the enunciation within the enunciation, that is, the quoted discourse within the apparently "free-flowing" discourse, and then I shall consider the verb *cogía*.

These passages, like most of the presumed internal monologues, are characterized by the quotations of the discourse of other characters and/or quotations of prior enunciations of the same character. While the ownership of this repeated discourse is not always indicated, the discourse itself is generally expressed within quotation marks or by means of some other stylistic device which allows us to recognize the enunciation as reiteration.[13] Such quotations are to be found in the two sections of Toto's interior monologue (chaps. 3, 5), in Teté's interior monologue (6), in Delia's (7), in Mita's (8), in Héctor's (9, although Héctor's is frequently without quotation marks), in Paquita's (10, again frequently without quotation marks), in Cobito's (11), in Esther's diary (12), and in Herminia's notebook (13, although significantly the only direct quotation here is the opening paragraph of the text, a citation from a newspaper). In view of the fact that in each of these cases the character is narrating only to himself, the logical question is why quote? Why would one quote someone else when one is talking or thinking to oneself? Since quoted words always represent a degree of authority and since, as I have shown, the *you* is always absent in these mono-dialogues, one must ask to whom is the monologuist demonstrating this authority?

Clearly, any quotation is an overt repetition and to quote is to acknowledge this duplication and concurrently to grant authority for the discourse to someone else. In general, we quote precisely for the purpose of employing this "authority" for our own ends. Quoted discourse, however, maintains an interesting, dual position; it simultaneously "belongs" to the one who quotes and to the one who is quoted. It is an intermediary step in which someone else's more authoritative and presumably more valid concepts are partially and/or gradually absorbed into the reiterator's system of ideas. The younger and less powerful, authoritative, or "official" the quoter is, the more credence he will place on that cited discourse, and, as he quotes, he acknowledges that the idea is both his and someone else's. Thus, at this level we might again employ the embroidery metaphor, for it is here that we are still able to discern the two layers, that is the fabric— someone else's idea, which in all likelihood developed from yet another person (and, thus, is still not "original")—and the stitchery—the repetition, the quotation marks. Quotation, then, points to both the self and the other, while the quotation marks indicate the dividing line between the two. At the same time, quotation also inevitably marks a step in the loss of innocence. One quotes in order to show oneself not naïve, not unknowledgeable.

The final step of this process is that one eventually ceases to acknowledge the other's contribution. The reiteration no longer has quotation marks; the speaker has usurped its authority and its ownership. It now belongs to him, and he has forgotten, intentionally or involuntarily, that it once belonged to someone else. Its "origin" is now buried, hidden from sight, as the other has been absorbed, assimilated into the self. What is repetition or other is no longer recognized as such. It now appears original, emanating from the self—a misconception which will lead to innumerable problems.

This repetitive process becomes particularly significant when one recognizes that much (perhaps nearly all) of our knowledge follows precisely the same path. All our language is learned in this manner, and many of our "facts" are absorbed via this path: quotation, repetition. Thus, quotation, while it underscores the quoted narrator, is also the first step in a process which will eventually usurp authority by covering and hiding its very source. What is left at the end of the third step is merely the presumption of authority, the myth of authority.

If one applies these theories to *La traición de Rita Hayworth*, several important points come to light. One realizes that the entire novel is a fictitious quotation. Every section is made up exclusively of the discourse of one or more characters, where the quotees are fictitious and the quoter has disappeared into the background, a dual situation which traditionally undermines the authority of the discourse and highlights the indifferentiation; apparently none of the characters is more nor less reliable, none of the ideas more nor less valid. It is precisely this lack of authority which makes many readers so uncomfortable with the text and which, as I shall show in the coming pages, is the message of the novel: there are no differences, all is discourse, mask, masked.

But let us return to the questions posed earlier. Why quote to oneself? Unmistakably, this question necessarily encompasses two questions. First, why cite someone else's words to oneself? And, second, why quote one-

self to oneself? In Chapter 3, during Toto's presumably interior monologue, he does both. The gesture of quoting to oneself seems to indicate a
need to remember exact words and phraseology in order to be able to
analyze and understand. It is clear that Toto does not quite understand
what has taken place; perhaps by remembering each word, each sentence
exactly as it occurred, he will be able to find the significant link that he may
have missed the first time—the link which will explain all that he cannot
comprehend. The reiteration also reflects the learning process itself (as I
have suggested). The student with the history textbook repeats to himself
the fact he finds there in order to imprint it, as it were, on his mind, so that
he cannot forget it. Toto apparently pursues something similar. By mentally repeating these concepts, not only is he attempting to comprehend
them, but also he is imprinting them on his "mind" so that he will not
forget them.

The quotation of the others' remarks, then, is related to the reiteration of
one's own comments. Again, Toto evidently attempts to understand, to
find the link between his words and the others'. I noted earlier that to cite
is to grant and/or to validate the authority of the one quoted, but, if the *you*
addressed is absent in the interior monologue, to whom is the interlocutor
validating this authority? The answer is now clear—to himself. If I grant
John a certain merit by quoting him, and this validity is confirmed by the
you to whom I am citing him, then by quoting myself, I am both granting
myself authority and power and simultaneously validating that authority.
By reiterating his own words to himself, Toto endeavors to raise his status
in his own eyes; self-quotation is a form of saying, "my words are important and worthy of repetition."

Ultimately, this entire theory of citations takes on particular meaning
when applied to the concept of women. One notes that much of the quotation in Chapter 3 is related to sex. It is not irrelevant that the male generally
learns about sexuality and women from someone else. What is learned is a
set of differentiations (differentiations whose comprehension was dramatized in *La ciudad y los perros*) which are cultural and which are given
credence by virtue of the "teacher" who is always wiser and generally
older. In Chapter 3 of the Puig novel this process unfolds. Pocha has told
Toto about the sex act; he quotes to himself and eventually absorbs what
she told him into his own set of concepts, forgetting the origin or authoritative basis for the information as it passes through the process of mythicization. In the end, his "knowledge," his "facts," about sex have taken on
legitimacy and authority by the mere gesture of repetition. The "original"
authoritative source (which clearly is never original since he/she too is
merely repeating—significantly, Pocha's words too are patently repetition)
is forgotten or lost. All that is left is what one "knows" to be true although
one is no longer sure why it is true. Ironically, then, his concepts, notions,
"facts," about women are not only mere linguistic creations, but indeed are

only quotations and repetitions. The significant paradox is that these "facts" (as demontrated by various characters, not just Toto) are the quotations of "authorities" whose expertise is dubious. Toto learns about coitus from a twelve-year-old girl who does not know much more about sex or men and women then he does, and, yet, she is his sage on the subject. It is she he quotes.

Significantly, it is at this point in his development, too, that Toto learns the emotion-evoking capacity of words. Although he still does not understand the significances or the referent for the word *cogía;* as he calls Felisa *"cara de cogía"* (p. 43) (" 'fucksface,' " p. 34), he discovers that the words elicit strong reactions in others (she strikes him). But the pertinent question here is why *cogía?* Why precisely this verb form? In addition to its double meaning as both "took" and a vulgarity for "fornicated," the word itself encompasses three specific aspects that seem relevant.

First, the verb is not always used as a verb; Toto's use of it as a noun reflects his basic lack of comprehension about the functioning of language. Although a linguist might see *cara de cogía* as a transformational use of *cara de cogida,* Toto does not, nor is it likely that such was the intent of its usage. The word he has heard is simply *cogía,* and while he may associate it with the *cogida* of the bullfight (an association I shall discuss in the coming pages), the word has been used by the young girl in the imperfect tense as a replacement for the conditional tense—" '*si* un muchacho se subía a la azotea mientras yo estaba dormida, me sacaba la frazada y *me cogía*' " (p. 41, emphasis added) (" '*If* a boy came up to the roof while I was sleeping, he *would* take off my blanket and fuck me,' " my translation). As Jespersen has noted, it is not unusual for a child to be confused about word usage;[14] as presented in the text, Toto is only six years old and is still trying to comprehend this thing we call language. Thus, one might presume that what is happening here is precisely what Jespersen has already noted: "Not infrequently what is said on certain occasions is taken by the child to be the *name* of some object concerned" (p. 116). The linguist goes on to give as an example a child's use of the word *pretty* as a substantive instead of the word *flower* and notes, "perhaps most frequently, a word is first for a child a proper name" (p. 117). Toto's use of *cogía* as a noun reflects a similar confusion.

Second, the verb, used in the third person, often without reference to its subject, implies anonymity on the part of the subject, and thus a certain universality; the subject might be anyone. Significantly, however, the verb is singular, and when a subject is expressed that subject is *he*—still indefinite, but distinctly male. Thus, in spite of the fact that in Toto's mind two people or two entities are involved in this act, only one acts, while the other is acted upon.

Third, and perhaps most interesting, however, is the temporal form of the verb—the imperfect tense. As we know, the imperfect is used to indicate repeated action in the past, thus underlining the repetitive nature of the act. Significantly, however, the imperfect is also used (as it often is in this text) as a substitute for the conditional tense in if-then/contrary-to-fact clauses, which takes us back to one of the principal linguistic leitmotifs of the novel—how things might be, but are not.

Undeniably, Pocha's presentation of this word reflects the portrayal of language in this text. On page 41 when she explains to Toto exactly what this *cogía* involves, one notes that in spite of her lengthy explanation, she still is not able to communicate the idea to Toto. Furthermore, she explains to Toto by beginning in the present tense, telling what happens in general terms (in an almost mythic present that forms part of the game, "let's pretend")—you/he does this, you/he does that *to me:* " 'yo estoy durmiendo en la azotea y estoy durmiendo tapada con una frazada pero sin bombachas puestas. Entonces vos sos un muchacho grande, y venís... y me hacés una cosa' " (p. 41) (" 'We make believe I'm sleeping on the roof and I'm asleep covered up with a blanket but I don't have any underpants on. And you are a big boy, and you come... and do something to me,' " p. 32). Thus she is directly involved in this act and includes herself in the story, perhaps as a representative of the female gender. Given her age (twelve) and the "let's pretend" aspect of the game, one simply presumes that she is creating a fiction. Midway through the sentence, however, she changes to the imperfect tense: " 'si un muchacho se subía a la azotea mientras yo estaba dormida, me sacaba la frazada y me cogía' " (p. 41) (" 'If a boy came up to the roof while I was sleeping, he would take off my blanket and fuck me,' " my translation), and the reader is left to wonder whether she might not be telling what *did* happen.[15] Or is she just telling us what would happen if . . . ? An identical linguistic process is demonstrated on page 42 (pp. 33–34, English) as Pocha continues her explanation of *cogía*: " 'el muchacho me *mete* el pito en el agujerito de la cola y no me *deja* ir, yo ya no me *podía* mover y se *aprovechaba* y me *cogía*' " (emphasis added) (" 'The boy *puts* his weeny in the little hole of my tail and he *doesn't* let me go. I [*couldn't*] move at all and he [*took*] advantage and [*fucked*] me,' " emphasis added). The result is a sense of both ambiguity and universality, and Pocha's narrative gesture, like that of the other characters, has been a movement from a generality which seems fictitious to self-inclusion which is accepted as fact.

But perhaps what is most apropos to this study is the manner in which this seemingly innocuous word (and Toto's seemingly naïve use of it) undermines the myth of innocence by being employed and presented in such a surreptitious fashion. Just as one might be inclined to presume that the descriptions or visions of the female in this or any text might be innocent to the extent that the narrator or author seems to have little or nothing to say about women per se—that is, a comment on women is not ostensibly the subject of the text—and to the extent that the narrator or protagonist himself might appear young enough or unwordly enough not to have formed a prejudicial view of women, one might be inclined to view Toto's use of the word *cogía* with a degree of self-delusion. But the treatment of the word in this text unequivocally contradicts this position and underlines the fact that semiotic usage is fraught with meaning and intention, overt or covert.

First, the use of the word belies the myth of innocence to the extent that even as Toto learns the word, and even as he fails to completely grasp its significance, he does, nonetheless, on some level, comprehend its connotations, or at the very least, its evocative powers, He may not know what it means, but he certainly does understand that it is a "bad" word as evidenced by his use of it, *cara de cogía*, when he is angry with Felisa and wants to hurt her. Second, the word's changing significance and connotations throughout the centuries call into doubt the possibility that the word might ever have been completely nonevocative. In fact, as Eusbeio R. Castex has noted in reference to the verb *coger*, "En principio sería un eufemismo; mas ese eufemismo se hizo tan patente, tan claro, que dejó de ser palabra decente."[16] It is particularly significant, too, that this word *cogía*, which as I shall show provides the axis around which the entire text gravitates, is based on a double-entendre, as is the entire text, beginning with the title.

In addition, the feigned innocuousness is further disavowed by the fact that an examination of the etymology of the morpheme *coger* exposes the verb's relationship to all the principal leitmotifs of the novel. For example, as one studies the etymological roots of *coger*, one discovers that it is directly related to *acollechar* which means "acorralar los ganados" (to drive cattle into a corral).[17] At the same time, at least one dictionary defines the verb as "copular, sobre todo el ganado vacuno" (to copulate, particularly cattle).[18] Not surprisingly, although certainly not conspicuously, one of the principal preoccupations of the entire Puig text is cattle,[19] and cattle unexpectedly relate to most of the other major concerns of the text. To cite an instance, the opening conversation of the text, which has been discussed in detail, continually returns to Mita, and it is Mita who leads us to the unconventional topic of cattle, for as already noted, *mita* in Argentina refers to a lot of cattle to be transported. Furthermore, two other sections of the novel, which are concurrent with the opening conversation and each other, center on the unexpected topic of cattle: "En casa de Berto, Vallejos 1933" and "Carta de Berto, 1933" ("At Berto's, Vallejos, 1933" and "Berto's Letter, 1933"). In fact, the principal leitmotifs which occur in the three sections are all directly related to the verb *coger*: the question of pregnancy and sexual relations; cattle, young bulls, veal; and economic problems.

The segment "En casa de Berto" opens with a statement regarding sexual relations: " 'Porque somos sirvientas se creen que nos pueden levantar las polleras y hacernos lo que quieran' " (p. 22) (" 'Just because we're maids they think they can pull up our skirts and do anything they want to,' "

p. 16), a statement which already links economics and coitus (if the servants were not poor and financially dependent presumably the masters would be less sexually abusive of them) and which undermines by anticipation Berto's statement in his letter that, unlike his brother, he is not a womanizer. Then, the older servant's admonition to Amparo (whose sister has been cast out of her home for having given birth out of wedlock) prefigures Pocha's words to Toto: " 'ya estás perdida si te dejás embromar por alguno' " (p. 22) (" 'You've had it if they pull the wool over your eyes,' " p. 16). Similarly, in this same segment, the arrival of the milkman subtly ties together all three topics to the extent that he discusses his cows and Berto's extramarital activities: " '¿De qúe se salvó el señor?' 'De que lo matara un marido cornudo' " (p. 26) (" 'What did Mister Berto get away with?' 'With being killed by a jealous husband,' " p. 19). Significantly, the word *cornudo* points to the cattle theme (and again undermines Berto's pretense of fidelity) and the economic problems (the characters discuss the milkman's successful survival in economic hard times, and we are subtly shown Berto's economic situation by the fact that he is unable to pay the milkman). Later in the same segment, after Amparo and Felisa again discuss women who give birth out of wedlock, Amparo talks to Toto and questions, "¿Cuesta más una cama o un novillo?" (p. 26) ("What cost more, a bed or a steer?" p. 20)—again juxtaposing coitus and cattle. The topics are even further associated by Amparo's desire to take home a *milanesa* (beef, veal) for her niece (born out of wedlock), because they are too poor (economics), and the child has never eaten one. The entire segment ends once again with Amparo's concern for the dead cattle which are bringing economic disaster on the family and thus indirectly on herself. Thus, throughout the segment cattle, coitus, and the economic situation are inextricably associated because of the linguistic patterns, in a manner which parallels Toto's associations between coitus and the movie he has seen. *Coger,* then, is insidiously employed for its evocative powers not only by Toto but also by Puig.

In analogous manner, the letter which Berto is writing to his brother during the course of the action in this same segment also makes multiple references to the three topics. Its physical location at the end of the novel suggests that it is intended to refocus attention on the three subjects. Berto emphasizes in his letter that the economic problems which he is undergoing are a result of the cattle dying, which is a result of the drought—it is not his fault or his inadequcy which is causing the problem. (Of this I shall have more to say later.) Furthermore, he speaks of Mita much as one might speak of any female bovine—"está gorda por la crianza . . . está redonda . . . tiene que pensar en alimentar al crío con el pecho" (p. 288) ("She's fat from breastfeeding . . . she's nice and round . . . she has to think of feeding the infant with her breast," p. 249). And, as I have suggested, he boasts of his marital fidelity, which apparently directly contrasts that of Jaime, his brother, yet contradicts what we have learned in earlier chapters: "Yo desde que conocí a Mita me olvidé de que existen las mujeres, te juro que no son macanas" (p. 291) ("Since I met Mita I forgot that women exist, I swear I'm on the level," p. 251); were this true, his maid would not complain as she does nor would the milkman speak of his escape from an angry husband. Thus, the novel structurally opens and closes with *coger* and its implications.

Finally, the association between *coger*, cattle, and the economic situation is highlighted by the fact that Toto learns about this *cogía* from Pocha as they are playing with the manger scene, a scene which again semiologically links babies, cattle, and perhaps even economic well-being, since Pocha's family has a manger scene and Toto's does not.

Thus, the apparently innocent use of *cogía* on the part of Toto and by implication on the part of the narrator is not at all guileless but rather fraught with connotation and evocative powers which lead us to the major concerns of the text, as evidenced by the fact that the word's etymology, an etymology which is probably neither totally conscious nor explicit on the part of the reader or the writer, also leads us directly to the main concerns of the text. In fact, the word itself with all its many connotations and its etymological inferences becomes in some sense a microcosm of or a synecdoche for the text. But, the etymology of *coger* offers yet other insights into the text and the depiction of the female.

The economic relevance of the verb *coger* is further implicated by Boyd-Bowman's study, from which one may conclude that the word was often employed in sixteenth-century Spanish America in reference to taking gold from mines.[20] Since *mina* is still used today in many parts of South America in reference to a female that one plans to or would like to dishonor, or has dishonored, and since one might easily understand virginity in anthropological terms as an economic value, *oro*, gold, it is not difficult to understand how *coger* might have evolved from its usage in relationship to removing gold from a mine to being understood metaphorically in relationship to sexual relations (i.e., remove gold, value, from a *mina*, female). Clearly, the other principal use noted by Boyd-Bowman, to collect crops, elicits a similar economic connotation and might subsequently lead back to the question of cattle and all its implications, since the survival of the cattle (and therefore the economic well-being of the owner) depends upon adequate gathering of crops (as evidenced in *La traición*).

Along the same lines, the female is evoked by the fact that the word *cosecha*, harvest, the collecting of crops, is believed to have derived from the feminine form of the past participle of *coger*'s etymon: *cogecha* (Corominas). Significantly, however, while Corominas provides us with an explanation of how the past participle came to be *cogecho*, he never addresses the question of its feminine form, either as *cogecha* or the current *cogida*.

Etymologically there are even more clues which point to the current significance of *coger* in the Río de la Plata countries and which make the word even more significant and less innocuous within the context of the novel and our perception of the female. Returning again to Corominas, one notes that one of the "aceptaciones raras" of *coger* is "dar (un golpe)" (to strike, to hit, to deliver a stroke or a blow). As an example, Corominas quotes Pérez de Hita, " 'Lison le *cogió* en descubierto del adarga un golpe por los pechos, tan bravo que *le metió la lança por el cuerpo*' " (p. 120, emphasis added). There is clearly little difficulty in perceiving the metaphoric relationship between this quotation and the sex act, and one wonders if it was this usage of the word which eventually led to its meaning in relationship to the *corrida*.

Perhaps it is in relation to the bullfight that *coger* most dramatically links itself to the major leitmotifs of the Puig text, for the bullfight again leads to the cattle leitmotif, while it also carries us in another direction to what the title has suggested is the major focus of the text. As I have indicated, the title of the novel links it to *Sangre y arena*, a novel about bullfighting which had been made into a movie—note the layers covering, and the movement away from, any possible discernible "origin" or source. In regard to the bullfight, *coger*, *cogida*, refers to a goring by the bull and in this sense is easily understood as a metaphoric representation of coitus (or vice versa) whereby the female is gored by this symbol of masculinity, or as Pocha expresses it, "perdida, terminada para siempre." To the extent that the bull is viewed today as a symbol of maleness par excellence (although this was not always the case), then, of course, the goring of the bullfighter will be viewed as defeat (and indeed it is, for he may well lose his life) by a greater masculine force. But once again, the bullfight which forms the model in this text is already supplementary, swathed in layers of fiction and re-creation, and merely contributes to Toto's confusion about the sex roles, since, as he views it, Gallardo's goring by the bull was provoked by doña Sol. Thus, to the child's mind, it is not the bull which is to blame, nor even Gallardo, but rather doña Sol, and on some semiconscious level, the subject of this verb, *coger*, changes and becomes feminine, just as it does as he plays *cogía* with Pocha and takes the female role himself.

Similarly, Toto's unexpected psycholinguistic or semantic association between the film he has seen and his introduction to sex leads him to identify coitus with punishment. Throughout Chapter 3, we watch him analyze his behavior, both good and bad, and insist that he is a *"pescadito bueno"* ("good little fishie") who ought not to be punished. Insistence on his position as *pescadito bueno* might be seen as the first step toward the assertion of his own masculinity, since the *bad* little fish is eaten by the hairy plant—obviously an undesirable situation for the little fish. "Goodness," then, might protect him from this fate.[21] More importantly, however, one notes that on pages 42 and 43 (33 and 34 in English) the little fish is used as a simile for Pocha ("si la Pocha se queda quieta como un pescadito"—"if Pocha stays still like a fishie") and the result of such behavior would be that "los pelos del chico . . . se la come toda" (p. 43) ("the boy's hairs . . . eats her all up," p. 34). Obviously, then, one would not want to be a bad little fish and subject oneself to such annihilation. Thus, perhaps we espy the beginnings of future value judgments, essentially unfounded and purely arbitrary, in regard to the differences between the sexes. The person that would allow this to happen to her (or him, which is not likely) is clearly, "perdida, está terminada para siempre, no se ve nunca más" (p. 43) ("lost, finished forever, she's never seen again," p. 34), and, this is precisely the position, in relation to femaleness, that each of the males in the text is trying to avoid.

Paradoxically, Chapter 3 also ends with Toto's imagination having divided him into a *pescadito* and a *negrita*, both of whom are pursued and die. The latter self-imposed incarnation is no doubt the result of his father's having called him "mi negrito," as he does in his letter to Jaime ("es un negrito precioso," p. 288) ("he's a handsome little bugger," p. 249— literally, little black fellow). The question, of course, is why has Toto converted *negrito* into its feminine form, and why is he both a *pescadito* (in his mind, one of the participants in the act of coitus) and a *negrita*? The answer again lies in his comprehension (or lack thereof) of the sexual act as well as his confusion between the sex roles. In Chapter 3, he perceives the hairy plant (which he later refers to as "planta de cogía," p. 45—"fucks bush," p. 36) as a somewhat obscure metaphor alternately for the male and for the female. The fact that when he and Pocha play *cogía* he assumes the feminine part while Pocha pretends to be the boy further confuses the roles of the two genders. Thus, from the very beginning, Toto tends to see himself as, and identify with, both male and female (although, as I have noted, he does see the latter as a less desirable position), in much the same way as he continually identifies with both the heroes and heroines of movies and novels. The fact that society has tended to bring women and children together and oppose them to males merely intensifies his confusion.

In other words, Toto is continually portrayed (as are most of the characters) as viewing himself as both self and other. The paradox is not so much that he sees himself in the two roles, which to our minds are contradictory, but rather that he sees no contradiction in the roles. Again, Toto appears to be undergoing the same lessons in life and language that were observed in *La ciudad y los perros*; he is learning to differentiate, to understand both psychologically and linguistically the difference between *I* and not-*I*, between male and not-male. In this vein he notes: "Mamá pega cachetadas que no duelen mucho y papá pega cachetadas que deshacen" (p. 37); "al Héctor también pero es más grande que yo, corre más ligero" (p. 36) ("Mommy slaps me but it doesn't hurt much but when Daddy slaps you he breaks you in two," p. 29; "Héctor too but he's bigger than me, he runs faster," p. 29). But it is not easy to distinguish, for in many cases the differences seem blurred or nearly nonexistent: "mami, y la pechera blanca de los hombres es igual que la tuya con la puntillita y la peluca blanca" (p. 31, here Toto seeks the differences between a figure of a person—that is, a representation, a metaphor—and a person) ("Mommy, and the men in white dickeys same as you, tiny lacing, white wigs," p. 24); "así el gitano cree que yo soy otro" (p. 35, here, he can be more than one while being one—all as a result of the misconception of the other) ("so the gypsy will think I'm somebody else," p. 27); "papá no tiene frío, se puso el poncho, era de tío Perico que se murió" (p. 36, his father and his uncle are clearly two distinct people, but the fact that they can wear the same poncho seems to imply that they, too, are almost interchangeable) ("Daddy isn't cold, he put on the poncho, it was Uncle Perico's who died," p. 28); "Mami te comiste un muñequito, yo me comí otro . . . ¿les duele a los muñequitos?" (p. 31, again Toto is trying to discover the difference between people and their representations) ("You ate a little doll Mommy, I ate another . . . does it hurt the dolls?" p. 24).

Thus, the movement through the text via Toto is a progression in differentiation and thus manipulation of words and language and a pseudo comprehension of women. (I say pseudo because it is clear that ultimately Toto understands very little). What is particularly pertinent is that Toto learns about women (and, of course, sex, sexual relationships, and sexual differences) as he learns about language; the two processes are intricately interrelated. As he puzzles on the meaning of the word *cogía*, he is simultaneously puzzling on language and women, that is, sexual difference, and his conclusions will eternally color his perception of women.

However, to explain the text as a history of the development of Toto, while accurate to a degree, is patently based on an overemphasis of some segments of the text and an underemphasis of others. Clearly, Toto is the linking factor, the character who seems to provide unity to the text insofar as he appears in some form in nearly every segment, but he is the protagonist, central figure, of only three of the sixteen individual segments—certainly not enough to establish overriding importance in the text. On whom or what, then, do the majority of segments focus?

The novel is divided into two parts of eight segments each. The reason for partitioning the novel neatly into two sections is unclear, but the first part is made up exclusively of presumably nonwritten discourse—dialogues, monologues, interior monologues or streams of consciousness, and so forth. Of these eight sections, two are "narrated" by Toto and the rest by various *female* characters. In Part Two, the eight segments are composed of three interior monologues or stream-of-consciousness discourses (via two male minds and one female mind) and five written compositions (notebooks, diaries, letters, compositions): one written by Toto, one written by Berto, and three written by other female characters. Toto, then, narrates only three of the sixteen segments, while ten of the remaining thirteen segments are narrated by female characters, and one is forced to acknowledge that the female plays a far greater role in the text than is immediately apparent or than critics have seen. One must wonder, in the light of the predominance of female *I*'s here, if the protagonist of the text is not Woman, and if Toto does not serve merely to represent the development of the male vision of that Woman. And, clearly, the evolution of this "male vision" is incomplete without the letter of Berto; Berto is, after all, in every way, what little Toto will come to be.

Those critics who have accused Puig of shoddiness or deliberate reader deception (and how can a writer do anything but deceive?) have missed the point of the letter.[22] Rather than labeling it withheld information, one must understand it as both a reconfirmation of what the careful reader should have already perceived throughout the text and as an indication of what Toto's future will hold for him; one certainly does not have to follow him through twenty or twenty-five more years to know where he is going. Thus, in addition to functioning as an end which forces us back to the beginning, the letter reaffirms the represented society's view of women by functioning as either a counterpart to Toto's interior monologue in Chapter 3 or as the reflection of the final step in the male psychic development.

The similarities between the letter and Toto's monologue are found principally in those points related to females and language. Berto writes and Toto speculates at precisely the same time of day—four o'clock in the afternoon, siesta time—and each does so out of boredom, for lack of anything else to do, anyone else to talk to. Essentially, then, each "talks" to himself; each divides himself into a speaker and a recipient, an *I* and a *you*. Berto's *you* may appear to be his brother, but like his decision not to send the letter, his statement that he does not expect an answer (although again this might be considered a cross-out and thus affirm that he does) merely underlines the fact that he had been talking to himself all along. Siesta time, then, with its forced silence and absence of a suitable partner becomes a time of self-dialogue, self-manipulation, and division of the one into two, as language becomes the means of self-gratification.

Thus, both Toto and Berto discourse precisely because Mita is absent, and Mita (again, the mother figure according to her name) is absent for economic reasons. Her absence, in turn, allows or encourages each of them to fantasize, to supplement, to embroider. Again, language is shown to be anything but innocent. Yet, for all their efforts at employing language to make the other present, both fail doubly. First, in spite of a certain consolation which results from the use of language, the other is still absent; secondly, the distance between the re-creation and the referent emphasizes even more pointedly the absence of that referent; Mita of the FW has little relationship to the Mita who appears in the CFWs. In fact, the portrayal of

her is distinct in each section of the text, and one might even wonder why
Mita has not been considered the main protagonist of the novel, since she
either appears in each section or has created (both in the sense of giving
birth and in the sense of educating, forming, within the fiction) the seeming textual focus, Toto. But, this absence of the mother and the evolving
preoccupation with her is not unique to Toto's discourse. Berto refers not
only to the absence of Mita but also to the absence of his own mother,
whose death presumably created his and his brother's problems. Additionally, the absence of the mother is apparent in many of the other sections.
Teté directs part of her discourse to her mother who is elsewhere; Cobito
talks in part to his absent mother; Héctor relates conversations between
himself and Mita, his surrogate mother, and refers to the death of his own
mother.

What is noteworthy about the absence of the female is that she is so
blatantly re-recreated, distorted, supplemented (embroidered) in the
minds of the male characters, who are consequently disappointed (or
would be disappointed) to discover that even within the fiction she does
not meet their ideals, their concept of her as they have re-created her. One
of the notions that permeates this text is that the other characters' perceptions of Mita have little to do with the "real" Mita (that of the FW). She is
simply not the perfect mother-goddess figure some of the other characters
would make of her; although it certainly does appear that she makes con-
certed efforts to meet the others' expectations, she generally falls short of
them. In fact, her position directly parallels that of Rita Hayworth in *Sangre
y arena*.[23] As I have noted, Toto feels that Rita has betrayed the young man
in the movie—a confusion on Toto's part between Rita and her character,
doña Sol, and a confusion that might be interpreted as a betrayal itself, but
a betrayal on the part of Toto who expects Rita to *be* what she is patently
only *pretending to be* to please the audience,[24] a misconception which again
confuses role, supplement, mask, with the one playing the role, the
masked.

But, there is a more profound level to this "betrayal." One cannot forget
that *Sangre y arena* is an American movie based on a Spanish novel; thus,
we already have two levels of translation, both linguistic and media. Furthermore, the movie that Toto "sees" is probably spoken in English and
has Spanish subtitles, another level of translation. If one carefully analyzes
the Blasco Ibáñez novel, one discovers that doña Sol did *not* betray the
young matador. Too often an emotional reaction to the novel, coupled with
identification with Gallardo, the protagonist, allows one to forget that from
the very opening pages of *Sangre y arena* he is portrayed as a *mediocre*
matador; the narrator of the Ibáñez novel states over and over that Gallardo is not particularly well-skilled in the art of bullfighting, but that he is
unusually courageous (or foolhardy, which may amount to the same).
Additionally, the narrator makes it perfectly clear to the reader that Gal-

lardo simply cannot and never will be able to fit into doña Sol's world. His rejection by her was to be expected, as was his death in the bull ring. He simply took one foolish chance too many. And it was his own pride, arrogance, and self-delusions, not her, which caused him to take that chance. The narrator of *Sangre y arena* repeatedly offers the possibility that Gallardo is *not* betrayed by the female but rather by his own dreams of glory and his own inadequacies—that is, by his own fantasies.[25] It is Gallardo himself, like Toto, who sees himself betrayed by her, and the reader must select one of the interpretations (the narrator's or Gallardo's) or somehow fuse them.

This selective interpretation as typified in Toto is demonstrated as one of the main concerns of the Puig text; from the opening section when the grandfather is going to kill a chicken for dinner, those same characters who are so anxious to eat the chicken are quite unwilling to see it killed. Their blindness is voluntary, as they psychologically refuse to acknowledge the source of that chicken on their table, in much the same way as Toto refused to acknowledge the "origins" of Gallardo's destined failure. Similarly, several of the characters (Berto and Amparo to mention just two) blame their own lack of happiness on the external, on the lack of economic security, and this, in turn, on the lack of rain.[26] Amparo observes, "nosotros tenemos que ahorrar, Totín, así tu papá nos compra los muebles y me quedo a dormir en la cama nueva. Cuando llueva va a crecer el pasto para que coman los novillos" (p. 30) ("we have to save, Totie, so your daddy will buy the furniture and I'll stay to sleep in the new bed. When it rains the grass is going to grow for the steers to eat," p.23); Berto writes, "con la sequía de este año en Vallejos no sé por donde empezar a rascarme" (p. 287) ("with this year's drought in Vallejos I don't know where to start scratching," p. 248). Once again the pattern is similar to that of *La vorágine* and *Doña Bárbara*: the characters impose what is internal to them on the external (which is not intended to imply that the external and internal do not merge at some point). They project their desires onto the other and then feel betrayed when the other does not conform to this ideal. The ultimate irony is that the very terminology associated with the female in this novel—*betrayed*—is precisely the act that the male is perpetrating on the female—*betrayal*: his imposition of his ideals upon her is his betrayal of her. No doubt the same "betrayal" is equally plausible with the sex roles reversed, but in this particular novel, it is the female who is erroneously viewed in the role of betrayer.

One wonders then if it is not this process which creates the textual as well as extratexual contradictions in which we tend to see women. Is this not why we tend to see women as heaven or hell, desired or despicable, mothers or prostitutes? Perhaps for all the pages of textual covering, embroidery, supplementation, efforts to impose the ideal upon her, that other "reality"—those other aspects not compatible with the cover—inevitably slip out, showing her to be at variance with what we had thought (hoped, demanded).[27] If this is so, then we must finally recognize that it is not the female herself who is contradictory. It is the discourse with which we try to cover her, shroud her, embroider her that is inadequate to the job and inevitably lets the fabric show through.

Conspicuously, too, Toto's monologue and Berto's letter expose the dread on the part of each male of emasculation, annihilation, effacement, obliteration, absorption—in short, all those fears listed earlier. The psychological basis of these anxieties and their manifestation is distinct in each, but the fears are essentially the same. Toto worries about being put into a skirt (apparently a fate worse than death) or being the little fish who is swallowed by the hairy plant. Berto worries about Mita witholding her salary from him and thus undermining his masculinity. (As we know, sex roles are directly tied to economics, and the male in twentieth-century, middle-class, Western society is, for whatever reasons, considered less masculine if he is unable to "properly" support the female).[28] Again, the fears are mythic in origin and projected onto the female to divert attention.

What also emerges in the comparison of the two sections is a perfect symmetry: Héctor/Jaime–Toto/Berto, inasmuch as Berto's attitude toward Jaime and his relationship to him is a direct parallel of that between Toto and Héctor. Both Héctor and Jaime are overt womanizers while Berto and son have an underlying sense of inadequacy in their rapport with women. The low self-esteem of each seems to have developed from an insistence that each was too young or too small. Toto's sense of confusion and/or inadequacy is at least in part due to Pocha's insistence "sos muy chico" ("You're too young"), a statement reiterated no less than four times (pp. 41–42). Similarly, Berto underlines the age difference between himself and his brother: "Vos ya eras un hombre, pero yo era un chico" (p. 290) ("You were already a man, but I was a boy," p. 251).

Perhaps, however, the most significant similarity between Toto's mental meandering in Chapter 3 and Berto's letter in the last section (in addition to the *coger*/cattle/economic links already noted) is the preoccupation with food, with eating. For example, Toto's monologue begins with a description of a candy box, which leads him to remember that he and his mother have eaten cookies in the shape of people, trees, and houses. He wonders if it hurt the *muñequitos* when he or his mother bit into them. From there he goes on to consider the canary eaten by the cat across the street and to worry a great deal that the bird that lives at his house might also be eaten. As he remembers his mother baking him a birthday cake, he wonders if the cat knows how to cook (since it ate the canary)—obviously he exhibits the same will to differentiate and assimilate we saw before. If people cook their food before eating it, why should the cat not do the same since both of us eat? At the school function, his father gets the sardine he wanted, and likewise, his father's cake has a cherry, while Toto's does not. The food leitmotif is continued in his encounter with Pocha. The manager he has gone to see is set up in the dining room; if he were bigger, he would cut Pocha's hair and make her eat her curls and dog excrement. As I have shown, the *cogía* becomes directly related to the concept of eating in the sense of ingestion, annihilation, and absorption; and, finally, Felisa is precisely in the process of preparing dinner when Toto calls her *cara de cogía*.

Similarly, Berto's letter makes several, although more subtle, references to the notion of food and eating. For example, in the second paragraph of the letter, Berto notes "Mita bien, mi Toto precioso, ya va para los ocho meses, *es una bolita de grasa*" (p. 287, emphasis added) ("Mita is fine, my Toto is a darling, he's almost eight months now, *a regular little butterball*," p. 248, emphasis added). A paragraph later, however, he goes on to complain that all the animals are dying and the financial climate is very bad. On the following page, he notes, in reference to Mita, "está gorda por la crianza, al fin ahora por el hijo se largó a comer como yo quiero que coma, y está redonda, antes se sujetaba de comer por la silueta, pero ahora que tiene que pensar en alimentar al crío con el pecho, se ha puesto a comer a gusto y está con el peso que debe tener, sabés que nunca me gustaron las huesudas. Mita es muy miedosa en la cuestión moneda, y si ella hace la digestión tranquila es porque yo no le dejo ver la gravedad de la situación" (p, 288) ("She's fat from breastfeeding. Now because of the child she finally started eating like I want her to, and she's nice and round, before she kept herself from eating for the sake of her figure, but now that she has to think of feeding the infant with her breast, she's eating like a human being and her weight is where it should be, you know I never liked the bony type. Mita is very worried about money, and if she has her meals in peace it's because I don't let her see how serious the situation is," p. 249). In both cases the metaphorical concern with eating or being eaten is directly female linked.

But eating is associated not only with women but also with economics. Obviously, the connection between women and economics is nothing original or unique; it is a relationship, an analogy, continually drawn by social anthropologists (women as units of exchange). While women as units of exchange *may* be a valid approach to primitive societies, the close relationship between women and eating or economics in this novel is not based on such a definition of the female. In fact, it is obvious that the relationship has quite a different basis. I suggest that eating, coupled with a wife and child that concretely and physically demonstrate the results of having eaten well, is directly related to the male's sense of success and his perception of his own masculinity. When Berto informs his brother that Toto is "una bolita de grasa" and that Mita "está gorda" what he is really saying is that economically he has been able to provide the financial support necessary to feed them to satiety. Thus, while the discourse overtly names the object, the *he* or *she*, it truly is pointing to the subject of the narration, the *I*. (The same, of course, can be said about the characters' descriptions of each other; the other, the object, is named and described but via this description we effectively learn most about the subject himself). Thus, Berto is indirectly reporting (or feigning) economic success on his part, prosperity for which he can be credited. The seeming paradox, of course, is that in the very same letter he negates this success (another cross-out), relating how economically difficult times are. Even as he does this, however, the reader (in this case presumably his brother, but in actuality himself) is meant to understand, infer, that in spite of the difficult times, for which he is not to blame, he, Berto, has succeeded in providing for his family and, thus, he is somehow superior (i.e., more masculine). This superiority is directly compared to his brother's status; in fact, one of the main objectives of the letter is to affirm his equality with his brother. His brother did not provide for the family's financial security when his mother died and, furthermore, insisted upon Berto's inadequacy to do so. It appears, then, that Berto's attitude toward food as it represents financial success and subsequent masculinity is not terribly different from Toto's preoccupation with food. In Toto's mind he who "eats" (metaphorically, as the plant) is more powerful, more dominant. Exactly the same semantic analogy is subtly demonstrated in Berto's letter.[29]

The other analogous aspect of the two discourses is, of course, the preoccupation with women. I have already discussed Toto's concerns as he "discovers" the opposite sex and coitus. Berto's concerns are not drastically different. Mita has given birth to Toto, which thus conclusively affirms Berto's masculinity as traditionally defined ("y ahora que soy un hombre y tengo un hijo" [p. 290] ["and now that I'm a man and have a son," p. 251]), but the fact that she continues to work and contributes her entire salary to the support of the family undermines that sense of masculinity and superiority. The conversation he hears between Mita and her sister draws attention to the problem. Thus, in many ways, he, like Toto, must be dependent upon Mita for the food he eats, a dependency he must justify: "yo no tengo la culpa si todo se me pone en contra" (p. 292) ("it's not my fault if the tide's against me," p. 252).

Thus, the letter at the conclusion of the book not only serves as a counterbalance to Toto's interior monologue but also underscores some of the most significant aspects of the book in general and women in particular. Of course, Toto's discourse had forewarned us and foreshadowed in metaphorical terms (that reaffirmed the movie or theatrical leitmotif) of what was to come in this final chapter: "el primer número no es el más lindo . . . el número más lujoso de todos es al final ¿cómo será el número más lujoso de todos? se sube el telón y queda otro telón brilloso y se sube ese otro telón y ya queda el último telón que quiere decir que ya va a empezar el baile más lujoso de todos y yo no me lo pierdo: ¡qué viento fuerte! y un portón se abre por el viento tan fuerte y se escapan la negrita y el pescadito, qué suerte" (p. 46) ("the first number isn't the prettiest . . . the fanciest number is at the end, what could the fanciest number be like? The curtain rises and there's another shiny curtain behind and this curtain rises and then there is the last curtain which means they're going to begin the fanciest dance of all and I can't miss it: what a strong wind! it's such a strong wind it opens the gate and the little black girl and the fishie get away, how lucky," p. 37).[30] Are we then meant to see the text, especially the final number, the letter, as a breath of fresh air that opens the door and lets the *negrita* and *pescadito* (traditional sex roles) escape?

Finally, the last segment, the letter, returns us once more to the verb *coger*. If one continues to trace the verb back to its presumed origins (which of course are not origins at all but merely the point to which our scholarship and written records reach), one discovers that the verb derives from the Latin *colligere*, to gather together, to collect (Corominas). Even more meaningful, however, is that if one takes one more step backward, one discovers that *colligere* is a derivative of *legere*, to gather, to pick, TO READ. In so many ways, then, the text has shown that learning about sex, sex roles, and sexuality is inevitably linked to learning about language and learning how to read (literally and metaphorically). Again, since neither reading nor language can ever be nor has ever been innocent, anything other than fraught with connotation and emotive significance, how can our understanding of sex roles and/or the opposite sex ever be anything but fraught with previous assumptions, that is, always already supplement, embroidery?[31]

7

José Donoso's *El obsceno pájaro de la noche:* Witches Everywhere and Nowhere

JUST as the witch is a being on the perimeters of society and distanced from the center, she would appear of little account and peripheral to both the *énoncé* and the *énonciation* of *El obsceno párajo de la noche* by José Donoso (Chile, b. 1925). Although critics have analyzed the novel in terms of social realism, mythic Latin America, and self-reflecting language, they have unanimously failed to recognize the importance of the figure of the witch as a structuring factor.[1] Nevertheless, without the witch, there would be no *énoncé* nor *énonciation*—"she" motivates or produces both. The novel, of course, combines two separate but parallel stories—that of the Casa de Ejercicios Espirituales de la Encarnación de la Chimba and that of the Rinconada. The links between the two stories are multiple: Mudito (Humberto), the Azcoitía family, and Peta Ponce. Both social structures exist, both stories came to be, because of the witch. The Casa functioned as a refuge for Inés's "saintly" ancestor after her involvement with the witch, and it now harbors the old, witchlike servants. In parallel fashion the Rinconada functioned as a refuge for Boy, offspring of the magical mating between Jerónimo and Inés and/or their doubles Mudito (Humberto) and Peta. Furthermore, Mudito, labeled the *séptima bruja* (seventh witch) resides in both houses and apparently narrates the story of both and the history of how they came to be. In other words, witchcraft and the figure of the witch are directly related to the very act of narration. Thus, once again it is a female figure around which the text centers, hidden as that center may be.

What are witches? Why are they women? Why are they feared? Why are they found at the center of a novel like *El obsceno pájaro*, a novel which has repeatedly been shown to be an analysis of language and literature as much as anything else? Is it possible that the figure of the witch is ultimately connected to language and the gesture of the baroque or neo-baroque writer?

As I shall show, the answer to this last question is a resounding yes—the image of the witch is a direct product of a gesture which parallels that of the baroque or neo-baroque writer as analyzed by Severo Sarduy, who has noted, "ser barroco hoy significa amenazar, juzgar y parodiar la economía burguesa, basada en la administración tacaña de los bienes. . . . Malgastar, dilapidar, derrochar lenguaje únicamente en función de placer—y no, como en el uso doméstico, en función de información—es un atentado al buen sentido, moralista y 'natural' . . . en que se basa toda la ideología del consumo y la acumulación. El barroco subvierte el orden supuestamente normal de las cosas" ("to be baroque today means to threaten, to judge, to parody bourgeois economy, based on the stingy management of property. . . . To waste, to squander language solely as a function of pleasure— and not as in domestic use, as a function of information—is a transgression against good, moral, 'natural' sense and reason . . . upon which all ideology of consumption and accumulation is based. The baroque subverts the supposedly normal order of things").[2] Sarduy continues his examination of the baroque by linking it to an eroticism which one also finds in the figure of the witch: "Juego, pérdida, desperdicio y placer: es decir, erotismo en tanto que actividad puramente lúdica, que parodia de la función de reproducción, transgresión de lo útil, del diálogo 'natural' de los cuerpos" (p. 101) ("Play, loss, waste, and pleasure: that is, eroticism as a purely playful activity, which parodies the reproductive function, a transgression of utility, of the 'natural' dialogue of bodies"). The Donoso novel and the female it depicts indeed represent a direct confrontation with and contestation of both bourgeois economy and parsimony as well as the Christian utilitarian view of eroticism.

Clearly, José Donoso's *El obsceno pájaro de la noche*, published in 1970 by Seix Barral, is not the first novel studied here to touch upon the topic of witches. This subject was already present in Gallegos's *Doña Bárbara* and Rivera's *La vorágine*. In the coming pages I shall show that in spite of the approximately fifty years which separate the earliest of these novels and *El obsceno pájaro* and in spite of the authors' totally different styles, purposes, or philosophies of art, the image and implications of the figure of the witch have changed very little.

But we are getting ahead of ourselves. Let us first consider what a witch is to the populace. The *American College Dictionary* (New York: Random House, 1964) defines witch in the following manner: "1. a person, now esp. a woman, who *professes* or is *supposed* to practice magic, esp. black magic or the black art; a sorceress. 2. an ugly or malignant old woman; a hag" (emphasis added). Similarly, *Webster's New World Dictionary* (New York: World, 1962) defines as witch "1. a woman *supposedly* having supernatural power by a compact with evil spirits; sorceress; the term formerly was also applied to men. 2. an ugly and ill-tempered old woman; hag; crone" (again, emphasis added). The common denominators in the two definitions are fourfold. First, although the term may formerly have been applied to men as well as to women, it now refers almost exclusively to women. Secondly, the magical or supernatural powers of the witch are no longer accepted as fact, as my italics emphasize. Thirdly, this power is not generally viewed as beneficent, but rather as maleficent. And finally the morpheme, as the second definitions imply, no longer refers only to those presumed to have some kind of special, supernatural, powers but can also refer to any unpleasant, *old* woman—I emphasize the adjective *old* and shall frequently return to it.[3] Thus both definitions tell us what any child over the age of five already "knows"; the facts (if, indeed, any exist) of witchcraft aside, a witch is an ugly, evil old woman who wears black and knows secret formulas that allow her to manipulate people and force them to do what she wishes. Significantly, in popular speech (as the dictionaries hint) any mature, assertive woman is likely to be called a witch if she has imposed her will upon the speaker or subjected him to her ill humor. In other words, although the word *witch* carries mostly negative connotations, the implications are definitely of power; she has the power, at the very least, to make life unpleasant. I further suggest that the source of that power is her negation of, and/or disregard for, socially accepted behavior and mores. Like the baroque writer, she lives outside of and in opposition to our rules for polite, civilized existence.

In the Donoso novel the implications and ramifications of the witch and witchcraft are vast and ultimately related to the many other aspects of the book which I have already studied.[4] Significantly, the novel opens and closes not with the figure of Mudito/Humberto, who might be considered the protagonist of the novel, nor with don Jerónimo de Azcoitía, who similarly might be deemed the protagonist of Humberto's book with the green cover, but rather with the image of old women and destruction. Significantly, the old women who live in the Casa de Ejercicios Espirituales de la Encarnación de la Chimba fill the pages of the text and, like the monsters of the Rinconada, exist at the center of the book (distracting attention in a manner I shall later discuss) but at the edges of the society portrayed therein and ultimately perhaps only within the fantasy of those who "perceive" them. In fact, the monsters and the Rinconada afford a refracted mirror image of the old women and the Casa; neither is quite what it seems, but each is intricately related to the other.

Among the many, many other ways this novel might be read, one can read it as a commentary on our reaction to old women, whom we often perceive as witches. It is a dramatization of hypocrisy and duplicity coupled with an inability or refusal to see beyond projected appearances. Indeed, it underlines a patent refusal to acknowledge that which we do not wish to see. Already in the first scene of the novel, the silence, the taboo, the interdiction, the masking to draw attention away from the forbidden subject is latent as Misiá Raquel remembers to inquire about her granddaughter's bridal nightgown which Brígida had been mending. Raquel's insistence about how the nightgown was torn, "En la luna de miel la rajó con el cierre de la maleta" (p. 11) ("The nightgown got caught in the zipper of her suitcase during the honeymoon," p. 3),[5] surely suggests a covering up, a refusal to acknowledge that "other," more erotic and more violent side of life. In many ways, *El obsceno pájaro* returns us to the ever-recurrent baroque theme of appearances versus reality, an opposition which is apparent from the first page and effectuated by the repeated use of ellipsis, which as Sarduy has shown is the principal figure of rhetoric used in the baroque.

The ellipsis, of course, is based on a missing element, and, thus, the result of the ellipsis is a displacement, a shift of attention; that is, rather than detecting the "original" element, one perceives its substitute. Thought of in these broad terms, the ellipsis is the basis of metaphor, synecdoche, metonymy, and allusion. In each case, the meaningful element which has been alluded to is missing, as the Holy Light is missing in the chapel, and our attention is shifted, first to a substitute element (the chapel becomes the site of the future holy birth), and ultimately to language itself, since, dialectically, once we recognize that there has been a substitution, we seek the "original" element and its point of contact with its substitute. But, in *El obsceno pájaro*, our attention is finally drawn away from both elements and shifted to the very fact of the substitution, that is, rhetoric and language, the invention. Before I discuss this final stage in the ellipsis and its relation to women, let us examine the first ellipsis of the text, an omission which will lead to the topic of the witch and the book's major ellipsis.

The novel opens, "Misiá Raquel Ruiz lloró muchísimo cuando la Madre Benita la llamó por teléfono para contarle que la Brígida había amanecido muerta. Después se consoló un poco y pidió más detalles" (p. 11) ("Misia Raquel Ruiz . . . shed many tears when Mother Benita called up to tell her that Brígida had died in her sleep. Then she calmed down a little and asked for more details," p. 3). In the pages which immediately follow, we learn that Misiá Raquel was ostensibly the mistress of the house in which Brígida was but a servant. When the latter became too old to serve, she was shunted off to the *Casa* to live out her remaining days. We also learn that at the *Casa* Brígida was one of the seven *brujas*. In this case as in all others in the text, the appearances of the situation are explained, and it is only much later, if indeed ever, that we learn that the "facts" of the situation had been silenced and things are not as we had believed.[6] In this case, the first chapter leads the reader to believe that Brígida was a poor servant to whom, from the goodness of her heart, Misiá Raquel had promised a lavish funeral as a reward for so many years of faithful service. Much, much later in the text, we discover, however, that on the contrary Brígida, although seemingly the servant, was a very rich woman who had "psychologically" enslaved Raquel and manipulated her into doing an infinite variety of tasks in the accumulation of her fortune. Thus, although Brígida herself owned vast quantities of real estate, she had refused to live in any of her houses or to manage her affairs, insisting instead on maintaining her position of pseudo-servant while Raquel, in the role of pseudo-master, in effect worked for her. Furthermore, the beautiful funeral was paid for and arranged by Brígida herself. And, rather than being terribly sad (as the tears would imply) at the death of her former servant, Raquel is supremely relieved (as we later learn) to be no longer at the mercy of Brígida. Her insincerity in this respect is apparent insofar as she does manage to console herself enough to ask for the details regarding the death, while, just a couple of paragraphs later, she dissolves her grief to the point of remembering to inquire after her granddaughter's nightgown. Apparently the nightgown is every bit as important as the death of the "servant" and thus doubly points to the hypocrisy, or covering up.[7] The text, then, patently underlines the dubious validity of language, which is apparently incapable of communicating anything other than itself. How, indeed, is one to handle a text whose very first sentences, written in what would appear to be the most innocent, direct, and transparent discourse, proves to be quite misleading and as opaque as the most complex baroque poetry? In a parallel manner, all the volumes of prose and treatises written over the centuries on the question of the witch might well function on a similar level of artifice and duplicity.

Already, then, in the opening pages is developed a pattern which can be observed throughout the text. The characters (usually women), who remain on the fringes of society and are spuriously powerless, pathetic figures, have become the masters and control the ostensibly powerful rather than vice versa. Appearances are not what they seem, but the text allows us to acknowledge this only much later. In so many ways, then, the manifest power is also a sham, an ellipsis, an absence. In fact, Myrna Solotorevsky has aptly shown that the text frequently uses the technique of accepting an overt metaphor or simile as fact, as the text continually turns back on itself, reassessing its prior statements.[8] Again, in a baroque style, it piles figures and tropes one on top of the other, burying the central absence and causing the figure or trope to be understood as the essence. As I shall show, this is precisely what occurs with the figure of the witch.

This entire question of power and appearance is directly related to the topic of the witch and accurately reflects the role of women as perceived and portrayed by Donoso—women who are always on the fringes of society, seemingly pathetic and helpless but ultimately extraordinarily powerful as a result of their roles of infinite servitude. As the text so frequently points out, servitude confers power on the server: "Desempeñando estos menesteres las viejas fueron robándose algo integral de sus patrones" (p. 65) ("By performing these tasks . . . the old women slowly robbed them [their masters] of an essential part of themselves," p. 49); "Los patrones las mandan a encerrar aquí [en la Casa] cuando se dan cuenta que les deben demasiado a estas viejas y sienten pavor porque estas miserables, un buen día, pueden revelar su poder y *destruirlos*" (p. 64, emphasis added) ("Their employers have them locked up here [in the *Casa*] when they realize how much they owe these old women and are terrified because, one fine day, these miserable creatures may show their power and *destroy them*," p. 48, emphasis added). Paradoxically, the servant of the servants (in this case, Mudito) is the most powerful of all: "Y al servir a estas rémoras, al ser sirviente de sirvientes, al exponerme a sus burlas y obedecer sus mandatos, voy haciéndome más poderoso que ellas porque voy acumulando los desperdicios de los desperdicios, las humillaciones de los humillados" (p. 66) ("And by serving these parasites, by being the servant of servants, by laying myself wide open to their mockery and obeying their orders, I'm becoming more powerful than they because I'm accumulating the waste products of the waste products, humiliations by the humiliated," p. 50). The power, then, lies not where it would appear—another ellipsis.

Doubtlessly, the use of the term *witch* (both Brígida and Mudito belong to the group of *siete brujas*) with all its negative connotations is the result of just such an inverted hierarchy of power. The position of fundamental servitude in which the female (particularly the socioeconomic class of female on which this novel centers) has existed in recent centuries has surely conferred upon her powers similar to those portrayed in *El obsceno pájaro*.[9] No doubt, the resentment of this ascendancy on the part of the masters results in their labeling her a witch—suggesting, of course, that the dominion is ill-gained and threatening. Nor is it irrelevant that throughout history witches have generally belonged to the lower socioeconomic classes— that is, classes which have served as domestics—rather than the class of masters.[10] Significantly, too, witches are often referred to as *"servants* of the Devil,"[11] an appellation which alludes to both a master/servant relationship and a male/female division to the extent that, to my knowledge, the Devil has never been portrayed as a female; his workers, servants, the witches are generally female, but the source of the power is understood to be male.

This inverted power hierarchy—inverted because it is the opposite of what it appears—is perhaps most patently dramatized in *El obsceno pájaro* in the images of the dogs, whose positions seem in many ways to reflect those of Jerónimo and Inés. Jerónimo is the master of four large, fierce black dogs, reminiscent of Alejo's black dogs in *El lugar sin límites* (canines which also destroy la Manuela, another servant on the periphery of society and potentially too powerful). Jerónimo's four black dogs are described: "Sus cuatro perros negros gruñen disputándose el trozo de carne caliente aún, casi viva. Lo desgarran . . . babosos los hocicos colorados, . . . los colmillos, fulgurantes los ojos en sus rostros estrechos. . . . mis cuatro perros negros como las sombras de los lobos tienen el instinto sanguinario

. . . de la raza más pura" (p. 188) ("Jerónimo's four black dogs snarl, fighting over the chunk of warm meat that's almost alive. They tear it to shreds . . . their red mouths foaming . . . their fangs bared, their eyes flashing from their narrow faces. . . . my four dogs as black as the shadows of wolves have the bloody instinct . . . of thoroughbreds," p. 152); in other words, like Jerónimo himself, they pertain to a level of nobility and reflect some of his power. The four dogs, however, stand in sharp contrast to the other dog that appears repeatedly in the text—*la perra amarilla.* The latter, of course, is female (presumably, the four ferocious black dogs are male), ugly, scrawny, and dirty. The black dogs eat raw meat; the yellow bitch eats anything, even garbage, and loiters in the most disgusting places among all types of debris. Although she is described (not unlike Peta Ponce) as a "garabato flaco, ansioso, voraz, insaciable" (p. 189) ("mere scrawl there, skin and bones, eager, voracious, [insatiable]," p. 153), she nonetheless manages to steal the piece of meat intended for the more regal animals and escape. She presumably is killed several times but always returns. Invariably connected to the female element of the novel, she, in her own, pathetic way, inevitably outsmarts and/or overpowers the reputedly more powerful (and usually male).

Unquestionably, the whole issue of the dogs is directly related to the topic of witchcraft in a multiplicity of ways. First, the story of the landowner with nine sons and one daughter inexorably links dogs—particularly the *perra amarilla*—to witchcraft. The dog always appears with the *chonchón* (about which I shall have more to say later) and was purportedly the incarnation of the nursemaid/witch: "la perra era la nana y la nana era la bruja" (p. 39) ("the bitch was the nursemaid and the nursemaid was the witch," p. 27), a statement which in its very format visualizes the textual (and baroque) gesture of wrapping everything with layers on top of layers and simultaneously underscoring that which is, that which was, and that which might be. Furthermore, dogs in general are often associated with the devil, Hades, the underworld, and Hecate, goddess of the underworld, queen of black magic, and patroness of witches. Even more precise in connecting the dogs to witchcraft, however, are the cited textual descriptions. Jerónimo's dogs are black, a color associated with evil to even the most naïve reader, and the description of their skirmish over the piece of meat resembles the devil's famed struggle for the soul of man. Like the devil, too, they are male, they have fangs, and their eyes flash. Similarly, the yellow dog exhibits many of the characteristics of a witch. As already noted she is female as are most witches. But, why yellow? I have shown elsewhere that the color yellow might be related to the story of the landowner insofar as the daughter associated with the dog has blond hair ("The Baroque, the Picaresque and *El obsceno pájaro*"). In addition, this term is employed for its evocative qualities. Yellow conjures up an image of age, of antiquity, of deterioration and decrepitude. People, like paper, seem to

become yellow with advanced age. Significantly, Peta Ponce and the original nanny, both of whom are embodied in the *perra amarilla*, are of indeter-
minate oldness; both seem to have existed for all of eternity, as have the
witchcraft and the sexuality they embody. The details of the description of
the yellow dog further parallel a hypothetical portrayal of a witch, since
she is labeled skinny and described as dirty and unkempt. The customary
image of a witch is a skinny, dirty old woman. And the use of the term
garabato not only accentuates her scrawniness but adds a note of awe and
dread evoked by the evil images the word carries. *Garabato* (gallows), of
course, would be psychologically associated with wrongdoing and death.

There is no doubt that the other terms used to describe the dog, already
metaphorically converted to a *garabato,* are even more pertinent to a discussion of witches: "ansioso, voraz, insaciable" ("eager, voracious, insatiable"). At first glance one is inclined to believe that these terms all refer to
the dog's hunger; a stray, she apparently does not eat regularly and for her
this *trozo de carne* ("chunk of meat") would be a special treat. A second
glance at the textual implications (coupled with other textual references),
however, causes one to pause and consider quite a different link between
the "original" nanny, Peta Ponce, the dog, and the traditional image of the
witch. All are products of an ellipsis, and all are directly connected with
incarnate sexuality (which as I shall show is but another ellipsis). The
words used to characterize the dog, "ansioso, voraz, insaciable," are also
the very words one might use to refer to her perceived sexual "appetite."
In this respect, the description of the dogs simultaneously leads us forward
(in the text, not necessarily temporally) to the conception of Boy, a conception which paradoxically produces one ellipsis while presenting itself as
the product of another ellipsis, and backward to the story of the landowner's daughter and that ellipsis which is central to the text.

The description of the dogs, found at the beginning of Chapter 12, in-
troduces the two chapters which relate the various possibilities for the
conception of Boy, and once again one sees that the *énonciation* mirrors the
énoncé insofar as both undermine the premise of power and hierarchical
authority. The text never provides us with the ultimate, authoritative version. Similarly, Jerónimo, the speciously powerful, needs only to impreg-
nate Inés as a final proof of his potency. Five years of wedlock have passed,
however, with no resultant pregnancy. Whether Jerónimo finally impreg-
nanted Inés, or Humberto impregnated her, or Jerónimo impregnated her
via Peta, or Mudito impregnated her via Peta, the yellow dog is a recurrent
element of the scene and apparently essential to the insemination. And the
result of this act is double. First, Boy is conceived, but he is a monster;
significantly, it has long been accepted in popular mythology that monsters are the fruit of copulation with the devil.[12] Are we then to understand
Jerónimo and his black dogs as the incarnation of the devil? But the other
result of the scene is perhaps more important and directly related to both

witches and ellipsis. After that night, Jerónimo becomes impotent, and it is at that point that Humberto/Mudito begins to convert into the *imbunche*, insisting that he has no sex. Are we then to understand the yellow dog's stealing of the "trozo de carne caliente aún" ("chunk of meat still warm") as a foreshadowing of what is to happen to Humberto and Jerónimo? The witch, of course, has long been credited with the ability to make the phallus disappear, and this is a topic Donoso repeats in *Tres novelitas burguesas*. In a parallel manner, the female too has been viewed traditionally as the physical product of an ellipsis (she is often viewed as an incomplete or atrophied male) while at the same time she generally has been credited with the capacity for inflicting this same ellipsis on others (specifically males). It is pertinent that one never hears the expression "castrating male," while "castrating female" is often applied to an assertive woman.

On the other hand, the scene might also be understood as what René Girard *(Violence)* has labeled the abolishment of differences. Differences, as he has shown, are generally man-made, imposed from the outside, supplemental, and not inherent. I would add only that they are also linguistic in nature, created by language, to the extent that they are an aggrandizement of the superfluous and nonessential. As Girard has suggested, differences are created when we focus on and make important some variation (the male/female physical difference?) which is inherently not as significant as we would make it seem. Differences, then, necessarily and by intent establish a hierarchy of power; as long as the differences are maintained and imposed, the hierarchy functions, and violence, in the form of total chaos, is forestalled. The abolishment of these differences, Girard insists, results in monstrosity.

Perhaps this is precisely the manner in which we are meant to read the renditions of Boy's conception, for what is monstrosity but the insertion of disorder and chaos into our neat, ordered, and civilized world? The conception of Boy, like the position of the witch, undermines our "normal," Christian, patriarchal, and civilized (and it is relevant that non-Christian is commonly considered noncivilized) hierarchical power structure with Jerónimo at the top and Peta Ponce at the bottom. That dark, chaotic, "other" world filled with all those aspects of life which Jerónimo refuses to see or acknowledge breaks through, and we are never to know (again the ellipsis) with whom the potency, the power, rested that night: Jerónimo, Inés, Mudito, or Peta. The result then could only be the inevitable monster with his chaotic appearance which "era la confusión, el desorden, una forma distinta pero peor de la muerte" (p. 229) ("was chaos, disorder, a different but worse form of death," p. 186).

Jerónimo subsequently creates a world based on another ellipsis. He removes from the center of Boy's world all references, all pointers to what one might consider a normal world, and an entire new hierarchy is set up, different from but parallel to the former. Eventually, this newly created world would be considered the norm; the ordered, civilized world thus becomes abnormal, chaos, and distortion. Clearly, this is precisely the problem with the *viejas* and the witches: fear that their world with its inherent "disorder" and indifference to masculine supremacy will eventually take over and replace the patriarch. If society indeed depends upon a hierarchy of differences and if one finally recognizes that those differences and the hierarchy they produce are arbitrary, then one has every reason to fear the witch, for her physical difference (ellipsis) from the male ruling class could as well locate her at the top of the hierarchy as at the bottom.

The ellipsis in the story of the landowner's daughter also points to the eroticism noted by Sarduy. Let us consider the "original" nanny, charged with raising the landowner's own daughter, the "female island" in the house of men, "inaccesible para ellos, pero *no peligrosa*" (p. 38, emphasis added) ("inaccessible to them but *not dangerous*," p. 26, emphasis added). According to the story (the unreliability of which I shall examine later), the girl has reached an age at which she has learned all those timeless "feminine" arts—sewing, embroidery, making preserves, managing the household, and the like. All has been taught her by the nanny who sleeps in the same room. In other words, she has reached that age which marks the completion of her childhood training in feminine arts, the age at which the young girl is ready to leave the home of the father for the home of another male and become a woman. Paradoxically, the arts in which she has been trained (sewing, cooking, etc.) ostensibly have no bearing on sexuality, but, at the same time, these are the very same arts which prepare her to live in another man's home as wife and mother, two terms which inherently allude to an underlying eroticism, a sexual being, as well-hidden as they may often be. Once again, these arts function like the bridal nightgown, designed to cover and reveal the eroticism. Thus the nanny, who has trained her in these more readily observable (*and mentionable*) arts, has by implication prepared her for her future role as an adult woman and sexual being (presumably children are asexual).

Significantly, the rumors that the girl and nanny were witches began simply as a result of "malos tiempos, años de cosechas miserables, de calor y sequía, de animales envenenados y de niños que nacían muertos o con seis dedos en una mano" (p. 35; a prefiguration of the monster son who was to be born centuries later) ("bad times . . . years of skimpy harvests, of heat and drought, of poisoned animals and children born dead or with six fingers on one hand," p. 24). It may seem absurd to attribute such fortuitous happenings to the workings of a witch, but for many centuries witches have been presumed, even by the supposedly intelligent, to be able to wreak just such havoc. In fact, in the late fifteenth century, Pope Innocent VIII issued a bull which would become one of the principal documents in the study of witchcraft and which stated:

. . . many persons of both sexes, heedless of their own salvation and forsaking the Catholic faith, give themselves over to devils male and female, and by their incantations, charms, and conjurings, and by other abominable superstitions and sortileges, offenses, crimes, and misdeeds, ruin and cause to perish the offspring of women, the foal of animals, the products of the earth, the grapes of the vines, and fruits of trees, as well as men and women, cattle and flocks and herds and animals of every kind, vineyards also and orchards, meadows, pastures, harvests, grains and other fruits of the earth; that they afflict and torture with dire pains and anguish, both internal and external, these men, women, cattle, flocks, herds, and animals, and hinder men from begetting and women from conceiving, and prevent all consummation of marriage.[13]

Surely, if a Pope could be so credulous, what are we to expect from simple *campesinos?*

The result, then, within the text was that "los ojos de los campesinos se dirigieron hacia el cacique en busca de alguna explicación para tanta desgracia" (p. 35) ("the peasants looked to the landowner for some explanation of all their misfortune," p. 24). Thus, times are bad, a series of gratuitous events probably unrelated are chronologically juxtaposed in the minds of the peasants and therefore linked, and they turn to the authority, the man of knowledge and power, to produce a reason for this apparent threat to the alleged order and neatness of their universe. (That the universe and the cosmos might ultimately be not ordered or less than perfectly ordered is not a concept that humanity/society has ever been able to accept fully.) But, of course, the cacique is unable to proffer the explanation, and the rumors of witchcraft begin: "porque como no encontraban explicación para tanta desgracia era necesario culpar a alguien" (p. 36) ("because the blame had to fall on someone," p. 24). Again, there must be a cause, an order. This basic need to blame someone, to find a rationale, coupled with the possibility of envy of the nanny's privileges, converts the nanny, and in turn the daughter, into witches. Thus, the creation of the witch, which in the final analysis is always linguistic, insofar as she exists only as long as, and to the extent that, we *say* she exists, is the result of an ellipsis, a void. She is created to fill in that lack of comprehension, that blank. And she is created by the *dicen* or *se dice*, expressions which feign authority and power but which, because they lack a specific, personal subject, ultimately prove totally unreliable and negate all that *se dice*. In this respect, the repetition of the expression merely underlines the problematic and precarious status of what has been rumored.

In a similar manner, it has been suggested that historically the creation of the witch figure was founded on just such an ellipsis. In his study of witchcraft, Edward Peters suggests that what were ultimately to be accepted as the "facts" of witchcraft may well have begun as a mere rhetorical exercise with little or no foundation in fact:

> Yet in the *Rhetorimachia*, Anselm lays out a barrage of accusations that appear familiar to historians of later accusations of magic, heresy, and witchcraft. What may have been well within the limits of rhetorical exercise, and was understood in that way in the eleventh century, influences later chroniclers and moralists in a setting in which the fictitious character of the work was ignored or forgotten. (P. 23)

Thus, the figure of the witch may well have originated in a void, as a filling in of previously empty space, just as the witch is created in *El obsceno pájaro* explicitly to occupy and eliminate the blank space. As I have shown in another place, the principal gesture of the baroque is an intentional and even frantic filling up of empty spaces in order to distract attention from the fact that behind the mask, the appearance, or the ostensible order, there is nothing ("The Baroque"). It is precisely this void that the baroque gesture attempts to disguise, and in this regard, it is fitting that baroque literature flourished in approximately the same historical period as the witch hunts and the publication of the multiple treatises on the art of witchcraft. Similarly, both society and religion are created precisely to cover up or explain away this potential void or chaos. Thus, magicians and witches have long been linked with heretics, antagonists of religion who threaten the structure of religion and ultimately society.[14] The codification of witchcraft, thus, seems to be an essentially baroque gesture which was intended to redirect attention away from that basic ellipsis.

Also, as I have demonstrated elsewhere, one of the focal points of *El obsceno pájaro* is an analysis of the use of language and a questioning of the validity of our interpretation of the "reality" comprehended by that language ("Amidst the Illusory Depths"). At every turn, Mudito reminds us that what we have before us is a linguistic creation, a group of signifiers which ultimately point only to themselves and not to anything outside of the text. Such, of course, is precisely the case with the morpheme *witch*. Paralleling the other silences of the text, this word too effectuates a shift of focus which obliterates the real center, the true protagonist. By calling someone else a witch, one shifts the attention away from the self and onto the other. Now the other is to blame for the self's problem. Thus the witch figure would seem to be the epitome of Girard's scapegoat or *pharmakos*, created by layers of *dicen*, layers of wrappings which are but the characteristics projected by others—pure supplement, as shown in Chapter 4.

But we still have not found the link between this witchcraft and eroticism, which is the greatest ellipsis of all. It is pertinent to note that nearly all of the "crimes" that Pope Innocent VIII attributed to witches were related to sexuality, fertility, and reproduction: crop failures, animal husbandry problems, stillborn children, abortion, sterility, impotence and so forth.[15] Similarly, the *Malleus Maleficarum*, written by Kramer and Sprenger (1st ed. ca. 1486), as authorized by Pope Innocent VIII, specifically states, "All witchcraft comes from carnal lust, which is in women insatiable" (cited in Masters, *Eros and Evil*, p. xx). The Donoso text, too, underlines the question of sexuality by noting similiar problems in the "bad times": bad crops, stillborn children, malformed children, and so forth. This mysterious undertone of sexuality carries over to the cacique's daughter in several ways. First, the purported truth about the daughter is learned, significantly by the elder brother as he is leaving the bed of his mistress. Angry that he is leaving so soon, she snarls at him, "Apuesto que tu hermana no ha llegado a la casa todavía. Las brujas vuelven cuando canta el gallo" (p. 37) ("I'll bet your sister hasn't gotten home. Witches come back at cockcrow," p. 25). The reference to his sister is, of course, of double implication. As shown in Chapter 5 above, to mention one's mother, that is, to make reference to her sexuality or immorality (the use of the expression implies that they are one and the same), is one of the greatest insults in the Spanish language. Unquestionably, to mention the sister is of parallel significance and carries the same implications to the extent that all the females of the family have traditionally been considered guardians of the family's honor and morality. In this case, the audacity of the lover to mention the sister, especially to name her in such an unhallowed setting (her bedroom), places the sister on the same level as the mistress and, thus, in the eyes of the brother denigrates her. Second, the lover suggests that the sister has not yet returned home, once again implying immoral or illicit activity and marring the honor of the family. As usual, the fact that the brother is there, engaged in an illicit affair, has no negative effect on the family honor, while the mere suggestion that the sister might not be safely locked in her room, threatens to destroy that honor. And, thirdly, of course, the lover overtly labels the sister a witch, who arrives home "cuando canta el gallo" ["when the cock crows"], another expression fraught with erotic implications.

The common link in all these situations, of course, is the silence, the overt absence of words that might allow us to understand the effacement, the masking, the erasure—in a word, once again, the ellipsis. What is *not* said, what is concealed, is ultimately what is vital to full comprehension. Patently, we are not dealing in the Donoso text with the cross-outs of *La traición de Rita Hayworth*, cross-outs which negated but which allowed the "subtext" or the antipode to show through. On the contrary, here we are confronting an erasure or obliteration which allows only the very merest trace of the concealed material to show through. What happened when the father entered the daughter's room; what did he see? One never knows for sure, and doubtlessly the message of the text is that one can never know, for the text effaces the incident as surely as the father's poncho obliterates the scene from the view of the others. Again the *énonciation* is such that it prevents the emergence of one version as more authoritative than the others. The textual traces which remain, however, all suggest that one is witnessing a social taboo—female sexuality, in whatever form. All of the textual elements related to this story point to just such a reading, and I shall show that all, by textual inference, point to the unspeakable— insatiable female eroticism, an insatiability which psychologists would suggest is a basic male fear, but which I shall demonstate is ultimately merely a question of power.

Although all the elements of the cacique story are tied to some type of eroticism, certain elements are repeated in other sections of the novel and are even more overt in their sexual connotations. A Freudian would no doubt note at this point that all aspects of life are ultimately linked to a latent sexuality. I do not necessarily agree and instead suggest that the tightly woven scheme of this text is, intentionally or not, definitely meaningful and underlines these links. The three elements which are most closely tied to some type of eroticism are the nanny, the yellow dog, and the *chonchón*.[16]

Of all these elements the *chonchón* might seem to have the least connection to our topic, and, indeed, perhaps outside the text it has none, but within the text, the link is ineluctable. The *chonchón* is first mentioned in the legend of the landowner's daughter, where it is described: "en las noches de luna volaba por el aire una cabeza terrible" (p. 36) ("on moonlit nights a horrible head would fly through the air," p. 25). In Chapter 7, one finds a similar description: "Mi cabeza vuela por el aire" (p. 111) ("My head flies through the air," p. 87). The mere repetition of these words might not be significant without the insistence on the act of flying, "vuelo, vuelo" ("I fly, fly,") and if Iris were not to scream in response, "el chonchón, el chonchón, el Romualdo es brujo y transformó en chonchón a mi gigante y sigo volando, volando liviano convertido en chonchón, volando" (p. 112) ("the *chonchón*, it's the *chonchón*, Romualdo's a witch and he turned my Giant into a *chonchón*... I fly from hand to hand," p. 87). It is this image and the subsequent repetition of the *chonchón* which ties it to unspeakable eroticism in two ways. First, the head of the Giant is indubitably an erotic figure inasmuch as Iris (alias Gina) has sexual relations with whoever wears the mask. She is incapable of distinguishing one young man from another once he has donned the papier-mâché head. She indiscriminately makes love with all of them, believing them to be the same person (if the mask, face, is the same, the inside must also be). Analogously, she scorns anyone not wearing the head. Thus, like the baroque artist, she allows her attention to be diverted (perhaps even willingly and intentionally) to the decorative surface, the mask, while patently ignoring whatever might lie beneath the mask. The sexual implications of the papier-mâché head are further underlined by the conversion of the nose into a phallus, as the boys kick the head back and forth as if it were a ball: "mi enorme nariz trans-formada en falo, soy un falo" (p. 114) ("my enormous nose, changed into a phallus. [I am a phallus]," p. 89).

At the same time, the scene returns us once more (although with su-preme subtlety) to the topic of the dogs in two different ways. First, the entire dispute with Romualdo over the head began simply because Tito, who had rented the head with the intent of having sexual relations with Gina, was thwarted in his desire because of the presence of the yellow dog (that same yellow dog who always accompanies the *chonchón*). The dog, by looking through the window of the car, spoiled his potential lovemaking with implied powers not different from those Pope Innocent VIII attributed to witches: "hinder men from begetting." This, of course, is exactly what the yellow dog did. Pertinent to this discussion too is Tito's brother's response to Tito's report that Gina "no me dejó" ("she wouldn't let me"). The brother responds, "Esa perra amarilla siempre anda siguiéndola y *dicen que* a otros cabros también les ha echado a perder el asunto" (p. 106, emphasis added) ("That yellow bitch dog's always trailing her around and *I hear* it loused it up for other guys too," p. 82, emphasis added). This comment coupled with the old women's discussion of Iris's puberty, or lack thereof, suggests the possibility that again, contrary to what the reader had been led to believe, Iris/Gina has never consummated a relationship, that the yellow dog may have always interrupted, and that this entire myth of her having had relations with the series of males (Jerónimo included) may be simply that: a myth, a story, a fabulation to protect the "masculin-ity," the self-image, of each of the males. Only Tito, the youngest of all and still completely inexperienced, is honest and candid enough to admit that nothing happened. Romualdo, in fact, responds to the brother's complaint by saying, "Si tu hermano fuera bien hombre, bien macho, se la hubiera culiado bien culiada no más" (p. 107) ("If your brother was a real man, a real stud, he'da screwed her good," p. 83). In this same vein, the *perra amarilla* was also present the night that Boy was conceived, and although that time it would appear that the dog facilitated consummation rather than hindering it, one must not lose sight of the fact that the result of the copulation and/or the yellow dog's presence was impotence for Jerónimo and sexlessness for Humberto.

In addition, this scene in Gabriel's bookstore directly parallels the de-scription of Jerónimo's *four* black dogs and reaffirms my interpretation of that scene. Here, significantly, the struggle is with *Los Cuatro Ases* and just as the four dogs "gruñen disputándose el trozo de carne. . . . Lo desga-rran" (p. 188) ("snarl, fighting over the chunk of warm meat. . . . They tear it to shreds," p. 152), the *Four* Aces "me rajan peleándose mi falo magnífico, en dos, en tres pedazos, ya no queda nada" (p. 115) ("tear me

apart, fighting over my magnificent phallus, now in two, in three, pieces...
nothin's left now," p. 89). Clearly, the expression, *trozo de carne,* could be
understood as a euphemistic metaphor for phallus.

Now, interestingly enough, Iris/Gina is just the same age as the cacique's
daughter, patently an age of nascent sexuality. Insofar as Iris/Gina not only
has "sexual relations" with the papier-mâché head (from her point of view
at any rate, her relationship is with the head), and insofar as she even calls
it *el chonchón,* the text insinuates that what the cacique saw as he entered
the room was indeed of a sexual nature. The story emphasizes that the
chonchón and the dog are always together. That the dog is outside the girl's
window implies the proximity of the *chonchón.* Furthermore, the yellow
dog is always outside the window beyond which some erotic activity is
taking place (or being attempted), underlining a division between inside
and outside which is ultimately illusory. I have already mentioned that she
follows Gina around and watches as she makes love (or tries to) with the
Giant's head, and she bays outside the window of Jerónimo's and Inés's
room the night she conceives Boy. Thus it is not unreasonable to conclude
that what the father sees is erotic in nature, especially since his resolu-
tion of the situation is to rush the girl off to a convent, an action which has
long been the accepted treatment of the young woman who mars the
family honor in such a fashion, as any one who has read the Golden-Age
honor plays will readily attest.

Ultimately, however, it is not the sexuality of the situations which is
pertinent but rather the taboo surrounding this eroticism, the imposed
silence, the ellipsis which again connects to witchcraft. The whole question
of witches in the story begins and ends with an ellipsis. The nanny is
labeled a *bruja* due to the lack of a better explanation for natural
phenomena, and the story ends with one of the major ellipses of the text—
the scene behind the cacique's poncho.[17] The father's refusal to acknowledge the nascent sexuality of his daughter (to the extreme of whisking her
off to a convent, a locus of asexuality) is ultimately not different from the
old women's insistence that Iris's pregnancy (if indeed she is pregnant) is
the result of another immaculate conception (i.e., ellipsis). The very notion
of an immaculate conception is clearly a denial of eroticism and sexuality—
the deliberate creation of an ellipsis. It is paradoxically revealing that eroticism or sexuality has traditionally been spoken of in masked terms or
omission. As I indirectly suggested in analyzing the scene with the dogs,
eroticism is often obliquely spoken of in terms of food, hunger. Just as it is
acceptable to speak of the "feminine arts" as cooking, and so forth, it is
somehow less offensive to refer to lasciviousness as hunger. Similarly, as
Cabrera Infante has noted, erotic literature *(la novela rosa)* depends upon
euphemisms (a form of ellipsis, a not naming), absence, interruption,
blank spaces, and typically at the moment of heightened eroticism, the

curtain is drawn, the book ends, or the scene shifts.[18] Might I add, the poncho is spread?

It is appropriate, then, that everything in and related to the *Casa* is already covered, past—ex. Everything used to be something else: the ex-convent, ex-chapel, ex-servants, ex-writer, ex-holy statues. Nothing is what it was or what it appears to be. All the signs, stripped of the surface qualities which made them significant, meaningful, now remain in an interim state—still retaining traces of these prior indicators (if only in the memory of the characters) while inevitably pointing to the paradoxical current absence of those past qualities. All in the *Casa* simultaneously points to the past, now absent, qualities while underlining the very fact that nothing is what it was. This, of course, is precisely the semiotic position in which we find all old people.

But, again, the basic problem with witches seems to be that they do the unspeakable, both literally and figuratively, by challenging these socially imposed, extraneous criteria. The Church (and society to the extent that its mores and values are shaped by the Church) would make of human sexuality a strictly utilitarian activity: the production of wealth in the form of children. The witch, or our image of the witch, on the contrary, negates this utilitarianism and uses eroticism as the baroque writer uses language, "solely as a function of pleasure." The fact that the witch is often old enough to be beyond her reproductive years underlines the unprofitability of her eroticism. Similarly, the sexuality and erotic activities of the old women in the *Casa* are all completely purposeless, if the objective of sexual activity is fertilization and subsequent childbirth, and perhaps produce a pejorative attitude in the reader (who may think in terms of "obscenity") because, like all homosexual activity, they produce nothing of material use. One of the traditional complaints against the purported sexual activity of witches is that it is indiscriminant in regard to heterosexuality or homosexuality. The fact that Mudito is allowed to sleep with Iris, but tightly bound by the six *brujas* to prevent any potentially fertile contact, surely reaffirms the notion of eroticism without a utilitarian goal.

Likewise, whatever the father saw in the daughter's room was in some way threatening to the house full of males. Previously they had been quite willing to allow the *isla femenina* to continue as long as they believed it "inaccessible to them, but not dangerous." Now, their insistence on eliminating this feminine island suggests that it has become somehow dangerous. But surely the "danger" resides in the daughter, not in the nanny, just as it resides in Inés, not in Peta, for as the text so repeatedly underlines, the essential, unchangeable part of the story is the poncho, the obliteration, which I call the silence and which "escamotea al personaje noble, retirándolo del centro del relato para desviar la atención y la venganza de la peonada hacia la vieja" (p. 43) ("makes the noble daughter vanish, thus removing her from the center of the story in order to shift the attention and vengeance of the farmhands to the old woman," p. 31). The text continues in a statement which might apply equally well to any of the old women, including Peta, "Esta, un personaje sin importancia, igual a todas las viejas, un poco bruja, un poco alcahueta, un poco comadrona . . . sirviente que carece de sicología individual y rasgos propios, sustituye a la señorita en el papel protagónico de la conseja, expiando ella sola la culpa *de estar en contacto con poderes prohibidos*" (emphasis added) ("A person of no importance, like all other old women, somewhat of a witch, bawd, midwife . . . servant, who seems to lack an individual psychology and characteristics of her own, she takes over the girl's leading part in the story and she alone expiates the heavy guilt that comes from *contact with forbidden powers*," emphasis added).

But what are these forbidden powers, what is the danger? Again, the answer seems to be female carnality, the unspeakable. Inés reputedly is as powerless before Jerónimo as the yellow dog is in the presence of the black dogs, and yet one manages to steal the *trozo de carne* while the other, by withholding sexual favors, "convinces" Jerónimo to allow Peta to remain in the household, an act which might also be seen as the metaphoric stealing of the *trozo de carne* if one wishes to understand the expression as a euphemism for phallus and phallus as a symbol of power. It is not irrelevant that the scene describing the dogs immediately follows the description of Inés's and Jerónimo's wedding night:

> Sabía muy bien cuánto la deseaba Jerónimo. Por eso, en la noche de boda, fríamente, con la cabeza despejada, cometió el pecado mortal de negarle su cuerpo a su marido, a quien ella también deseaba. Y se lo hubiera seguido negando durante toda la vida si hacia el alba su cuerpo implacablemente desnudo junto al de Jerónimo no hubiera incendiado la lucidez de su marido. Ella logró triunfar: él se lo prometió todo, lo que quisiera, lo que le pidiera. (P. 186)

> (She was aware of how much Jerónimo desired her. And so, on her wedding night, with a clear head, coldly, she committed the mortal sin of denying her body to her husband, whom she also desired. And she'd have gone on denying it to him for the rest of her life if, toward dawn, her body, implacably naked beside him, hadn't set fire to her husband's lucidity. She won; he promised her everything, anything she wanted, anything she asked for. [P. 151])

Surely there can be no doubt that it is just this type of power that the male of our species eternally fears and that provokes him to employ the term *witch*.

In the final analysis, the problem with both witches and old women is a question of language, power—not supernatural powers, but rather powers inherent in knowledge. Throughout the centuries knowledge and sexuality have been implicitly linked. The entire story of the Garden of Eden and the Fall alternates between whether Eve's sin was sexual in nature or was her acquisition of knowledge, or both. Witches (as epitomized by the old women and, in fact, by Eve herself) refuse to silence what society has deemed unmentionable. They speak of, know of, and allow to surface all those sides of life which polite civilization would have banished—sexuality is ultimately just one of those aspects. The witches and old women concede that things are not what they appear; they acknowledge another side to all, a dimension we would prefer to ignore. In the cacique story the focus is shifted away from essences, leaving us with masks, wrappings, appearances. The witch knows—that is her sin; she sees beyond the poncho, and from the civilized point of view this knowledge is power and thus intimidating, since it threatens to allow the thinly shielded chaos to break through and run rampant. This chaotic, dark side of everything, in which the witch seems to function aptly, is reflected throughout Donoso's work in that uncivilized chaotic world always on the brink of bursting through. It is focused, in fact, in the epigraph of the novel, which underlines that life is composed of both the ordered and the unordered, the "civilized" and the chaotic. Significantly, the epigraph's reference to the obscene bird of night is directly and immediately related to this entire discussion of witches.

Bruja, the Spanish word for witch, has another frequently acknowledged meaning: it also refers to a type of owl, no doubt the bird of night referred to in the epigraph and, of course, the very bird popularly associated with witchcraft. Similarly, the *bruja* of popular mythology seems to have taken many of its characteristics from those freely associated with the bird: wisdom and a link to death. No doubt this link with death is the connotative result of the fact that it is a bird which appears only at night, and death has long been related to the night, the darkness, the unknown. The etymology of this morpheme, however, leads to some very pertinent and indeed provocative notions.[19] According to the *Diccionario de la Academia* of 1726, as cited by Roque Barcia in the *Diccionario general etimológico de la Lengua Española* (Madrid, 1881), *bruja* is an owl-like bird that "tiene el instinto de chupar a los niños que maman" ("has the instinct to suck nursing children"). Surely, many of the pejorative connotations of the expression *bruja* when used to refer to a female derive from the fact that the same term is used to refer to a bird believed to harm infants; the connotations, along with the signifier, are simply applied to a different signified. Psychologically, it is only a short step from a bird or woman who destroys the young to one who prevents the young from being born or causes them to be born deformed (read, of no productive use to society). Again, the crimes seem to be knowledge (wisdom to accomplish these feats) coupled with the inhibition of productivity. Similarly, the female has always understood better than the male those aspects of life connected with childbirth (thus, she is afforded a certain wisdom he lacks), and she has always been reluctant to turn her offspring over to society (the patriarch) and allow him/her to be expended in war or other socioeconomic exchange patterns.

Now, the bird of night referred to in the epigraph is mentioned specifically in a context of chaos and violence, a context which is unquestionably meant to be seen as the framework for the novel: "life . . . flowers and fructifies on the contrary out of the profoundest tragic depths of the essential dearth in which its subject's roots are plunged. The natural inheritance of everyone who is capable of spiritual life is an unsubdued forest where the wolf howls and the obscene bird of night chatters." Thus, the dog *(la perra amarilla)* and the bird *(la bruja,* Peta Ponce, the old women) are both symbols of this other world that our religious or civilized world would cover up and the bridges which link the two worlds. The dog clearly exists on a level somewhere between the wildness, bestiality, and untamed nature of the wolf (to the extent that a dog is a domesticated wolf) and the tame, refined, "genteel" society of man. The dog is neither civilized man enmeshed in his comedy nor the untamed wolf, but spans the gap, just as Peta Ponce bridges the space (hence her name, Ponce, from the Latin *pons,* bridge) between the aristocratic civility of the Azcoitía family and the savage, disordered chaos. The witch, significantly, is the point at which the two sides of the coin meet, semiotically pointing to both much as the saint so often referred to in the text exists somewhere between the two sides of the coin. Indeed, both saints and witches (heretics) supposedly have powers; it is merely a question of whether or not these "powers" are acceptable to our system of values or religion. Notably, Santa Teresa de Avila, in her mystic trances, was often accused of heresy.

Significantly, the bird chatters and the wolf howls; neither communicates anything but disorder. But, the bird is labeled obscene and again allied to the witch, for while the bird's only apparent sin is its chattering, this is precisely the threat of the witch and the old women—they refuse to be silent and stifle that other world. It is significant that one possible etymology of the English morpheme *witch* leads us back to the word *victim.* The suggestion, of course, is that because they "know," they must die, even if only metaphorically.

In conclusion, then, we must finally realize that the witch is but one more example of this series of endless reflections. If, as Donoso posits throughout the text, all we have are surfaces reflecting other surfaces, then the witch must merely echo our own chaos, which rests not as far below the surface as we might hope and which ultimately forms a part of that surface. To this extent she is the product of our own projections and negations of our "natural inheritance." Like Eve she mirrors our own evil, and like Mudito's Swiss chalet she insinuates the possibility of both an inside and an outside, but the duality is illusory—inside and outside are one. Ultimately, the witch is but an insignificant old woman (as in the cacique story), a void, an empty signifier which retains a trace of that past, but which we wrap up in layers of covering, supplementation. As a semiotic symbol then the witch is the product of self-projection mediated by desire, plus physical presence mediated by linguistic associations, as I have shown. Expressed as a formula:

$$\text{WITCH} = \frac{\text{self-projection}}{\text{desire}} + \frac{\text{physical presence}}{\text{linguistic association}}$$

There can be little doubt either that since evil tends to be sexually oriented, as R. E. L. Masters has noted, it is necessarily projected outward by the male who, attempting to conceal or deny his own concupiscence (which he inevitably views as the threat of the noncivilized, nonrefined, animal heritage), will project it onto her, blaming her for the desire he feels (a process which again parallels sacrifice, as studied by Girard).

This projection, of course, is already inherently present (although very subtly) in the rib story to which I have so frequently returned. Although Eve would appear to be the incarnation of all evil, if one examines the story quite literally one must see it as an unintentional parable of our relationship with the witch. The story says that Eve, symbol of evil, sexuality, and knowledge, *was removed from Adam* in the form of a rib; once removed from him, the evil (which since it was taken from him must be his own, now projected outward) would seem to live outside him. Similarly, Masters has suggested that the witch and devil are merely excuses for our own behavior, "to kill a witch . . . was to kill also, for the moment, the lust that intolerably tormented him" (p. 149), and that, in fact, the writings on witchcraft are merely licit pornography (p. 147). Thus, man's own lust is projected on the female (it is significant that most of the witches tortured and killed were female, while all the Inquisitors were male), but that lust must soon return as do the *perra amarilla* and the witch in whatever form she may take. Thus, the witch in *El obsceno pájaro* fully dramatizes what was mere suggestion in Gallegos's novel, as doña Bárbara "menaced" the civilized and masculine world.

Thus, the "danger" of the witch is the danger of the novel and of Mudito, narrator of the text and the *séptima bruja*, who is empowered with all those abilities we credit to a witch—power to change his form and that of others, to make of others what he will, to create where nothing exists and to destroy where something does—powers in a word, of language. The dangers clearly are threefold. They include first an eroticism which as Girard suggests is directly linked to violence and chaos and which as we have seen is directly related to power to the extent that these females can use the eroticism to control the male; second, knowledge and acknowledgment that this apparent "order" (ultimately a linguistic creation) is only surface sham which hides a chaos of nothingness; and third, a seeming ability to live outside of, beyond, this male-imposed order. Unlike the males, as exemplified by Jerónimo's creation of the Rinconada and the Church's creation of an almost infinite order, the witch or the old women seem able to accept and live with the chaos and lack of order. Thus, the witch is no doubt the true heretic who challenges or perhaps just ignores the patriarchal authority of our society and religion, thus undermining the very foundation of society as we know it, for she understands, as did Henry James and as does Donoso, that "the natural inheritance of everyone . . . is an unsubdued forest."[20]

8

Women, Language, and Cats in Luisa Valenzuela's *El gato eficaz:* Looking-Glass Games of Fire

> Más remoto que el Ganges y el poniente,
> Tuya es la soledad, tuyo el secreto.
>
> . . . .
>
> En otro tiempo estás. Eres el dueño
> De un ámbito cerrado como un sueño.
>
> Borges, "A un gato"

WOMEN, cats, and language. An absurd triad? A meaningless medley? Perhaps so before Luisa Valenzuela's *El gato eficaz,* but certainly never again.[1] In fact, with the publication of the novel in 1972, history has repeated itself, and once again a woman is to blame—she has opened Pandora's box and all the evils have escaped into the world. But this time doubly so. In the text, evil is disseminated in the form of black *gatos de la muerte* (cats of death) which are bound to destroy the white *perros de la vida* (dogs of life). On another level, the text itself is the Pandora's box from which the evil issues in the sense of a feminine protest against the masculine developed world, a world often poorly organized (in spite of the seeming order spoken of in the last chapter), poorly structured, and certainly squandered. This protest takes the form of a recognition of and emphasis on the female powers, which like those of *El obsceno pájaro* are often hidden and generally scorned in the world outside the text but ever present and potentially dangerous. In less metaphoric terms, one finds in the Valenzuela novel a twentieth-century version of the many myths which are imposed upon the female of our species—myths that the woman herself is not always loath to accept.

It has repeatedly been said that the purpose of poetry (and I use the term in the Greek sense of the word) is to discover or to create previously unrecognized or unacknowledged relationships which enhance our comprehension of our physiological and psychological world.[2] In this one short, poetic novel, Valenzuela has told us more about ourselves as women and more about our intricate relationship to the language we so casually take for granted than we would have believed possible. As a result, in the coming pages I shall be forced to effectuate a triple reading of the novel which will encompass only three of the many exegeses the text itself demands. The first reading will focus on the mythology which has traditionally linked women with the figure of the cat. The second will examine the myths and rituals which surround women in the game of chess. These two readings will in turn demand a simultaneous third reading which will examine the points of contact between this text and a much older and seemingly innocent text which also revolves around a female chess player, Lewis Carroll's *Through the Looking Glass*. This last approach will demonstrate that the Valenzuela novel offers a much more direct analysis of the same points touched upon by this earlier but equally dangerous English text.

But first let me note that the novel itself is a very nearly perfectly wrought work. Although it superficially appears loosely written and organized, careful reading and attention to detail reveal its clever and sensitively artistic juxtaposition of the intricate and curious links between cats, women, language, and ritual games. At every turn the novelist questions and analyzes the novelistic form and the feminine role, both of which are the products of multiple myths that the author examines, demystifies, and undermines. At this point, it would be appropriate to give a synopsis of the novel, but in attempting to organize one, the reader soon discovers that to do so is very nearly impossible, for the novel negates or defies almost all of our traditional concepts of novel. *El gato eficaz* has no plot in the conventional sense of the word. Instead, it is a subtle and poignant dramatization and analysis of some of the basic problems of contemporary feminine life, which engulf us in a modern sense of loss, isolation, and impotence. Ultimately, as the narrator herself states, "Aquí no ha pasado nada, ni pasará ni pasa" (p. 89) ("Nothing has happened, will happen, or is happening here").[3] Also, with the exception of the narrator herself, there are no characters in the historical sense. Even the narrator, who by her own definition is a "cómplice de un gato de la muerte. Un vil gato basurero" (p. 9) ("accomplice of a cat of death. A vile garbageman [refuse heap] cat"), defies most of the rules we generally try to impose upon a narrator. Her voice moves about and incorporates itself into various forms, various bodies. Much like the voice of Mudito in Donoso's *El obsceno pájaro de la noche*, it is ever new and ever changing while ironically always the same—demonstrating, of course, that linguistically the referent for the first-person pronoun is inevitably multiple and fluctuating.[4] At one point, the narrative *yo*, which is always conscious of its role as chronicler, even decides it would prefer to be a male and changes sex; nevertheless, she soon becomes bored with the "masculine" games and reverts back to female. At other moments the narrator is the *yo* of the diary and the confession, while it simultaneously embodies the *yo* of the confessor and, thus, must absolve itself of its sins. In still other places, it personifies an entity which, like the reader or critic, peruses the prose of others, and at some points it even becomes the hidden, abstract *yo* of the scientific or informative essay. Thus, Valenzuela has cleverly managed to group a number of different forms of writing that have traditionally been thought to function in very different capacities and a number of different first persons which have conventionally been thought to be masculine. Juxtaposed as they are, however, it soon becomes evident that the disparity of the functions is but another illusion and that ultimately there is very little fundamental distinction between journalistic and novelistic writing—all forms of writing operate on similar levels of supplementation. Thus, as the narrative first-person pronoun concurrently exemplifies women, the creator, and the novel itself, or writing, the narration, which, from the start, has lost its traditional center and innocence, becomes the pure free-play to which Derrida has referred,[5] and the text is a game, but like Borges's game, a deadly serious one.

Furthermore, the first-person pronoun in *Through the Looking Glass* (1876) maintains a parallel if indeed problematic stance. In that text it represents Lewis Carroll, the alter ego of the Reverend Charles Lutwidge Dodgson, Alice of her waking world, and Alice of her dream world. That is, it functions on various levels of authority and power. Alice's opening conversation with her kittens in fact ponders the question of the punishments awaiting her, a question which surreptitiously slips in and out of the Valenzuela text and a question which implies the existence of a greater authority or power than that of the speaker. The games which one finds in Valenzuela are epitomized in Carroll in the linguistic puns as well as the game of chess, populated with characters from other nursery rhymes. Thus, just as the Valenzuela novel is populated with characters from ancient myths (both Greco-Roman and Aztec), *Through the Looking Glass* is populated with characters from children's myths—nursery rhymes.

In a similar fashion, a kitten provides the structural framework for *Through the Looking Glass*, which begins with a discussion of whether the white kitten or the black kitten was to blame (again a question of culpability which permeates the Valenzuela text) and ends, of course, with Alice shaking the black kitten awake and positing her philosophical question to it. It is appropriate that the feline figure in *Through the Looking Glass* should be a kitten since Alice is but a child, not an adult female as the full-grown cat would suggest in *El gato eficaz*. The fact that Alice's kittens are specifically black and white also points to the Valenzuela text (or vice versa), but of this I shall have more to say later.

What are some of these intricate relationships and myths that link women, cats, and language and with which Valenzuela so cleverly toys? The feline figure has long played a role in mythology and literature. Its characterization has traditionally been one of power, and it has often been coupled with the concept of women. Consider for example the Sphinx of classical mythology, part woman, part lion, part bird, holder of the secret and slayer of all Oedipus's predecessors who failed to unravel the riddle.[6] The analogy is not gratuitous but, in fact, this concept is immediately pertinent to the novelistic material and the notion of game. At the end of *El gato eficaz*, the narrator, not unlike the Sphinx, entreats her reader to go back and "descubra las claves de este juego, alínee las piezas—blancas perrovidas, negras gatomuertes—y retome los ciclos" (p. 119) ("discover the clues to this game, line up the pieces—white dog-lives, black cat-deaths—and continue the cycles"). Thus, in this sense the cat and women are tied to the game of chess (of which I shall have more to say), a game which creates its own drama and with rules so complex, only she who understands them completely is able to play the game successfully and win. Oedipus, as we know, solved the riddle of the Sphinx but still lacked that more relevant information about his parentage that might have been his salvation.

In addition, the cat, in the form of the lion, often appears in the Bible. While not overtly female oriented, it nonetheless appears as a symbol of either God or the devil—that is, as a supernatural being with extraordinary power over life and death, a power which, as already shown in earlier chapters, is often considered female.[7] And, in the New World, the *Chilam Balam*, the *Popol-Vuh*, and the twentieth-century beliefs of the Brazilian tribes studied by Lévi-Strauss, all link the jaguar to supernatural powers and the underworld of death.[8] But it is perhaps in contemporary Hispanic literature that the cat has appeared in the strangest places with the most peculiar significance. Consider, for example, the affiliation between Fuentes's Aura, Cortázar's Talita, Sábato's Alejandra and cats.[9] In each case, the portrayal of the female character is complexly dependent upon the image of the cat.

There are, of course, numerous examples of this sort, but in the interest of expediency let us acknowledge that the cat as a metaphor for women in *El gato eficaz* is a commonplace, and certainly not original in and of itself. In the metaphors of our everyday language, for the most part we speak of felines as "she" and scorn the "cattiness" of women. What is unique and innovative in Valenzuela's novel is that the reader is now forced, for perhaps the first time, to question the basis for this metaphor and its implications; one is compelled not only to seek the points of contact between cats and women but inversely to consider the significance of the aggregate of the mythology which surrounds women as a result of the metaphor.

The question that one is prompted to ask, then, is why this strange bond between women and cats. Man, of course, has long viewed the female in connection with animals. Throughout the centuries he has repeatedly asked himself if she can possibly even have a soul (soul, of course, being the characteristic which distinguishes humans from animals). This novel seems to imply that the psychological association of women and animals is the consequence of a fundamental and continual process of differentiation. As Michel Foucault *(Les mots et les choses)* has noted, the self can identify itself only as it recognizes and separates itself from the other. And, as discussed at length in the chapter on *La ciudad y los perros,* our comprehension of the world and our language itself are ultimately based on our ability to differentiate between X and not-X, between the same and the other. We have two words for two objects because they are somehow not identical. Now, for man the other, or not-man, has had two forms: the animal and the female. Thus, although obviously woman is not-animal, the fact that both animals and women can be defined as not-man or as man's opposite assuredly produces some of the overlapping of connotation between the two terms, woman and cat.

But why do we encounter the underlying insinuation of the supernatural and death surrounding both the female and the animal? Again, I suspect that the evolution of the connotation can be linked to the notion of the other, which because of its very quality of alienation and separation, is shrouded in mystery and produces fear and anxiety—fear of the unknown and what is different or not understood because it is different, apprehension of a potential or imagined power which threatens to destroy the self. Thus evolves the correlation between the other (in this case animals and women) and supernatural powers, witchcraft, and death, to which I have so often referred.[10]

Nevertheless, in *El gato eficaz* this link between cats, women, the supernatural, and death is toyed with, carried one step further, and eventually transposed to language and the novel itself. As the narrator notes, "Fuego, juego, así soy yo, me ocupo de una letra hasta el mismo dibujo" (p. 67) ("Fire, game, that's what I am, I concern myself with a letter, even it's very design"). In fact, the expression *gatos de la muerte* which predominates in the novel is clearly the result of a linguistic game. In this text it appears that the term *vida perra,* or *vida de perros* (dog's life), is construed in a rigorously literal manner and subjected to a little linguistic "witchcraft," if you will. In other words, the colloquial, metaphorical phrase *vida de perros* (life of dogs, dog's life) is inverted to produce the new expression *perros de la vida* (dogs of life). In turn, this new term finds its dialectical opposite in the phrase *gatos de la muerte*—cats being the opposite of dogs and death being the opposite of life. As one might imagine, the *gatos de la muerte* are friends, companions, and allies of the female narrator. The irony is that it was she who imported the *perros de la vida*, but, although they are enemies of the *gatos de la muerte*, for some reason the dogs are unable to recognize the cats. Thus, the opposition between the two plays on our traditional, simplistic notions of good and bad in that the cats are black and evil, although intelligent, while the dogs are white and morally superior to the cats but less intelligent. The concept of dialectical opposition and the notion of separating the self from the other is emphasized even further, as the narrator states, "Puedo fácilmente dividir en dos al mundo (p. 17) ("I can easily divide the world in two").

Valenzuela then goes one step further with the linguistic game and connects the cats and dogs to the actual physical aspects of writing. The white dogs evoke the blank, white page, the tabula rasa, pure and virginal, which promises potentially infinite and perfect worlds. But the black cats, apparently necessary to produce these worlds in the form of writing, black lettering, soon enter, besmudge, and pervert the pure white page, with the resultant loss of purity and innocence and thus the destruction of those promised, ideal worlds.[11] Significantly, because the narrator has allowed the *gato de la muerte* to sleep upon her neck, she discovers that she now has "una quemadura negra en la garganta" (p. 109) ("a black burn on her throat"). Thus, cats and women are metaphorically linked to corruption and in turn to sexual lust and writing (both of which corrupt men, apparently), a connection which again points back to the discussion of witches in the last chapter. In this sense, then, once again the female and her cohorts commit the original sin, and once again, the destruction of the promised paradise is not only her doing but also the result of a mysterious mixture of eroticism and metaphysics (quest for knowledge).[12]

Now, inasmuch as the punishment for this corruption must be banishment from the paradise and ensuing death, one is reminded of Julia Kristeva's theory of narration itself: that the soiling (in the form of writing) of this pure, white page is a passage through death.[13] *El gato eficaz*, in this manner, would appear to be a perfect illustration of Kristeva's theory that the author must pass through a symbolic death in her conversion to narrator. Thus, in *El gato eficaz* the narration both begins and ends with death. In the beginning the loss or death of a male companion is bemoaned, and the narrator grapples with the fact that she will never see him again, *in spite of* his promise to her that "nos veremos mañana" (p. 8) ("we'll see each other tomorrow"). But again, the words lose all significance with the absence of the referent and the *yo*. That is, once that first person ceases to exist, any words implying his participation are necessarily invalid. In some ways it appears to be this death which prompts the writing of the text, and the writing in this respect fills a void, an absence as noted in the last chapter. In addition, the novel ends with the following reference to death:

"Jaque mate otra vez, que me mate de lejos. Me mate, memite, me imite: sólo en un renacimiento reside mi esperanza" (p. 119) ("Checkmate again, may it kill me from afar. Kill me, 'mythitate' me, imitate me: my only hope lies in a renascence"). In this manner, the text emphasizes the position of narration as death, but as death which results in rebirth and hope, so that void is filled with something else, some type of supplement. To a large degree, one of the prime purposes of the text is to play with our myths and our traditional concept of women in order to destroy them, but the goal of the destruction is the subsequent creation of a new image, hopefully more constructive. In other words, unlike so many contemporary novels, Valenzuela's novel is not destruction for the sake of destruction; rather, *El gato eficaz* is constructive destruction. As the text states, "Mueren de allá para acá, del otro mundo a éste" (p. 12) ("They die from there to here, from the other world to this one").

Shortly before the final statement expressing the hope of renascence, the narrator had reminded us that she is now *imprinted* on the male retina (the blank page) and that she is now pure recollection, memory, and thus indestructible. Such was precisely the gesture of *María,* but, of course, the narrator had already recognized her position as pure representation when she stated, "El papel es trampa, yo soy trampa toda hecha de papel y mera letra impresa" (pp. 109–10) ("The paper is a trick, I am a trick all made of paper and simple printed letters"), a statement which underlines my insistence on the female as literary creation, supplement, inside and outside of fiction. Thus, the author passed through this symbolic death as she became narrator and converted herself into a series of words and signs (black "female" marks on the white "male" page or retina), just as all mankind passes through a symbolic death and metamorphosis as it becomes caught up in and reduced by its mythologies and supplementations. But the new essence or image seems to be firmly imprinted, whether one wishes to acknowledge it or not. The narrator also discloses to us that she is now a mixture, a composite that he "trata de remover en el caldero de su mente para hacer de mí una masa informe que ya no lo perturbe" (p. 118) ("tries to stir up in the cauldron of his mind to make me into a shapeless mass that will no longer bother him") but that "Nunca habrá de lograrlo" ("He'll never be able to"). Thus, as one *referent* is destroyed, a new one is born.

From early mythology, then, the cat is no longer just a cat and woman is no longer just woman, but instead both have been enveloped in supplement and connotation that ultimately have very little relationship to "catness" or "femaleness." That is, from the earliest traceable moment one sees the sign moving away from its referent and already becoming pure supplement. This movement away from the referent is paralleled, if in fact not dramatized, in the metamorphosis which the narrator undergoes. On one level we return to the more primitive story in which animals talk, but in which the notion of speech among animals is but a reflection of an innocent confidence in the ability of the word to capture the referent. Paradoxically, at the same time the text demonstrates a preoccupation with the word which no longer presents (makes present) its referent. As already mentioned, the very first pages of the novel are preoccupied with the fact that although he said "nos veremos mañana," his death has removed the referent from that first-person pronoun and made those words meaningless. The entire discourse then becomes a game which toys with the concept of supplement and removal from the referent and illustrates how this removal develops and transforms itself into a new "reality," in which we are no longer capable of seeing the supplement as supplemental (as other) but in which again we are inclined to see the supplementation, substitution, as the *inherent essence* of the thing itself.[14] What begins as obvious supplement or adjective soon dominates as the referent disappears.[15]

In this sense, the whole notion of other has been transferred to language itself as one recognizes the distance between the signifier and the signified, a distance fraught with supplementation and power, and Valenzuela forces us to acknowledge that the signifier itself *is the other*. And thus we circle back to the basic mythology which surrounds the cat and the other and realize that if the cat is a signifier for women it too must somehow be other. And of course, it is, for women certainly are not cats. In this sense, the myth itself is supplemental and dangerous to the extent that we had failed to recognize it for the supplement it is and the distance it holds. It is dangerous because at some point we stop recognizing the metaphor as metaphor and begin to accept it as innate and inherent to the thing itself. This, of course, is precisely what has occurred with the image of woman.

The image of the cat, then, stands as the epitome of the plurality of the sign, too often overlooked or forgotten. And, of course, the more plural the sign the greater the role of the supplement, for when the signifier implies several signifieds, the supplement functions as the selector and imparts meaning. The text ultimately chides the self-indulgence of women as we allow ourselves to first be supplemented or displaced (which may be inevitable) and then to be created by that language which is already supplemental. The use of the cat as the principal metaphor is appropriate in that there are few other words or expressions in Spanish so fraught with meaning and so frequently used as part of metaphorical expressions.[16]

Thus, Valenzuela demystifies some of the metaphors and the mythology surrounding women. In effect, the narrator recognizes that she, like all narrators, is a supplement of a supplement of a supplement, and she notes, "desde aquí me observo jugar a ser mirada con mi propia mirada" (p. 106) ("from here I watch myself play at being watched by my own gaze"), and concludes the novel as noted, "Jaque mate otra vez, que me mate de lejos. Me mate, memite, me imite: sólo en un renacimiento reside mi esperanza" (p. 119) ("Checkmate again, may it kill me from afar. Kill me, 'mythitate' me, imitate me: my only hope lies in a renascence"). The rebirth, clearly, is a second reading of the novel, which like the Phoenix rises from the ashes again only to be slain once more, but as the text indicates, "El peligro de estos bichos [los gatos de la muerte] no es la muerte, como indica su nombre, sino algo más sutil y más dañino: la clarividencia" (p. 29) ("The danger of these critters [the cats of death] isn't death, as their name indicates, but rather something more subtle and destructive: clairvoyance").

This dangerous clairvoyance or insight becomes apparent only at the conclusion of the text where the final words, much like the concluding words of *Through the Looking Glass,* compel us to go back and read the text once more, seeking meaning on another level. The second reading of the novel forces us to reexamine even more of our cultural assumptions—whence that dangerous clairvoyance or insight.

On the last page of the novel, the narrator declares that she awaits "un nuevo solidario como vos que descubra las claves de este juego y alínee las piezas—blancas perrovidas, negras gatomuertes—y retome los ciclos" (p. 119) ("a new associate like you to discover the clues to this game, line up the pieces—white dog-lives, black cat-deaths—and continue the cycles"). I accept the author's challenge and shall attempt to do as she asks: discover the key to the puzzle and extend the metaphor of the game to see where it leads us.

There would be no doubt that Valenzuela is referring to chess here even if she had not continued with the words, "Jaque mate otra vez." The image of the white *perrovidas* and the black *gatomuertes* of which I have spoken already evokes the chess pieces, usually black and white, colors which differentiate the two chess "armies." The morphemes *vida* and *muerte* which one encounters in the terms *perrovidas* and *gatomuertes* also would seem particularly appropriate to signal the chess game, since life and death are figuratively associated with these colors and since a chess match presumably must continue until one army symbolically annihilates or defeats the other by surrounding the king—that is, one army finishes the game "dead," conquered, the other, "alive," conquering.

This discussion of chess necessarily leads us back even further to Carroll's *Through the Looking Glass,* where the chess pieces are not black and white but rather red and white. Significantly, however, the kittens, which Alice insists are the incarnations of the queens, are black and white. I suspect that the change in chess piece colors here is the result of a double motivation. First, of course, some chess sets (like checkers sets) are black and red, rather than black and white, so the use of red pieces would not be totally inappropriate, although the combination of red and white is inventive (and Carroll was known to continually strive for an innovative twist to all). Furthermore, surely Alice could not be portrayed as either a red or a

black pawn (and eventual queen), because of the negative connotations of
those colors; she must be presented as white, pure, and innocent—her
innocence is, indeed, one of the themes of the text. Given, too, that the
question of slavery was quite a sensitive issue during the period in which
Through the Looking Glass was written, Carroll may have wished to avoid the
racial implications of black kings and queens. At any rate, what is most
pertinent to this discussion is that Alice, not unlike the Valenzuela narrator, sees the kittens not as kings, but as queens—that is she associates
them with female figures, not male. This stance also suggests indirectly
what Valenzuela continually points out—that the female in both works is
believed to be transformable and metamorphic, while the male is perceived
as constant and immutable.

However, one must consider the significance of the chess game within
the confines of the novels and those of the contemporary feminine situation. We know that chess is one of the oldest games still played today.[17]
Invented around A.D. 500 in India, exactly how or when it was conceived is
not known, but there are a multiplicity of myths surrounding its origin. It
is particularly relevant that many of these fables center on a female figure,
the *mater dolorosa,* whose name varies according to the version but whose
story and role remain basically unchanged. According to the legends, there
was a war between two brothers during which one of the brothers was
accidentally killed. The surviving son created the game to explain this
death to his mother, to exonerate himself, and/or to console her.[18] In other
words, the game was invented for a woman, by a man closely associated
with the death of her son and motivated by her affliction or disconsolation
in the face of the absence or death of the male. It is pertinent to note also
that the leitmotif of the mother mourning the loss of the son seems linked
to an even older myth—that of Isis and Osiris, a myth and its subsequent
rite in which one son kills the other in order to seize the power of the
kingdom; in the myth, this act too results in the perpetual affliction of the
mother, the queen.[19] In effect, since the bull which was worshiped as part
of the rite of Isis was black with a white square on his forehead (according
to Bulfinch), it is certainly possible that the myths of the invention of chess
might have originated here since the chessboard is but a series of white
squares on a black background (or vice versa).[20] In a similar manner, the
psychologist Norman Reider ("Chess, Oedipus and the Mater Dolorosa"),
among others, has suggested that the fables of the origin of chess and the
game itself both reflect the residue of an oedipal story or situation—that is,
once again, the game is perceived as the result of a conflict between two
men for the favors and powers which rightly belong to the mother, the
queen.[21] In this respect, the female has played a role which has remained
essentially hidden and has rarely been recognized but which is also essential and revealing. Ironically, the female, that is, the queen, was not a
member of the *dramatis personae* of this theater/game during some one
thousand years. But here perhaps lies her importance.

As any psychologist would tell us, what is not manifest and overt but rather appears to be hidden can be as significant and equally important as that which is overt. Thus, if one wishes to associate the game with the rite and the myth, one must recognize that all that remains of this ancient rite is the ritual control over the movements of the chess pieces—the rite itself has been lost—and the myth or myths which are linked to the game are but the words which accompany the representation, words which neither explain nor give the reasons for the rite, but which simply describe and narrate.[22] And significantly, as René Girard has noted in his study *Violence and the Sacred*, the true meaning and significance of the ritual is always hidden to its participants—they always believe it to be other than what it is. Or as Borges has expressed it in a more poetic format: "Cuando los jugadores se hayan ido, / Cuando el tiempo los haya consumido, / Ciertamente no habrá cesado el rito" because, as he affirms in another sonnet, "También el jugador es prisionero / . . . de otro tablero / De negras noches y de blancos días."[23]

And what does all of this have to do with Valenzuela's novel? Everything. As I have already noted, the novel itself is pure play and presents itself as a series of linguistic and/or conceptual games as the author herself continually reminds us that what we face is a game: she speaks of constructing puzzles (p. 11), states, "Por eso juego" (p. 67) ("That's why I play") and that she herself is a game (p. 67), and even goes so far as to entitle a section "Juguemos al fornicón" (pp. 68–70) ("Let's Play Fornication"), a section in which she furnishes us with the rules for playing not chess but coitus. This notion of play ties in neatly with the myth of the *mater dolorosa* when one realizes that all the games of the novel, like chess itself, materialize as a consequence of the absence of the male. The second sentence of the novel notes, "El le dijo mañana nos veremos y ella de inocente le creyó" (p. 7) ("He told her we'll see each other tomorrow and she, innocent, believed him"). Although it is suggested that he has died ("¿Por qué entonces entró en el improbable baño de los túneles y dejó que otro hombre le sorbiera la vida?" [p. 8] ["Why then did he enter the improbable bathroom of the tunnels and let another man suck the life out of him?"]), we never discover for sure what happened to him, and for our purposes it does not matter.[24] What is relevant is that the novel is crisscrossed by his absence, perhaps like any game or like the life of any female. And, in more general terms, what is pertinent to this discussion is the link between the game and the death of the male, a link which in turn is connected to the ancient myths and the invention of chess.

The legends of chess and the *mater dolorosa*, like the game itself, begin and end with the death of the male, explicit or implicit, metaphoric as it may be. According to the myth, the game of chess was created after the death of the son, and the game reenacted the events which lead up to his death, a representation which, of course, also ended with a new dramatization of the murder. The chess game today also ends with the death or the possibility of the death of the king.[25] And, clearly, at that moment, one can once again reinitiate the cycle and begin a new game; thus, the chess match not only ends with death (metaphoric as it may be) but also begins once again as a result of this death. And this repetition, a cycle as inescapable as that of any rite, leads us directly to *El gato eficaz*, since the novel too terminates with the death (although perhaps again metaphoric) of the narrator, who concludes with the words, "Jaque mate otra vez, que me mate de lejos. Me mate, memite, me imite: sólo en un renacimiento reside mi esperanza" (p. 119) ("Checkmate again, may it kill me from afar. Kill me, 'mythitate' me, imitate me: my only hope lies in a renascence"). Clearly, all rites, like the myth of the origin of chess and like the myth of Isis whose ritual had as its goal the resurrection of Osiris, the dead son and husband, are precisely this: an imitation, a re-presentation, which engenders the rebirth and hope. The difference is that in the novel the death is not just that of the male but also that of the female, mother of this game, who can also be resuscitated in another game (reading).

Thus, although *El gato eficaz* might appear not to be in conformity with the myths, since the "death" is that of a female rather than a male, this feminine death does coordinate with the game and with the legend of its origin in a subtle fashion. According to several versions of the myth, the mother, after witnessing the games and the dramatization of the demise of her son, fell into despair and died herself (Reider, p. 454). Viewed in this manner, both the myths and the novel demonstrate three steps in common: (1) the death (absence) of the male, (2) the game which serves to explain his death, to distract her or to alleviate her grief, and (3) *the resultant death of the female.* If one accepts Norman Reider's theory, that game is therapy which includes a simulated version of the crime (p. 450) and add to this Girard's theory that the participants in the ritual believe the meaning to be other than what it is, then one must ask if the crime might not be the death of the female rather than that of the male (as we have always presumed), a death which he provokes.

Numerous psychological studies have analyzed the Oedipus complex and insisted that the violence directed against the father is almost always hidden, but it is appropriate to suggest that perhaps this violence is also directed against the mother, who, in the oedipal situation, is inevitably violated, symbolically or virtually.[26] After all, to violate the mother or marry her (which may well be the same thing in a more attenuated form) is nothing more (or less) than another form of mitigating or overthrowing the power she has over the son. Once the two are married or she is violated, her power or supremacy remains in his hands, and she, at least in her previous form, mother, is annihilated. Thus, it might be more valid to perceive the Oedipus myths as the son's usurpation of the powers of the mother and his subsequent affirmation of autonomy and sovereignty. And it is precisely this irony which Valenzuela appears to have discovered, underlined, and denounced when she says, "Jaque mate otra vez, que me mate de lejos" (p. 119) ("Checkmate again, may it kill me from afar"), or even earlier in the novel when she declares, "Muevo una pieza, es jaque mate y el muerto soy yo qué bueno" (p. 67) ("I move a piece, it's checkmate and the dead one is me, how nice"). Nevertheless, she assures us, "vuelo a desarmar lo armado" (p. 80) ("I fly to disarm the armed [uncock the cocked]"), and here one finds the possibility of that rebirth to which she has referred, because it is only the recognition of the myth's underlying significance that allows her to deconstruct the structure which subjects her. And, in effect, if the chess game points to the death of the queen, she (in the novel, at any rate) has already been reborn.

Indeed, one can validly protest that today the queen begins the chess-match at the side of the king and is, in effect, the most powerful piece on the chess board: to capture the queen leads almost inevitably to checkmate, that is, to the fall of the king. But it was not always this way. When the game originated, there was no female on the chessboard nor anything that might represent her. The piece which is today called the queen was then a masculine counselor with very limited powers. The most frequently diffused and accepted theory is that the piece changed from a counselor to a feminine figure in the fifteenth or sixteenth century because of the homophony between the Arabic word *fierge* that comes from *ferz*, counselor, and the French word *vierge*, maiden—words which are differentiated by only one letter (Davidson, *A Short History of Chess* p. 28). Thus the woman entered the game purely by chance and a linguistic quirk—a feat that she has never accomplished in the Spanish card deck. It was also during this period that the queen gained many of the powers which she has today (Davidson, *Short History*, p. 14). In effect, as William Hone declared with great surprise in the year 1832:

> Strangely inconsistent with our ideas of propriety and probability, the queen is the chief character in the contest. She is not merely the soft excitement of the war who bids her king go forth with her blessing; no, she is the active, undaunted, indefatigable leader of an army, herself a host![27]

But Hone, among others, ignored a fundamental and pertinent characteristic: the king is inviolable; he is never truly captured nor removed from the chess board during the match (Golombek, *Chess*, p. 19), while this is patently not the case with the queen. She is captured and removed from the board as quickly as possible. Also, there is only one king (in each army of course), and he is never replaceable. On the contrary, the feminine counterpart is not only substitutable but also imitable, like the narrator who at the end of the novel points out, "me imite: sólo en un renacimiento reside me esperanza" (p. 119) ("imitate me: my only hope lies in a renascence").

In the game, the pawn who passes through the eight horizontal squares and arrives at the other vertical extreme is crowned queen in spite of his presumable masculine gender. If one wishes to understand the game as a metaphor of life, this would suggest that anyone can become queen, but one is born king, and he is not interchangeable. That is, once again one sees that the feminine powers are easily seized or transferred, or at least we pretend that they are.

Again, *Through the Looking Glass* offers a clue to the interpretation of *El gato eficaz*. In the earlier novel, eight of the twelve chapters are devoted to Alice's endeavors to traverse the eight squares of the chess board and become queen. It is precisely the result of these efforts, as portrayed in the Carroll text, which make this apparently innocent text ominous. *Through the Looking Glass* is clearly a continuation of Alice's "adventures," and, as we all know, adventure novels present a hero who passes through a series of adventures or trials to return home and claim his princess, his kingdom, and his reward. Now Alice, like the Valenzuela narrator, passes through the required trials, arrives at the goal, and is "queened." But Alice is a little *girl*, not a heroic knight (male) in shining armor, so the end of her story, like the end of the Valenzuela novel, is *not* a kingdom but an awakening (and a rude one at that). And awaken she does, only to find herself right back where she started, all her efforts for naught, shaking a kitten, wondering about her own existence, her own reality (did she dream the red king or did he dream her?), and having no one pay any attention to her, not even the kitten who is too busy licking its paw to answer her questions. Ironically, even don Quijote when he awakens from his heroic dream is treated with sympathy, but not Alice. And herein, I suggest, lies the danger of Carroll's text and the message of Valenzuela's: both poignantly dramatize just how far little (or big) girls' dreams take them—nowhere. Valenzuela's novel might well have been addressing Alice, with her fascination for the looking glass, when it admonishes, "nunca vuelvas a dejarte enamorar por un reflejo" (p. 21) ("never let yourself fall in love with a reflection again"), thus suggesting that we cease our acceptance of these reflected supplementations.

There can be no doubt that Valenzuela's manipulation and play with the notion of chess returns us once again to the center of that novel where the game of the text, its references to various other games, and the link between these and the ancient mythology become even more patent. The narrator states, in what is almost the exact physical center of the text, "Quiero detenerme a veces para descubrir que todo lo vivible puede ser jugable" (p. 67) ("I like to stop sometimes and discover that everything livable can be playable"), and continues, "Muevo una pieza, es jaque mate y el muerto soy yo" (p. 67) ("I move a piece, it's checkmate and the dead one is me"), words laden with significance for every woman. From here, the narrator leads us in a very subtle fashion to the myth of Prometheus, saying, "Salgo por el mundo a llevar el mensaje del juego, igual que Trometeo. Fuego, juego, así soy yo, me ocupo de una letra hasta el mismo dibujo y la corto a mitad de un camino ascendente" (p. 67) ("I go out through the world to carry the message of the game, just like Trometheus. Fire, game, that's what I am, I concern myself with a letter, even its very design, and I cut it halfway up its path"). Clearly, this change of one letter was precisely the accident which allowed the queen to enter the chess match centuries ago, but at this point one must ask what Prometheus has to do with all this. We already know that he brought fire to the world, fire that he stole from the gods, and that between *fuego* (fire) and *juego* (game) there is only one letter of difference, a letter with which Valenzuela plays and a letter which perhaps signals what awaits anyone who does not play this game of life well and according to the established rules, but there is another, much more important link between Prometheus and our author, so playful yet serious.[28]

According to Greek mythology, Prometheus was one of the Titans, a race of giants who inhabited the Earth before man. He created man from a bit of dirt or soil mixed with water. The legend says that Prometheus and his brother, Epimetheus, were charged with the creation of man and with providing him all the facilities he would need for life on Earth. But it is said that Epimetheus distributed all the possible gifts and characteristics to the animals, so that when he got to man, he had nothing left to bestow upon him. For this reason, Prometheus was forced to steal fire from the gods and give it to man so that the latter would have something which would make him superior to the animals. In this manner, the myth of Prometheus links itself to that of Isis and Osiris, of which I have already spoken, since the latter also furnished the gifts of civilization to man.

Nevertheless, in the myth of Prometheus, in order to punish the brothers for stealing fire and chastise man for having accepted the gift, the gods sent the first woman, Pandora. Pandora, it seems, was created in heaven and each god contributed something toward her perfection. Her name, in fact, means woman of all gifts. Upon being sent to Earth, she was accepted with great joy by Epimetheus, but from this point on the versions vary. Some say that the gods sent a jar with her, others say that the jar was already in Epimetheus's house, and still others say that it was not a jar at all but a box. At any rate, as we all know, victim of her curiosity, Pandora opened the jar or the box and all the vices escaped into the world, which accounts for today's world, filled with all forms of evil, sickness, war, and the like. In other words, all the bad that we find in the world today is present because of the intrepidity of the female.

Thus, like Alice, we find ourselves back in the Garden regardless of all our efforts to escape from it, for the most curious aspect of this myth of

Prometheus clearly is the repetition of the same theme in the story of Eve, who also caused us to lose our innocence, and paradise, because of her curiosity. The irony of this representation of the woman, an irony which has been lost in the more recent story of Eve, is that in the final analysis, the female was not to blame for anything. It was man, as well as Prometheus and his brother in the Greek myth, who did not conduct himself appropriately and who committed crimes and nonsensical acts. Had man not accepted Pandora, gift of the gods, had Prometheus not stolen fire, had Epimetheus not given all positive characteristics to the animals (had he used a little foresight), the brothers would not have found themselves in such a situation. Furthermore, the myth demotes Pandora from the woman of all gifts to the producer of all evil. But, as already indicated in the chapter on *La ciudad y los perros,* since the tendency of Western civilization is to divide everything into opposite and bipolar notions, if the man wishes to and in effect must see himself as the incarnation of all good, then all bad must be personified in his polar opposite—the female. It would appear that it is very difficult to accept the possibility that both might embrace the good as well as the bad. That is, once again, what is within the male is projected onto the female and as a result appears to emanate from her. And, once again, her image becomes supplementary to the extent that it is superimposed by his projections. But the narrator of *El gato eficaz* resolves the problem in an efficient manner; she notes, "Ya no es libre [él], me jacta de decirlo. Libre soy yo después de haber dejado mi imagen en sus manos y no tener así que andar cuidándola como hace la gente que no sabe entregarla. Puedo ahora hacer lo que yo quiera, él cuida de mi imagen" (p. 118) ("He's no longer free, I'm proud to say. I'm the one who is free ever since I left my image in his hands and haven't had to go around worrying about it like those who don't know how to hand it over. Now I can do whatever I want, he takes care of my image"). And this would appear to be the only logical thing one might do, since, as she bitingly admonishes, "Ésta es la historia de él, lo reconozco, las construcciones las hago en su homenaje. Desarmo algunas partes con ingentes esfuerzos . . . y toda yo soy piedra desollada a causa del esfuerzo y desarmar los laberintos" (p. 79) ("This is his story, I admit it. I compose the structures as a homage to him. I dismantle some parts with enormous efforts . . . and I'm all flayed stone because of the effort of building and dismantling labyrinths"). Thus, she encourages him to do what he wishes with her image since as Borges has affirmed, "También el jugador es prisionero / . . . de otro tablero / De negras noches y blancos días." But, like Alice, the narrator of *El gato eficaz* cannot win; like Alice she has played the game by the rules, done what she has been told, and tried to conform, but for naught. She too has ended up where she started. As Valenzuela notes, "Podríamos detenernos a aspirar pero cuesta trabajo. . . . Podríamos detenernos juntos a aspirar un momento, tener aspiraciones de futuro, cosechar esperanzas que se sumen, y no puedo seguir: de golpe me doy cuenta que es la cobardía que nos mueve a respetar los pactos a no romper esquemas, y eso me da asco" (p. 116) ("We could stop to take a breath [aspire] but it's a lot of work. We could stop together to take a breath [aspire] for a minute, have future aspirations, reap hopes that are sinking, and I can't go on: suddenly I realize that it is cowardice which encourages us to respect pacts not to destroy the structures and that disgusts me").

In conclusion, then, it is evident that the game with which the narrator plays is a metaphor which dissimulates, attenuates, and sublimates the basic violence which for so long has been imagined as directed against the male but which is now shown to be directed against the female. In this manner, Valenzuela has once again opened Pandora's box, but this time she has opened it metaphorically in the form of her mouth, an orifice which she, elsewhere, has labeled the most dangerous part of a woman.[29] But, as the myth of Pandora concludes with hope which did not escape from the box, and as the chess match always ends with the possibility of another match, the novel too ends on a note of hope. The narrator lets the male worry about and take care of her image (since it seems to matter so much to him) and allows that he "[la] mate, [la] mite [convert into myth], y [la] imite" so that she can be reborn from the ashes of this *fuego/juego*, like the Phoenix who is reborn from his own funeral pyre, in order to play again.[30] After all, as the narrator states, "vivir es un juego y hace falta osadía" (p. 67) ("to live is a game which requires audacity"). Perhaps the audacity lies in refusing to accept the rules of the game as they are written and refusing to let the subtle, even disguised, violence continue.

Thus *El gato eficaz* has juxtaposed all the topics examined in the last seven chapters—otherness, differentiation, mythology, language, supplementation, absence, death, violence, sacrifice, evil—and has shown that all are interrelated. I would hope that the Valenzuela text indicates the path that the novel of the future will take and in this sense provides a logical concluding point for a study of the female character.

Conclusion

A S this analysis of the portrayal of the female during one hundred years of the Spanish-American novel concludes, what is most important for us to bear in mind and what is far too often overlooked is that her portrayal has not always nor necessarily been totally pejorative even in those novels written by men (e.g., Puig, Donoso, Vargas Llosa).[1] What has been noted, however, is that like Eve she is regularly depicted as absence, either significantly distanced from the writer, narrator, protagonist, and reader, or nonexistent, even within the fiction. From *María* through *El gato eficaz* our texts have unanimously demonstrated that this absence has been a necessary condition for writing, narrating, and reading: Efraín could not write until María ceased to be; Cova did not write his memoirs until Alicia was no longer at his side; and Toto "wrote" while his mother was elsewhere, working or napping. Because that absence (like a vacuum)[2] accordingly demands to be filled, draws into itself that which surrounds it, and strives thus to become nonabsence, the blank space (the female character) is ineluctably subsumed by a projection of the writer (historically, most often male) who "writes" her both literally and metaphorically.[3] Thus, whether she is viewed as good or bad, she is a reflection and/or aggrandizement of the male. He has created her at least in part so that he can be afforded a suitable mate or enemy (depending on the work and the period) who will glorify him. In chivalric romances, the hero needed an exemplary mate to prove his own value and excellence; *Doña Bárbara* has suggested that he needs an equally suitable enemy for the same reasons. At the same time, however, whether she is depicted as good or evil, she often represents an extrication of the good or evil within him, as was the case with the witch and with the nefarious Eve, the rib taken from Adam.

Nevertheless, as has been repeatedly illustrated, she is but a projected reflection of the writer/reader, a linguistic concoction, pure supplement whose essence or referent (signified) has been lost or never existed apart from the writers' and the readers' psyches. It has been demonstrated too that her supplementation is effectuated as much by the reader as by the writer. Even Eve is as much the outgrowth of what we and her other readers throughout the centuries have read into her. Although we have seen that the literary female is often the progeny of the *se dice* or *dicen*, it

186

might easily be demonstrated that she is equally the product of the *se lee* or *leen*. Again, consider doña Bárbara, who is not, in fact, presented nearly as negatively as her readers have long insisted. Repeatedly, then, language and rhetoric have created and imposed themselves on our image of the female, overshadowing any possibility of extratextual referentiality. Sometimes this has been intentional (e.g., Santos Luzardo), sometimes quite coincidental (e.g., Toto). Throughout history, it is our image of the texts, our reading of the female, which has had far greater impact than the texts themselves or any being in the world. Be it the story of the Fall or Adam's rib, be it doña Bárbara or our perception of the witch, in each case our cognizance has been colored by what we thought we were going to see, by what we were told we would experience. In other words, each reading and our subsequent reaction has been predicated on and conditioned by a previous reader, by the other. Thus, the female is not only inevitably other, but even our experience of her is shaped by yet others. She is thus doubly removed.

There can be little doubt, then, that the contradictions we seem to find in the novelistic female's portrayal, contrariety that we have come to understand as inherent to her rather than to her depiction, representation, recreation, are all products of the supplement not recognized as such. That is, we as readers have made linguistic, semantic connections (connections, to be sure, often prompted or encouraged by the writer) which have no basis in fact. We have allied signified A with the unrelated signified B because their signifiers have some similarities (etymological, phonic, semiotic, etc.) or relationship, and we have effaced or forgotten the gratuitous nature of the signifiers and their arbitrary relationship both to each other and to their signifieds. Thus, we have associated barbarism with a woman named Barbara because of the semantic link, just as Toto erroneously tied the fish-eating plant to coitus, and the narrator of *Todo verdor* linked women and the moon.[4]

So, as promised, we circle back to the Garden and to my original question: why is the Spanish-American novel so nearly devoid of memorable female protagonists? Examination of the novels has generated several possible explanations. Apparently the Hispanic, because of his culture and religion, tends to view women in more neatly polarized terms than many other national or ethnic groups. Our texts have suggested that to him she is either the Madonna or the prostitute, Heaven or Hell, Mary or Eve, and nothing mediates these two extremes. Clearly, both antipodes are sociolinguistic creations, and the fact that no mother (not even his own) is quite as perfect as he would have her, and no prostitute is quite as bad as he would deem her, is lost somewhere in the process of supplementaton to which I have so often referred. The end result, of course, is that because he must perceive her as one of the two polarities (he has, after all, been told by the authorities that she is either . . . / or . . .), and because he cannot experi-

ence her in reality as either, she is always irrevocably absent, always remote from him and ultimately unfathomable. This extraliterary situation
perpetuates and is perpetuated by the literary presentation of the female.

Thus, regardless of how much he may wish his fiction to center on her,
he is substantially foiled on two levels. First, since the female being with
whom he comes into contact in the world is neither totally prostituted nor
totally a Madonna figure, as already suggested (as much as he attempts to
impose one extreme or the other on her—e.g., Toto, Jaguar, Humberto), he
never manages to comprehend the total woman, the female who is a mixture (as is all humanity). Since he lacks this knowledge, his text truly
cannot focus on anything but his imagined projection of one pole or the
other, just as Toto's partial knowledge led to various erroneous conclusions about sex. Second, as he depicts one antithesis or the other, he must
by necessity produce flat, colorless, unidimensional characters because he
envisions them as such: the Virgin Mary *or* Eve. Great and memorable
characters (both male and female) throughout history are precisely those
who are not unidimensional but rather complex, ambivalent, paradoxical,
filled with self- or inner conflict: Quijote, Madame Bovary, the brothers
Karamazov, Temple Drake, and so forth.[5]

How do we explain such a dichotomous view of women to begin with?
Clearly, as noted, at least part of the problem is linguistic. We have words
to describe and name the Madonna figure and the prostitute, but we have
no word with which to name that being who might mediate the two. On
another level, it would perhaps be easy to blame the Catholic Church, for
there can be no doubt that the Church exercises great influence on Hispanic life, and surely the Hispanic view of women mirrors that of the
Church: Eve or Mary, Hell or Heaven. Were this the only root of the
problem, however, we would have to presume that those writers influenced by Protestantism or Judaism would have an even more limited
view of the female since these two groups lack the Virgin Mary as a
significant personage; the female figure of these two religions is, unfortunately for our purposes, Eve.[6] On the other hand, the answer may lie in the
fact that as delineated in our novels, the Hispanic family is even more
female-dominated than many non-Hispanic families. Our texts have
shown that, from his earliest moments, the male child is almost completely
surrounded by females (mother, servants, sisters) and that the father tends
to be absent, rarely participating in the family life. Indeed, father figures
were conspicuously absent or never mentioned in many of the texts
studied: we know little or nothing of Cova's father; Santos's father was
killed when he was young; Nicanor's father is not mentioned; Juan Preciado's is absent; and most of the young men in *La ciudad y los perros* have
been raised principally by their mothers. As Dorothy Dinnerstein has suggested, our sexist, human malaise cannot be corrected until our child-
caring arrangements become less female-controlled and are shared by the
two sexes.[7]

But the answer to the question of the absence of memorable female protagonists may be even more closely related to the third question posited at the beginning of this study: why is it that even those novels whose titles promise female protagonists ultimately focus on other topics or characters? Clearly this diversionary tactic will occasion a scarcity of memorable female protagonists, and here indeed the novels have spoken for themselves as promised. Doubtlessly, one of the main issues of each of the texts (intentionally or not on the part of the authors) was the power, covert though it often was, of the female. In fact, it would be relatively facile to characterize each of the novels as a dramatized, albeit unwitting, exposition on covert female power. María's primacy rested in her ability to reject the suitor, Efraín, as did Alicia's. The latter, of course, possessed the additional power to prevent Arturo from seeing or having control over his progeny (read, property). Doña Bárbara similarly threatened Santos's property and dominion. Agata, although completely powerless, pathetic, and full of inner strife, nonetheless, in the eyes of Nicanor at least, held occult powers which allowed her to understand things he could not (translate, she was more intelligent than he, and intelligence is power).[8] Pedro's mother governed his activities (to the extent of interrupting or distracting his sexual fantasies), and Susana had the power (subtle though it was) to deny his existence, disobey his law. Similarly, Dolores clearly held sway over the activities of Juan, to the extent of being the agent who sent him to his demise in Comala. Catalina uses her power by refusing to forgive Artemio and denying him the witness his existence requires. In *La ciudad y los perros* the women motivated the males' entrance into the academy and effectuated their struggles to prove themselves nonfemale as they were subjected to the supremacy of various females and their abilities to reject the males. *La traición de Rita Hayworth* centered on the male's latent but surfacing fears of women, as did *El obsceno pájaro*. Finally, of course, *El gato eficaz* taught us that woman's powers are no longer covert but overt. Not only has she broken out of her prototype, but she has recognized her latent potency, capabilities long covered and denied, which can be used only once she recognizes that her figuration, as tailored by him, is inherently suppressive. She regains that power, however, once she leaves her image in his hands and refuses to concern herself with it (i.e., once she denies his supremacy):

Libre soy yo después de haber dejado mi imagen en sus manos y no tener así que andar cuidándola como hace la gente que no sabe entregarla. Puedo ahora hacer lo que yo quiera, él cuida de mi imagen. . . . Ahora él encierra mi imagen y la abriga con su cuerpo que también era parte de mi imagen. (P. 118)

(I am the one who is free ever since I left my image in his hands and haven't had to go around worrying about it like those who don't know how to hand it over. Now I can do whatever I want, he takes care of my image. . . . Now he locks up my image and shelters it with his body that was also a part of my image.)

If feminist theorists such as Merlin Stone *(When God Was a Woman)* and Elizabeth Gould Davis *(First Sex)* are correct when they suggest that much of the Eve story was produced by religious leaders in order to defame women in general and thus undermine and expunge the power of the previous matriarchal religions, then again the biblical story has provided an interesting paradigm for the Spanish-American novel, since the question of the female here is also power related. Basically, the female power portrayed in our texts is of a triangular nature, perhaps again an inadvertent mirroring of the Garden situation (Adam/Eve/serpent–God/Adam/ Eve) and/or the Virgin Mary's triangular role. In our novels we have seen that as mother the female controls the male child's life, and on some level he resents this domination, this authority. As sweetheart she has the power to reject him, a rejection which becomes a sign of potential destruction or diminishment of his self-image, his masculinity as it is defined in the Western world. Nevertheless, it was demonstrated in the texts that he is offered the possibility of retribution via the ritual sacrifice, the marriage rite, for once he marries her, he spuriously terminates her reign over him, and he becomes the dominant being as he usurps her power (as in the oedipal situation). Thus, as dramatized in our novels, the power structure can be visualized by means of a triangular diagram:

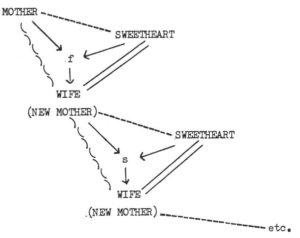

Unquestionably, in hierarchical terms and from the perspective of the male character, the mother remains on a somewhat higher plane than the sweetheart, but both hold sway over him (f, father, or s, son) as the arrows indicate. The male character, however, possesses or at least seems to maintain power over the wife who will become the new mother and reinitiate the power triad. Obviously, the son would wish to emulate the father and repeat his perceived primacy. The son, nevertheless, has only observed the father's dominance in relation to the wife/mother and has not witnessed the father's powerlessness before his own mother and sweetheart. Thus, once again, partial vision creates a myth, larger than life, and the son, because he finds himself powerless before the mother and the sweetheart, needs to overcompensate with the wife in order to meet his perceived ideal (myth). When the father figure is absent, as he so often was in these novels, that perceived patriarchal power is even more hyperbolized and mythicized.

The question of power gains even greater significance when we examine it in relation to the question of that absence of memorable female protagonists which results from the novelistic shift of attention away from the female characters. Our texts obliquely posit that the male never feels quite secure in this power he ostensibly holds and must therefore continually authenticate his supremacy to himself. His previous powerlessness seems ever ready to break through the thin mask of potency and adequacy he has donned. In this respect our texts all point to the conclusion that the writing itself, the narrative process, becomes a form of exorcism, a ritual designed to invalidate and/or obliterate that covert or latent female power. If one denies her potency and primacy, perhaps she will become less powerful—perhaps the word will create the situation one wishes to find, and, indeed, on some level it does. Thus, I return again to my point of origin and insist that the writing process itself and the subsequent reading it demands (that is, the portrayal of the female) is a process of mythmaking in which the reality is substituted by wishful thinking. Thus the female needs to be verbalized, made present, but written and read in a way that banishes her to the past, which is considered more primitive. By doing so, the writer somehow recaptures that lost paradise, those origins, while at the same time he highlights the glories of his masculine (that is, nonfemale) present. Simultaneously, as he writes or reads her, he makes her nonthreatening and nonother. Once written and read, she is an extension, an offshoot of himself, spawned by him, a part of him, himself outside of himself (just as Adam's rib became Eve). Thus, her perceived power (which may well be but another projection, myth) is exorcised, eliminated, usurped by him since she is now his invention. Once again, the male defies biology and gives birth to the female.

Thus at the center of the literary depiction of the female we encounter the question of power which is generated by the linguistic trap of envisioning and thus idealizing the world in terms of polar opposites. Because our language tends to offer only antithetical extremes, one inevitably views oneself as either the conqueror or the conquered, the winner or the loser. The Hispanic emphasis on *machismo* merely intensifies this polarity. Similarly, once the entire issue of winners and losers is articulated by means of a sexual metaphor (as it is in most Western cultures but perhaps more so in Hispanic countries) then the male/female interrelationship, by linguistic implication if nothing else, becomes a question of power, of winners and losers.[9] Unquestionably, the Hispanic's view of the history of his culture magnifies such polarities. More than any other Western group, the Hispanic views his beginnings as a conquest. From what he understands as the origins of his civilization, he was the conquered and perhaps must eternally strive to compensate for that initial loss, that metaphoric "original sin."

Hopefully, with the advent of more and more frequently read women writers such as Luisa Valenzuela, we can eventually debunk these mythic antitheses and begin to recognize other possibilities.[10] The world does not have to be viewed in terms of polar opposites, winners and losers, and it is time to learn to recognize that such figures and tropes are merely that— linguistic creations which lead nowhere but keep us ever entrapped in that lost Garden which perhaps never existed.

Notes

Introduction

1. All biblical quotations are from the Revised Standard Version (New York: Thomas Nelson, 1953).

2. Most biblical scholars seem to agree that the rib story postdates the version of Chapter 2. For a discussion of this and references to source materials see Theodor Reik, *The Creation of Woman* (New York: McGraw-Hill, 1960).

Throughout this study I have intentionally limited the references to biblical scholars and explicators of the Adam and Eve story. This study is not intended to be an analysis of the biblical story as such. Since we lack access to the original texts, this would be a fruitless gesture. Rather, I am more interested in the metaphorical ramifications of the story and its parallelisms in more recent literature. I see the story as a paradigm for the portrayal of the female in other literary works and not as a text to be studied in and of itself.

3. Mary Daly, for example, in *Beyond God the Father* (Boston: Beacon, 1973), hereafter referred to as *Father*, points out how far-reaching and ubiquitous the myth truly is. In *The Church and the Second Sex* (New York: Harper, 1975), hereafter referred to as *Church*, Daly echoes Katharine Rogers, who notes in her history of misogyny in literature that many misogynists "have appropriated or misappropriated for their own purposes" these biblical texts. See *The Troublesome Helpmate* (Seattle: University of Washington Press, 1966), p. 3. Rogers also suggests that the Jahvist story is particularly damaging to women since it implies not only that woman does not exist in her own right but also that she is not created in God's image but rather in man's. Thus, she is a reproduction of a reproduction even as early as this.

Merlin Stone in *When God Was a Woman* (New York: Harcourt Brace Jovanovich, 1978) also underlines how pervasive the Adam and Eve myth is in today's society (p. 7) and sees the myth as an undermining of female power and authority as well as a justification for male dominance. As early as 1958, Robert Graves expressed similar views in *Adam's Rib* (New York: Thomas Yoseloff, 1958), p. 12.

Taking a somewhat different stance, Phyllis Trible offers a most positive, female-affirming reading of the Genesis story. See "Eve and Adam: Genesis 2–3 Reread," in *Womanspirit Rising*, ed. Carol P. Christ and Judith Plaskow (New York: Harper & Row, 1979), pp. 74–83.

Clearly, once again the problem lies not in the story itself but rather in the ways in which we have come to read and interpret it. Such, of course, is precisely the problem with the novels examined here.

4. According to Reik, biblical commentators acknowledge that Genesis was written at different points in history by two different groups of people: the earlier group who called God *Elohim,* and a later group who called God *Yahweh* (p. 18). The "rewriting" of the creation story has also been discussed by Naomi Goldenberg, *Changing of the Gods* (Boston: Beacon, 1979), as well as by Merlin Stone and Mary Daly as noted above (n. 3).

5. *Man's World, Woman's Place* (New York: Dell, 1971), p. 26.

6. Most feminist critics agree that even when the biblical image seems positive, as is the case with Mary, the model is so far beyond the reach of the average woman that it produces negative ramifications anyway.

7. In a parallel manner Lloyd M. Graham, *Deceptions and Myths of the Bible* (New York: Bell, 1975), suggests that the entire question is one of translation.

8. Jacques Derrida, *De la grammatologie* (Paris: Minuit, 1967).

Chapter 1. The Love Story

1. Some of the scholars who have commented on *María* include the following: Donald F. Brown, "Chateaubriand and the Story of Feliciana in Jorge Isaacs' *María*," *Modern Language Notes* 62 (1947): 326–29; Sonia Karson, "La estructura de *María* de Jorge Isaacs," *Revista Hispánica Moderna* 34 (July–October 1968): 685–89; Valerie Massón de Gómez, "Las flores como símbolos eróticos en la obra de Jorge Isaacs," *Thesaurus* 28:117–27; C. Enrique Pupo-Walker, "Relaciones internas entre la poesía y la novela de Jorge Isaacs," *Thesaurus* 22 (1967): 45–59; Seymour Menton, "La estructura dualística de *María*," *Thesaurus* 25 (1970): 251–77; Donald McGrady, "Función del episodio de Nay y Sinar en *María* de Isaacs," *Nueva Revista de Filología Hispánica* 18 (1965–66): 171–76; Mario Carvajal, *Vida y pasión de Jorge Isaacs* (Santiago de Chile: Ercilla, 1937); Ernesto Posada Delgado, "El paisaje en *María* y en *La vorágine*," *Boletín Cultural y Bibliográfico* (Bogotá) 10 (1967): 880–84; Germán Arciniegas, *Genio y figura de Jorge Isaacs* (Buenos Aires: Eudeba, 1970).

2. Throughout, I shall be using the terms *story* and *narration* in a very specific and restricted sense. I shall use "story" in much the same sense it was used by the Russian formalists, that is, the history, the tale communicated by means of the narration. Thus "narration" will refer to the narrative process, the telling, the ordering of events, narrator interruptions, etc.

3. Tzvetan Todorov develops the theory of *énoncé* as opposed to *énonciation* in *Littérature et signification* (Paris: Larousse, 1967). In this study I have sometimes used narration as a synonym for *énonciation* and narrative or story as a synonym for *énoncé*.

4. In all probability these names are also symbolic. Salomon was the wise Hebrew king (wise enough to turn his only daughter over to Christians to be raised properly?) and Sara was the wife of Abraham and mother of Isaac.

5. See M. Esther Harding, *Woman's Mysteries* (New York: Putnam, 1971), p. 156. The first edition of this book dates from 1935.

6. Helen Diner notes the same myth. *Mothers and Amazons*, trans. and ed. John Phillip Lundin (New York: Doubleday, 1973), p. 29.

7. See Valerie Massón de Gómez's study of the symbolism of the flowers, "Las flores."

8. All quotations are from the Losada edition (Buenos Aires, 1966). English quotations are from the Harper edition (New York, 1890), trans. Rollo Ogden.

9. Although technically the Holy Spirit is neither male nor female, "he" forms part of the otherwise male trinity, and it would rarely occur to anyone to depict or envision "him"/it as a female although it has on occasion been suggested that the god figure is a female.

10. See Vicente Cicchitti, "María y su magnificat," in *La mujer símbolo del mundo nuevo* (Buenos Aires: Fernando García Cambeiro, 1976), pp. 11–18. In the same collection, see also Graciela Maturo, "La virgen, anunciadora del tiempo nuevo," pp. 32–50.

11. Elizabeth Gould Davis develops an interesting theory which suggests that much of the early Church's success was a result of the incorporation of the virgin mother and her subsequent supplantation of the pagan virgin goddesses. See *The First Sex* (New York: Penguin, 1971), pp. 243–51.

12. Many of the early moon goddesses were viewed as essentially tetramerous: the full

moon, the waning crescent, the waxing crescent, and darkness. In this sense, they were the very symbol of temporal continuity and motion. See Helen Diner, *Mothers.*

13. José Donoso, *El obsceno pájaro de la noche* (Barcelona: Seix Barral, 1971), p. 182; *The Obscene Bird of Night*, trans. Hardie St. Martin and Leonard Mades (Boston: Nonpareil, 1979), p. 147.

14. José Mármol, *Amalia* (México: Porrúa, 1974). First edition was in Buenos Aires, 1855. The emphasis is mine. The English translations are my own.

15. Obviously, at this point in history it was not acceptable to think that perhaps there can be no Truth apart from language and that perhaps this Absolute Truth cannot exist.

16. Even though the picaresque hero may not be totally admirable, he nonetheless encompasses many of those masculine virtues such as adventure, spirit, intelligence, etc.

17. This statement, of course, ignores the ironic treatment of "heroes" which has predominated in much of the literature of the last thirty years.

18. Throughout this essay I shall persist in using the term *love story* not in spite of, but rather because of, its popular connotations. Regardless of how we embellish it, the love story (at least today) is a tale of the people. I also use the term to avoid any confusion with the notion of romance (as discussed by Northrop Frye and others), which encompasses a much broader spectrum of adventures and themes than does the love story. Thus I shall understand as love story any verbal work (its actual form as a novel, short story, narrative poem, or drama is not relevant to my purposes) whose principal concern and purpose is the dramatization of the development (or frustration) of a strong emotional and eventually carnal tie (love) between two characters.

19. See Northrop Frye, *Anatomy of Criticism* (Princeton, N.J.: Princeton University Press, 1957). Note, however, that when Frye uses the term *romance* he is not talking about the love story (although it would be included within Frye's notion of romance). Instead, he defines romance as "not the historical mode . . . but the tendency . . . to displace myth in a human direction and yet, in contrast to 'realism,' to conventionalize content in an idealized direction" (pp. 136–37).

20. Madonna Kolbenschlag, *Kiss Sleeping Beauty Good-bye* (New York: Doubleday, 1979) focuses on the inert quality and waiting posture of the traditional fairy-tale heroine.

21. Her position by the window is no doubt significant, although open to several interpretations. One might view her as guarding the opening of marital bliss and happy home life or as nearing the window which separates life from death.

22. Interestingly, she does not reject him, for if she did then we would have no story, and the purpose of the story is to embellish her—her rejection would imply his unworthiness and thus defeat the purpose.

23. A similar movement takes place in Alejo Carpentier's *Los pasos perdidos.* See Roberto González Echevarría, "The Parting of the Waters," in *The Pilgrim at Home* (Ithaca, N.Y.: Cornell, 1977), pp. 155–212.

24. This movement from a fraternal to an amorous relationship underlines what might be seen as latent incestuous desire in the text. As Brooks has noted, "Throughout the Romantic tradition, it is perhaps most notably the image of incest (of the fraternal-sororal variety) which hovers as the sign of a passion interdicted because its fulfillment would be too perfect, a discharge indistinguishable from death. . . ." See Peter Brooks, "Freud's Masterplot: Questions of Narrative," *Yale French Studies*, nos. 55–56 (1977): 297.

25. See Claude Lévi-Strauss, *Tristes tropiques*, trans. John Russell (New York: Atheneum, 1972), pp. 286–97.

26. Jacques Derrida, analyzing the "Writing Lesson," suggests, "l'origine de l'écriture répondait à une nécessité plus 'sociologique' qu' 'intellectuelle.' " See *De la grammatologie*, p. 190.

27. There can be little doubt that don Juan must be one of the most misogynous of literary

characters. Curiously, Lederer implies that don Juan may also be most fearful of women: "because to them [the don Juans] love, the lasting commitment, stands for being swallowed up by woman." See Wolfgang Lederer, *The Fear of Women* (New York: Harcourt Brace Jovanovich, 1968), p. 236.

28. Perhaps an all too typical example of this attitude can be found in Espronceda, who adored and exalted Teresa until he discovered that she could not live up to the superhuman expectations he had for her. Thus, because she did not meet the unrealistic and totally idealized concept he had created, he scorned and degraded her. "Mas ¡ay! que es la mujer angel caído,/o mujer nada más y lodo inmundo." See José de Espronceda, "Canto a Teresa," in *Presentación y antología de los siglos XVIII y XIX expañoles,* ed. Lucía Bonilla and Juan Agudiez, vol. 1 (New York: Las Américas, 1966), p. 251.

29. Katharine M. Rogers has noted, "The nineteenth-century idealization of self-sacrificing womanhood provided a vehicle for covert misogyny insofar as it assumed the subjugation of women and demanded self-renunciation from them." See *The Troublesome Helpmate,* p. 194.

30. Ancient myths seem to suggest that virginity was not valued until fairly late in Western history. Elizabeth Gould Davis suggests that it was not valued until the advent of the patriarchal Judeo-Christian civilization (*First Sex,* p. 158).

Chapter 2. Women and Nature

1. In *Recopilación de textos sobre tres novelas ejemplares,* ed. T. Pérez (Havana: Las Américas) there are a number of articles on *Dona Bárbara* by Raimundo Lazo, Edmundo Valadés, Mariano Picón Salas, Raúl Roa, Ulrich Leo, and others, as well as many articles on *La vorágine* by Arturo Torres-Rioseco, Horacio Quiroga, Eduardo Neale-Silva, Leonidas Morales, Edmundo de Chasca, Antonio Curcio Altamar, and Oscar Collazos, among others. In this collection see especially, Mariano Morinigo, "Civilización y barbarie en *Facundo* y *Doña Bárbara*," pp. 412–39, and José Antonio Fidalgo, "Criollismo e ideología en Gallegos," pp. 461–70.

There are vast bibliographies on both Gallegos and Rivera; I list only a few works which have the greatest bearing on this topic: Alfred Coester, "Maelstroms, Green Hells and Sentimental Jungles," *Hispania* 16 (March 1933): 43–50; John Englekirk, "*Doña Bárbara,* Legend of the Llano," *Hispania* 31 (1948): 259–70; Mario Llerena, "Función del paisaje en la novela hispanoamericana," *Hispania* 32 (1949): 499–503; Juan Bosch, "De *Don Quijote* a *Doña Bárbara,*" *Humanismo* (Mexico) 3 (August 1954): 31–35; Gustavo Correa, "El mundo metafórico de *Doña Bárbara,*" *Actas del Sexto Congreso del Instituto Internacional de Literatura Iberoamericana* (Mexico: Imprenta Universitaria, 1954), pp. 227–33; Ernest A. Johnson, "The Meaning of *Civilización* and *Barbarie* in *Doña Bárbara,*" *Hispania* 39 (1956): 456–61; Donald G. Castanien, "Introspective Techniques in *Doña Bárbara,*" *Hispania* 41 (1958): 282–88; Alfonso González, "Onomastics and Creativity in *Doña Bárbara* and *Pedro Páramo,*" *Names* 21:40–45; Orlando Araujo, *Lengua y creación en la obra de Rómulo Gallegos* (Caracas: Ministerio de Educación, 1962); Glen L. Kolb, "Aspectos estructurales de *Doña Bárbara,*" *Revista Iberoamericana* 28 (January–June 1962): 131–40; Glen L. Kolb, "Dos novelas y un solo argumento," *Hispania* 46 (1963): 84–87: Felipe Massiani, *El hombre y la naturaleza venezolana en Rómulo Gallegos* (Caracas: Ministerio de Educación, 1964): S. E. Leavitt, "Sex versus Symbolism in *Doña Bárbara,*" *Revista de Estudios Hispanicos* (Alabama) 1 (May 1967): 117–20; Raúl Ramos Calles, *Los personajes de Gallegos a través del psicoanálisis* (Caracas: Monte Avila, 1969); Margarita Peña, "El diablo, aliado y socio en *Doña Bárbara,*" *Mundo Nuevo,* no. 48 (June 1970): 65–69; A. Michalski, "*Doña Bárbara,* un cuento de hadas," *PMLA* 85 (October 1970): 1015–20; Hilda Marban, *Rómulo Gallegos: el hombre y su obra* (Madrid: Playor, 1973); Ernesto Porras Collantes, "Interpretación estructural de *La vorágine,*" *Thesaurus* 23 (May–August 1968): 241–79; Joan R. Green, "La estructura del narrador y el modo narrativo de *La vorágine, Cuadernos Hispanoamericanos*, no. 205 (January 1967): 101–8; Juan Loveluck, "Aproximación a *La vorágine*," *Atenea* 39 (July–September 1962): 92–117; Otto Olivera, "El romanticismo de José Eustacio Rivera," *Revista Iberoamericana* 17 (December 1952): 41–61; Jorge Añez, *De "La vorágine" a "Doña Bárbara"* (Bogotá: Imprenta del Departamento, 1944); Olga Carreras González, "Tres fechas, tres novelas y un tema: Estudio comparativo de *La vorágine, Canaima y Los pasos perdidos*," *Explicación de Textos Literarios* 2:169–78; José Angel Valente, "La naturaleza y el hombre en *La vorágine* de José Eustacio Rivera," *Cuadernos Hispanoamericanos*, no. 67 (July 1955): 102–8; Randolph Pope, "*La vorágine*: Autobiografía de un intelectual," in *The Analysis of Literary Texts: Current Trends in Methodology*, ed. Randolph Pope (Ypsilanti, Mich.: Bilingual, 1980), pp. 256–67.

2. I list but a few of their works published during this period. Darwin's *Origin of the Species* was published, of course, in 1859, but in the ensuing years he published *The Expression of Emotions in Man and Animals* (1872) and *The Descent of Man, and Selection in Relation to Sex* (1871). Some of Sigmund Freud's major works were also published during this period: *Interpretation of Dreams* (1900), *Psychopathology of Everyday Life* (1901), *Three Essays on the Theory of Sexuality* (1905), *Totem and Taboo* (1912–13), *Beyond the Pleasure Principle* (1920), *The Ego and the Id* (1923), and "The Passing of the Oedipus-Complex" (1925).

3. The outstanding exception to this statement is William Bull, who in his excellent study of the novel, arrives at many of the same conclusions I have. See "Nature and Anthropomorphism in *La vorágine*," *Romanic Review* 39 (December 1948): 307–18. Randolph Pope's study also calls into question the trustworthiness of Cova's vision.

4. Edmundo de Chasca, "El lirismo de *La vorágine*," in *Recopilación de textos*, p. 115. The emphasis is mine.

5. Antonio Curcio Altamar, "Un nuevo mensaje," in *Recopilación*, p. 141, my emphasis.

6. Several other critics substantiate my insistence on Cova's dementia. Valente ("Naturaleza") calls him a *loco* (p. 104); Loveluck labels him psychopathic and unstable ("Aproximación" p. 108); Pope's entire thesis points to Cova's inability to see what is before him.

7. All pages references from the Spanish *La vorágine* are taken from the Losada edition (Buenos Aires, 1972). The English text is from *The Vortex*, trans. Earle K. James (New York: Putnam, 1935). I have used the Espasa-Calpe edition of *Doña Bárbara* (Buenos Aires, 1964) and the translation by Robert Malloy (New York: Peter Smith, 1948).

8. Richard Ford, "El marco narrativo de *La vorágine*," *Revista Iberoamericana* 42 (July–December 1976): 573–80. Ford also substantiates my theory of Cova's unreliability.

Similarly, Randolph Pope concludes, "Cova es el intelectual, capaz de sobrevivir a un cambio tan radical y brusco, pero conserva en lo posible elementos del pasado y una actitud distante que le impide integrarse a los nuevos grupos que encuentra y con los cuales se siente solidario. Finalmente, su calidad de poeta le concede una visión estéticamente reflexiva que lo mantiene en una sensibilidad diversa a la de sus compañeros, pero que le permite escribir una obra de lectura atractiva para otros intelectuales y poetas que pueden observar en Cova una imagen instructiva" (p. 266).

9. Mejia has noticed that Cova's concept of love is superficial. See William Mejia B., S.J., "La mujer en la obra riveriana," *Boletín Cultural y Bibliográfico* 10 (1967): 161.

10. Bull also notes that the compulsions and fears which drive Cova are within him but projected outward, particularly onto the jungle ("Nature and Anthropomorphism," p. 311).

11. See Luisa Valenzuela, *El gato eficaz* (Mexico: Mortiz, 1972), p. 106. All translations are mine.

12. Bull also suggests that the vortex is Cova's tortured mind ("Nature," p. 309).

13. In any fictionalized narration, the single *énonciation* imparts at least two *énoncés*: one is presented with what metaphorically might be seen as two layers of story. One layer is what the narrator is apparently trying to tell us, while the other is what the author is trying to tell us by "allowing" the narrator to contradict himself. The game of the text (when these two *énoncés* are not identical) rests in the readers' attempts and capacity to "uncover" the latter.

14. This tension is not only reflected in Rivera's own work but may be the result of the opposition between these two world views (both of which he seems to find nearly equally acceptable).

15. Significantly, *Madonna* is another term erroneously employed by Cova or Rivera and as a result will henceforth be subject to misleading interpretations.

16. Jacques Derrida has observed, "L'écriture est dangereuse dès lors que la représentation veut s'y donner pour la présence et le signe pour la chose même" (*Grammatologie*, p. 207).

17. Significantly, René Girard has maintained that without this differentiation violence must erupt in order to establish a hierarchy of differences. It would not be difficult to analyze the entire text in these terms. See *Violence and the Sacred*, trans. Patrick Gregory (Baltimore: Johns Hopkins University Press, 1979).

18. Paradoxically, Lorenzo's explication of the *centauro* is not completely accurate, for the *centauro* is a mythological beast, half man and half horse. Thus, the *centauro* would literally represent the mixture of man (civilization) and nature (barbarism) within one entity.

19. Derrida, of course, has quite competently demonstrated the absurdity of what we call a natural or original state. See the chapter on Rousseau in *De la grammatologie*.

20. It is only in recent years, and especially in the United States, that progress and the forces of civilization have been seen as something less than utopian.

21. I must trust other scholars to analyze and debunk the validity of the very notions of "male principle" and "female principle" and note only in passing that in my opinion the "principles" are already based on what society has defined as male and female and in this respect are quite removed from the inherent, biological principles they try to suggest. That is, they are already social derivations and not "original" at all.

22. Sigmund Freud, *Civilization and Its Discontents*, trans. James Strachey (New York: Norton, 1962), p. 50. The work was originally published in German as *Das Unglück in der Kultur* (Vienna: Internationaler Psychoanalytischer Verlag, 1930).
The paragraph I cite continues, "—those very women who, in the beginning, laid the foundations of civilization by the claims of their love. Women represent the interests of the family and of sexual life. The work of civilization has become increasingly the business of men, it confronts them with ever more difficult tasks and compels them to carry out instinctual sublimations of which women are little capable."

23. Nevertheless, as Glen L. Kolb has noted, Lorenzo never was "un hombre en el sentido completo de la palabra." See "Aspectos," p. 134.

24. Indeed, Michalski notes that the chapter in which doña Bárbara is labeled *devoradora* is presented as a fairy tale ("Doña Bárbara," p. 1015).

25. It is revealing, however, that doña Bárbara's powers are presumed to be contingent upon a *male* force (*el Socio*).

26. Casey Miller and Kate Swift, *Words and Women* (Garden City, N.Y.: Anchor, 1977), pp. 80–91.

27. Miller and Swift's notions about surnames, of course, are far more applicable to women of the United States than to women of Hispanic countries, since the latter often do retain their maiden names or even the names of their mothers.

28. The links between *Doña Bárbara* and *Don Quijote* have already been noted by a number of scholars.

Chapter 3. Women and the Not-So-Golden Silence

1. Myron I. Lichtblau, *El arte estilístico de Eduardo Mallea* (Buenos Aires: Juan Goyanarte, 1967), pp. 15–16.

2. Enrique Anderson Imbert, *Historia de la literatura hispanoamericana*, vol. 2 (Mexico: Fondo de culture económica, 1970), p. 291.

3. All quotes are from the Espasa-Calpe edition (Mexico, 1951) and the John B. Hughes translation, *All the Green Shall Perish* (New York: Knopf, 1969).

4. What seems to be paradox and contradiction may, in effect, represent an attempt to capture that essentially human quality which is not easily stated nor portrayed.

5. Cf. the visible and invisible Argentina in *Historia de una pasión argentina*.

6. Cf. the Guillén brothers in *Enemigos del alma* and Nicanor and Sotero in *Todo verdor*.

7. I am not overlooking the fact that this type of temporal intermeshing of the specific with the vague is typical of the Bible or perhaps any sacred scripture.

I also acknowledge that the fairy-tale beginning tells us that we are about to hear of a world so removed we can never know it. Nevertheless, it is doubtful that the child hearing the tale recognizes this, and it is equally possible that the reader of the Mallea novel will never directly know the world described therein.

8. I have used two quite different sources for my statements on fairy tales: the more official *Grimm's Fairy Tales* and an assortment of inexpensive, children's editions of the various fairy tales. The use of the latter is based on my suspicion that more children are initially exposed to fairy tales via these editions than via the more official *Grimm's*. The opening quoted comes from *Snow White and the Seven Dwarfs* (New York: Prestige, 1976), p. 1. See also *Grimm's Fairy Tales* (New York: Pantheon, 1944).

9. Rapunzel, at birth, is turned over to Dame Gothel, while the miller in "Rumpelstiltskin" turns his daughter over to the king and no mention of her mother is ever made.

10. I am not implying that such is the case in the extratextual world. It is significant, however, that in the world of fairy tales it is the mother (who, because she is female, is presumed to be skilled in interhuman relationships), who imparts this knowledge and skill to her female child.

11. Andrea Dworkin, *Woman Hating* (New York: Dutton, 1974), p. 41.

12. See "Amidst the Illusory Depths of the First-Person Pronoun and *El obsceno pájaro de la noche*," *Modern Language Notes* 93 (March 1978): 280–81.

13. In fact, the very function of the editorial *we* is to create a bond between discourser and listener (recipient)—a bond which implies that both have the same opinion and which is designed to forestall negative response.

14. It is probably significant that in *La vorágine* the jungle is called "esposa del silencio, madre de la soledad" (p. 97) ("wedded to silence, mother of solitude," p. 127).

15. At this point, as at many others in the novel, the reader is uncertain as to whether one is to understand the words as indirect discourse of the character or as opinion of the narrator. Since it is very nearly impossible to ascertain the "ownership" of the words, I shall simply assume that they can be attributed to both the narrator and the character.

I should also note that although Mallea seems unwilling to grant Agata complete intellectual superiority, other female characters in some of his other works are openly granted that intellectual ability.

16. The association of the woman and the moon with all its implications has been discussed by M. Esther Harding, *Woman's Mysteries*, among others.

17. Another possibility never posited by the text is that the infertility is Nicanor's. Throughout there is a subtle, underlying presumption that Agata is to blame—a presumption which recalls the more primitive days when the male's part in conception was not understood. (In fact, some early peoples believed that moon rays caused impregnation.)

18. I use the opposition human/natural based on the notion that, as a result of the "forces" and changes produced by civilization and acculturation, what is today "human" is not necessarily "natural" in the strictest sense of the word. See Shulamith Firestone, *The Dialectic of Sex* (New York: Bantam, 1971), p. 10.

19. Nevertheless, the use of the metaphor of nature is not unique to this novel and indeed recurs throughout the works of Mallea.

20. There are several recent studies which demonstrate that language is still a male strong-

hold. See, for example, Casey Miller and Kate Swift *(Words)* and Robin Lakoff, *Language and Woman's Place* (New York: Harper, 1975).

21. I suspect that the alleged predominance of economic relationships among the "primitive" tribes, as described by the anthropologists of the nineteenth and twentieth centuries, may well reflect the preoccupations of the anthropologists rather than those of the tribes.

22. Juan Carlos Ghiano, *Constantes de la literatura argentina* (Buenos Aires: Raigal, 1953), p. 123.

23. I am inclined to disagree with Grieben, who sees the end as optimistic, and add that if one is to accept Sanchez's analysis of new life after death, then one must understand the novel as a negation of the Christian concept of rebirth, for Agata's new life, as I have noted, is but a repetition of her former and only offers temporary reprieve. Thus, the rebirth is but eternal condemnation. See Carlos F. Grieben, *Eduardo Mallea* (Buenos Aires: Editoriales Culturales Argentinos, 1961), p. 22; and Porfirio Sánchez, "Aspectos bíblicos de *Todo verdor perecerá*," *Romance Notes* 14 (1972): 469–75.

24. See Frank Kermode, *The Sense of an Ending* (New York: Oxford University Press, 1970), especially the chapter entitled, "World Without End or Beginning."

25. I think specifically of the conclusion of "Atomo verde número cinco," which is the story of things disappearing, leaving their owners with only words and no referents. The story concludes with the two characters alone, almost animalistic, running off into the night of the "inmenso escenario vacío." See José Donoso, "Atomo verde número cinco," *Tres novelitas burguesas* (Barcelona: Seix Barral, 1973), pp. 105–88.

26. Although Madonna Kolbenschlag's *Kiss Sleeping Beauty Good-bye* came into my hands several years after the writing of this chapter, it is interesting to note that many of her conclusions concur quite nicely with mine, and vice versa.

Chapter 4. Voices from Beyond

1. Juan Rulfo, *Pedro Páramo* (México: Fondo de cultura económica, 1969); Carlos Fuentes, *La muerte de Artemio Cruz* (México: Fondo de cultura económica, 1970). Translations are from *Pedro Páramo*, trans. Lysander Kemp (New York: Grove, 1959) and *The Death of Artemio Cruz*, trans. Sam Hileman (New York: Farrar, Straus and Giroux, 1964). Much of what I say here could also be said about Fuentes's *Aura* (Mexico: Era, 1970). English translations from *Aura* are mine.

2. Only if one knows the identity of the speaker and only if one accepts that speaker as an authority, as in the commandments from God in the Bible, can one accept the second-person future tense as a valid command. Cf. "Thou shalt not. . . ."

3. Paul Di Virgilio discusses the use of pronouns in *La muerte de Artemio Cruz:* "The technique exploiting the personal pronouns as an area of discovery detaches the textual language from a more traditional context for reference and authority generating a certain sense of autonomy in the narrative language which surpasses the reader's conventionalized expectations." See *"La muerte de Artemio Cruz:* The Relationship between Innovation in the Role of the Personal Pronouns in the Narrative and Reader Expectancy," *Revista Canadiense de Estudios Hispánicos* 5 (Fall 1980): 93.

4. The significance of the female figures in Carlos Fuentes has received considerable critical attention. See, among others, Richard J. Callan, "The Jungian Basis of Carlos Fuentes' *Aura*," *Kentucky Romance Quarterly* 18 (1971): 65–76; Lanin A. Gyurko, "The Image of Woman in Two Novels of Carlos Fuentes," *Research Studies* 43·1–18; Lanin A. Gyurko, "Women in Mexican Society: Fuentes' Portrayal of Oppression," *Revista Hispánica Moderna* 38 (1974–75): 206–29; Gloria Durán, "La bruja de Carlos Fuentes," in *Homenaje a Carlos Fuentes*, ed. Helmy F. Giacoman (Long Island City, N.Y.: Las Américas, 1971), pp. 242–60; M. Kasey Hellerman, "The Coatlicue-Malinche Conflict: A Mother and Son Identity Crisis in the Writing of Carlos

Fuentes," *Hispania* 57 (December 1974): 868–75; Linda B. Hall, "The Cipactli Monster: Woman as Destroyer in Carlos Fuentes," *Southwest Review* 60 (Summer 1975): 246–55. Rulfo's work has also been considered from this perspective. See, among others, María Luisa Bastos and Sylvia Molloy, "La estrella junto a la luna: Variantes de la figura materna en *Pedro Páramo*," *Modern Language Notes* 92 (March 1977): 246–68; José de la Colina, "Susana San Juan, el mito femenino en *Pedro Páramo*," *Universidad de México* 19 (April 1965): 60–66; Liliana Befumo Boschi, "La mujer en *Pedro Páramo*," in *La mujer símbolo del mundo nuevo*, ed. Vicente Cicchitti et al., pp. 138–52.

5. The studies on *Pedro Páramo* are far too numerous to list here. I refer the reader to a bibliography.

6. See Alan S. Bell, "Rulfo's *Pedro Páramo*: A Vision of Hope," *Modern Language Notes* 81 (March 1966): 238–45.

7. Since the original punctuation was not always respected in the translation, I have superimposed Kemp's translation with the original punctuation in this section where I discuss punctuation.

8. Myth, of course, is merely a religion we do not share.

9. The reader will note that I consistently use the male gender when referring to religious personages. I do this consciously and intentionally since all of today's major religions are patriarchal. Recent archaeological findings have shown conclusively that goddess worship did indeed exist, but we know far too little about these religions (usually disparagingly referred to as sects) to be able to state with any degree of knowledge whether or not they were structured on this same pattern.

10. The studies on *La muerte de Artemio Cruz* are too numerous to list here. Again, I refer the reader to a bibliography.

11. The few males with whom he has contact are also dead, but this world is principally populated with women.

12. See Julia Kristeva, *Le Texte du roman* (Paris: Mouton, 1970), especially p. 82.

13. This has already been noted by Ada Teja, "*Pedro Páramo*: Dialéctica e historia," *Chasqui* 4 (February 1975): p. 54. Narciso Costa Roa notes, "El efecto que se logra consiste en contaminar el mundo de los vivos con el mundo de los muertos, acentuando el ambiente fantasmal del relato, disminuyendo la distancia entre los límites que separan ambos ámbitos." See "El mundo novelesco de *Pedro Páramo*," *Revista chilena de literatura* 11 (April 1978): 43.

14. Floyd Merrell would surely disagree here, for he has noted that Catalina's problem is that "basically she does not realize that all choices are not simply binary." See "Communication and Paradox in Carlos Fuentes' *The Death of Artemio Cruz*: Toward a Semiotics of Character," *Semiotica* 18 (1976): 339–60.

15. Much contemporary feminist criticism and psychology is based on the theory that from the perspective of the infant the female represents both desire and a barrier to that desire.

16. The following, among others, have seen female significance in the moon images: Julianne Burton, "Sexuality and the Mythic Dimension in Juan Rulfo's *Pedro Páramo*," *Symposium* 28 (Fall 1974): 228–47; Bastos and Molloy, "La estrella"; Befumo Boschi, "La mujer."

17. The snake is often studied in relationship to the earlier goddess religions and seen as a symbol of those religions. See among others, Merlin Stone, *When God Was a Woman* (New York: Harcourt Brace Jovanovich, 1978).

18. Similarly, the male frequently associates his sexual experience with a female with a form of death.

19. Paul, for example in reference to the Adam and Eve story, states, "For Adam was formed first, then Eve; and Adam was not deceived, but the woman was deceived and became a transgressor" (1 Tim. 2.13–14).

20. Rosario Castellanos's version of the story of Adam and Eve offers a much more sympathetic interpretation of the Fall. See *El eterno femenino* (Mexico: Fondo de cultura económica, 1975), pp. 73–85.

Lloyd M. Graham, *Deceptions and Myths of the Bible*, posits that the entire problem is one of translation—a theory which corresponds with my interpretation of the female problem.

21. Although he has not delved deeply into the subject, Lanin Gyurko has recognized Fuentes's characters, particularly Regina and Catalina, as sacrificial victims. See "Women in Mexican Society."

22. Robert P. Matthews is one of the few commentators of Fuentes's work who addresses the question of violence. Although he does not analyze it from my point of view, he does note that "La violencia indiscriminada penetra a todos los niveles de la sociedad mexicana" and suggests that Fuentes sees the history of Mexico as "una sucesión de actos violentos." See "Las ideas de Carlos Fuentes: Desde lo mexicano hasta lo universal," *Revista Nacional de Cultura* 201 (November–December 1971): 47–60.

Matthews tends to view the violence, however, in much the same manner as the characters inasmuch as he overlooks the basic violence of the texts and sees instead only certain manifestations. Because Consuelo/Aura kills a goat, he sees the text as "la elaboración del concepto de la crueldad innata del hombre" and "una imagen de la estética de la crueldad que forma parte del ritmo armónico de la vida" (p. 49).

23. The incestuous nature of the relationship between Susana and Bartolomé is confirmed on pages 91–94 when she speaks of the cat who later seems to be an incarnation of her father, by saying, "Se la pasó haciendo circo, brincando de mis pies a mi cabeza" (p. 92) ("It just had a circus jumping from my feet to my head," p. 86). On pages 93–94, in the middle of the discussion on the cat, she is informed of the death of her father and responds, "Entonces era él" ("So it was my father," p. 88).

José de la Colina has also noted the incestuous relationship between Susana and her father, observing that when the two returned to Comala, their relationship was thought to be that of husband and wife, not father and daughter ("Susana San Juan").

24. This tendency to place the blame on women is clearly, although unobtrusively, dramatized in *Pedro Páramo*. In the scene with the incestuous couple, it is *she* who is marked by sin, *she* whom the bishop admonishes, *she* who dissolves into mud before Juan's eyes.

25. This dualistic status of goddess and object of scorn—prostitute—who can absolve her attackers seems to be the basic premise of pornography as studied by Andrea Dworkin in *Woman Hating* and Elizabeth Janeway in *Man's World*. Janeway posits, "the pornographers are looking with rage at the women who denied them their earliest pleasures, and in their subjection of them they are seeking revenge. But, as we have seen, they do not dare take their revenge unless they can do so with the full agreement of the woman" (p. 66).

26. See "*La muerte de Artemio Cruz* y Unamuno: una fuente de Fuentes," *Cuadernos Americanos*, no. 177 (July–August 1971): 200.

Significantly, too, González is one of the few critics who has referred to the possibility that Artemio is a twin, a fact which would tie the novel even more closely to Girard's theory of sacrifice.

27. *El laberinto de la soledad* (Mexico: Fondo de cultura económica, 1959), chap. 4.

28. It is not pertinent that Fuentes has chosen to use a mulata rather than an Indian as victim of the violation. The violation is the same.

29. José de la Colina notes that Juan, in fact, carries the picture of his mother as if she were the Virgin or his beloved ("Susana San Juan," p. 61).

30. Gyurko too has observed that Artemio (not unlike Pedro Páramo) builds his economic empire in an attempt to compensate for the loss of Regina ("Women in Mexican Society," p. 209).

31. From the opening page the text suggests that it is the woman who is necessary in order for him to see himself reflected: "abro el ojo derecho y lo veo reflejado en las incrustaciones de vidrio de una bolsa de *mujer*" (p. 9, emphasis added) ("I . . . open my right eye and see it reflected in the squares of silvered glass that encrust a *woman's* purse," p. 4, emphasis added).

Chapter 5. *La ciudad y Los perros*

1. There are many excellent studies of *La ciudad y los perros;* a few of the better known are Rosa Boldori, *Mario Vargas Llosa y la literatura en el Perú de hoy* (Santa Fe, Argentina: Colmegna, 1969); Emir Rodríguez Monegal, "Madurez de Vargas Llosa," *Mundo Nuevo,* no. 3 (1966): 62–72; Wolfgang Luchting, "Los fracasos de Mario Vargas Llosa," *Mundo Nuevo* nos. 51–52 (1970): 61–72; Luis A. Diez, *Mario Vargas Llosa's Pursuit of the Total Novel* (Cuernavaca: Centro intercultural de documentación, 1970); J. L. Martin, *La narrativa de Vargas Llosa, acercamiento estilístico* (Madrid: Gredos, 1974); José Miguel Oviedo, *Mario Vargas Llosa: la invención de una realidad* (Barcelona: Barral, 1970); Luis Aguero et al., "Sobre *La ciudad y los perros,*" *Casa de las Américas* 5 (May–June 1965): 63–80; Frank Dauster, "Aristotle and Vargas Llosa: Literary History and the Interpretation of Reality," *Hispania* 53 (May 1970): 273–77; G. R. McMurray, "Form and Content Relationships in *La ciudad y los perros,*" *Hispania* 56 (September 1973): 579–86; Alberto Escobar, "Impostores de sí mismos," in *Homenaje a Mario Vargas Llosa,* ed. Helmy F. Giacoman and José Miguel Oviedo (Long Island City, N.Y.: Las Américas, 1971), pp. 125–33; Jorge Lafforgue, "*La ciudad y los perros,* novela moral," in *Homenaje,* pp. 99–123; Pedro Lastra, "Un caso de elaboración narrativa de experiencias concretas en *La ciudad y los perros,*" in *Homenaje,* pp. 37–44; José Promis Ojeda, "Algunas notas a propósito de *La ciudad y los perros,*" in *Homenaje,* pp. 287–94.

2. P. 120. All English quotations are from Mario Vargas Llosa, *The Time of the Hero,* trans. Lysander Kemp (New York: Harper, 1966). Spanish citations are from *La ciudad y los perros* (Barcelona: Seix Barral, 1971), p. 105.

3. The French terms *énonciation* and *énoncé* are an effort to avoid the inevitable ambiguities of their English translations. *Enonciation* refers to the production (the act itself) of the linguistic units, and *énoncé* indicates the totality of that which is produced (i.e., the statement, the message).

4. At this point one might include a Freudian or even Jungian analysis of the child's identification with the parent of either sex, but such is not the purpose of this study.

5. See "*The Time of the Hero:* Liberty Enslaved," *Latin American Literary Review* 4 (Spring–Summer 1976): 35–46.

6. It is apropos that the structural anthropologists concentrate on the exchange of women and goods (economy) while the structural linguists make analogies between the exchange of words and economic systems.

7. See Michael Foucault's chapter on representation in *Les mots et les choses* (Mayenne; Gallimard, 1966).

8. Derrida has noted that to name is to inscribe in a system of differences (*Grammatologie,* p. 164), and, as Octavio Paz has noted, "La función significativa del fonema consiste en que designa una relación de alteridad u oposición frente a los otros fonemas. . . . Todo el edificio del lenguaje reposa sobre esta oposición binaria." See *Claude Lévi-Strauss o el nuevo festín de Esopo* (Mexico: Mortiz, 1967), p. 17.

9. This does not apply, however, to proper names in the world outside of fiction, since as Derrida has emphasized (*Grammatologie,* pp. 157–73), proper nouns in the world are not proper at all but shared. The fact that two people have the same proper name does not presuppose any similarity.

10. The exception to this general rule, however, might be found in the Russian novel, where in many cases the character does combine oppositional signifiers; that is, he may be both beautiful and ugly. In these novels, however, there is some type of strange congruity to these oppositions and a recognition that the polarities are only linguistic.

11. This portrayal of Jaguar is also somewhat Jungian, since for Jung the external mask is masculine whereas the dark, hidden unconscious is feminine. Obviously, the characterization of Jaguar fits precisely this mold.

12. This notion is well developed by Martin *(Narrativa)*. I would disagree with Martin only in regard to his notion of "original" innocence. He develops this notion of innocence very much as Lévi-Strauss does, and I would apply the same objections to Martin that Derrida has registered against Lévi-Strauss. See *Grammatologie*, pp. 149–202.

13. Joel Hancock interprets this play on light and shadows somewhat differently. See "Animalization and Chiaroscuro Techniques: Descriptive Language in *La ciudad y los perros*," *Latin American Literary Review* 4 (Fall–Winter 1975): 37–48.

Chapter 6. Manuel Puig's *La traición de Rita Hayworth*

1. Roland Barthes has noted that "Impossible, ici, d'attribuer à l'énonciation une origine, un point de vue. Or cette impossibilité est l'une des mesures qui permettent d'apprécier le pluriel d'un texte." See *S/Z* (Paris: Seuil, 1970), p. 48.

2. Manuel Puig, *Betrayed by Rita Hayworth,* trans. Suzanne Jill Levine (New York: Avon, 1973), p. 5. Subsequent English quotations from this edition. Spanish citations are from *La traición de Rita Hayworth* (Barcelona: Seix Barral, 1971), p. 9.

3. I have already spoken in earlier chapters about novels which fail to deliver the female protagonists their titles promise.

4. The difference between fictitious and nonfictitious discourse is that the latter believes it has an extratextual referent; the former sometimes *pretends* it does.

5. Thus, in Wayne Booth's terms, they would be categorized as unreliable narrators (*The Rhetoric of Fiction,* Chicago: University of Chicago Press, 1961). I have discussed a more linguistic definition of the unreliable narrator in Chapter 2, but here I am referring to the characters who are not the principal narrators of the novel (I suggest, in fact, that there is *no* principal narrator here), and whose distorted view is patent to the most naïve reader.

6. Embroidery always represents something pretty and attractive, with positive connotations. It never includes the unpleasant or the sordid.

7. Perhaps this identification is physical as well as verbal, but I shall leave the Freudian, oedipal study of this novel to others.

8. The exception to this lack of communication is, of course, the reader. Much is communicated to the reader, although he understands only what he is able to comprehend by innuendo, by means of his intuitive, wider vision.

9. José Ortega y Gasset, "Unas gotas de fenomenología," *La deshumanización del arte* (Madrid: Revista de Occidente, 1967), pp. 27–32.

10. Claude Lévi-Strauss speaks of a similar phenomenon in "Leçon d'écriture," in *Tristes tropiques*.

11. Even in the biological symbol ♀, the cross might easily be considered an X tipped on its side. While there is temptation to speculate on the origins of X (the cross-out, negation) as a genetic symbol for women, I shall not.

12. In Latin countries, it seems, a young man is most likely to be physically introduced to coitus at the hands of an older woman, the prostitute.

13. There are several devices which indicates quotation. For example, although Héctor's discourse lacks quotation marks, there is little doubt about what belongs to him and what belongs to someone else: "Que cantamos con mi tía siempre mientras lavamos los platos, me dice" (p. 155) ("that me and my aunt always sing while we wash the dishes, she says to me," p. 133). The same is true of Paquita's discourse: "¿por qué se vino papá? qué tonto, pero eran pobres y acá somos tan ricos que con una mano nos tapamos lo de adelante y con la otra lo de atrás. Pero papá nunca va a saber que tengo un pecado mortal" (pp. 173–74) ("why did Dad come here? how silly, but they were poor and here we're so rich we can hardly afford the rags on our backs. But Dad will never know I have a mortal sin," p. 150). In addition, the use of a question in the *you* form frequently signals an indirect quotation.

14. Otto Jespersen, *Language: Its Nature, Development and Origin* (New York: Norton, 1964), p. 116.

15. Although technically the imperfect could not narrate a single, completed action in the past, it could tell what was happening or what happened more than once. Similarly, there may be some doubt here on the part of the reader as to Pocha's comprehension of the differences between preterit and imperfect, since she is only twelve.

16. Eusebio R. Castex, *Tópicos lexigráficos* (Buenos Aires, 1927), p. 16, as quoted by M. L. Wagner in his review of the book in *Revista de Filología Española* 20:176–77.

17. Joan Corominas and J. A. Pascual, *Diccionario crítico etimológico castellano e hispánico*, Vol. 2 (Madrid: Gredos, 1980), p. 120.

18. Martin Alonso, *Enciclopedia del idioma*, vol. 1 (Madrid: Aguilar, 1958), p. 1113.

19. My conclusions regarding the evolved meaning of *coger* are quite compatible with those of Américo Castro who suggests that the predominance of the word's sexual connotations evolved because "en la lengua rústica, adquirió ocasionalmente el significado de 'cubrir el caballo a la hembra' " and the predominance of *ganadería en la pampa* resulted in its application to humans. See *La peculiaridad lingüística rioplatense* (Buenos Aires: Losada, 1941), p. 126.

20. Peter Boyd-Bowman, *Léxico hispanoamericano del siglo XVI* (London: Tamesis, 1971), p. 197.

21. This clearly reflects the position of the Church, particularly that of some of its early "fathers." If one were "good," i.e., celibate, one would be "saved" from the inevitable destruction and decay associated with death. Thus, logically it is a short step from mankind's desire to deny death to a belief that denying women, i.e., sexuality, remaining celibate, is denying decay. Therefore, woman is decay.

22. Alfred MacAdam, for example, states, "The family study . . . is rendered meaningless by the last chapter." See *Modern Latin American Narratives: Dreams of Reason* (Chicago: University of Chicago Press, 1977), p. 3. In another place he says, "The dislocated chapter may be understood either as an episode not essential to the plot, and therefore important only as information about the plot's prehistory, or one of the events which indeed pushes the action to its conclusion." See "Manuel Puig's Chronicles of Provincial Life," *Revista Hispánica Moderna* 36 (1970–71): 51. Similarly, David Southard notes, "Only then—at the very end of the novel—does the reader receive confirmation of what has already been deduced. Because the letter makes the reader return to the beginning, it is anti-climactic." (He has previously stated that anticlimax in Puig is reader deception.) See "Betrayed by Manuel Puig: Reader Deception and Anti-Climax in His Novels," *Latin American Literary Review* 4 (Fall–Winter 1976):23.

23. The relationship between the names of the two characters is perhaps suggestive (especially to Toto). Rita Hayworth's real first name was Margarita. The one-letter difference between Rita and Mita may well be significant in the mind of a child.

24. Implied here is another problem: there is a patent difficulty on the part of the characters in accepting each other in more than one role. For example, it never seems to occur to anyone that Mita might play the roles of mother, sister, wife, provider, and whatever else *without* any real contradiction, just as Rita could be doña Sol *and* Rita without conflict.

25. To prove the validity of this reading of *Sangre y arena* would require another complete chapter. I offer but a few passages of the novel as evidence of the validity of the reading. See Vicente Blasco Ibáñez, *Sangre y arena* (Buenos Aires: Espasa-Calpe, 1968) and *Blood and Sand*, trans. Mrs. W. A. Gillespie (New York: Dutton, 1922).

> los lidiadores . . . exponían la vida por algo más que el dinero. Sus incertidumbres y terrores ante lo desconocido los habían dejado más allá de las vallas. Ya pisaban el redondel; ya estaban frente al público: llegaba la realidad. Y las ansias de gloria de sus almas bárbaras y sencillas, el deseo de sobreponerse a los camaradas, el orgullo de su fuerza y su destreza, les cegaban, haciéndoles olvidar temores e infundiéndoles una audacia brutal.
> Gallardo se había transfigurado. (P. 29)

(They were risking their lives for something more than money. Their doubts and terrors

of the unknown had been left outside the barricades. Now they trod the arena. They were face to face with their public. Reality had come. The longing for glory in their barbarous, ignorant minds, the desire to excel their comrades, the pride in their own strength and dexterity, all blinded them, making them forget all fears, and inspiring them with the daring of brute force.
Gallardo was quite transfigured. [P. 41])

Era un torero que prometía 'hule', según expresión de los aficionados; y el tal hule era el de las camas de la enfermería.
Todos creían que estaba destinado a morir en la plaza de una cornada. (P. 30)

(He was a torero who promised 'hule'—according to the expression of the aficionados, and such 'hule' was likely to lead to a bed in the Infirmary.
Everyone thought he was destined to die, gored to death in the Plaza. [Pp. 42–43])

Valor y audacia eran lo necesario para vencer [according to Gallardo]. Y casi a ciegas, sin más guía que la temeridad, ni otro apoyo que el de sus facultades corporales, había hecho una carrera rápida, asombrando al público hasta el paroxismo, aturdiéndolo con su valentía de loco.
No había ido, como otros matadores, por sus pasos contados, sirviendo largos años de peón y banderillero al lado de los maestros. . . . Lo importante era subir de prisa, y el público le había visto comenzar como espada. . . .
Le admiraban por lo mismo que tenían su desgracia como cierta. (P. 30)

(Bravery and audacity only were necessary to ensure victory. Almost blindly, with no other rule than his own temerity, no other help than his own bodily faculties, he had made a rapid career for himself, forcing outbursts of wonder from the people and astonishing them with his mad courage.
He had not, like other matadors, risen by regular steps, serving long years as peon and banderillero at the "maestros'" side. . . . The great thing was to rise quickly, and the public had seen him commence at once as espada. . . .
It admired him for the very reason which made a catastrophe so certain. [P. 43])

Su suerte estaba echada. Matar toros o morir. Ser rico. (P. 48)

(His fate was decided. He would kill bulls or die. He would be rich. [P. 74])

¡Ay, esa mujer! ¡Como lo ha cambiao!... ¡Es otro! Sólo quiere ir con los señoritos ricos." (P. 146)

(Ay! that woman. How she has changed him!... He is another man! He only cares now to go with rich people. [P. 225])

Al irse la *gachi* rubia, había commenzado la mala suerte para el torero. . . . Su ánimo, sostenido unas veces y agobiado otras por los espejismos de su superstición, creía esto firmemente. (P. 202)

(when the fair-haired gachi left him his ill luck began. . . . His superstitious heart believed this most firmly. [P. 293])

Las preocupaciones profesionales resurgieron en su pensamiento. Todo lo malo que le ocurría era porque no se 'arrimaba' ahora a los toros. (P. 208)

(All his professional anxieties arose again in his mind. All the evil which was happening to him was because he did not now throw himself on the bulls. [P. 300])

Todo esto representaba la degradación de la familia, la tristeza de los suyos. Gallardo avergonzábase de que tal cosa pudiera suceder. Era un crimen privarles de lo que tenían,

luego de haberlos acostumbrado al bienestar. ¿Y qué era lo que debía hacer para evitarlo?...
Simplemente 'arrimarse' a los toros: seguir toreando como en otros tiempos... ¡El se 'ar-
rimaría'! (P. 212)

(All this represented degradation to the family, and Gallardo felt ashamed that such a
thing could possibly happen. It would be a crime to deprive them of what they enjoyed,
now they had become accustomed to ease and comfort. And what ought he to do to prevent
this?... Simply to throw himself on the bulls, fight as he had fought in former days... and he
would throw himself! [P. 305])

Thus, clearly one sees that (1) Gallardo was not a particularly skilled *torero*, merely a daring
one, and (2) he took the last foolish chance in the bullring in order to return to the glory and
riches (cf. the economic preoccupations of Berto) of prior times. If one carefully reads the first
description in the novel of one of his fights (Chapter 1), one must note that there is very little
difference between this fight and his last.

26. As Jeffrey Mehlman has pointed out in the introduction to his translation of Jacques
Derrida, "Freud and the Scene of Writing," *Yale French Studies*, no. 48 (1972): 73–74, through-
out Derrida's work the "very distinction between inner and outer is thrown into question."
This is precisely what happens in this novel.

27. I am not attempting to oversimplify here, nor do I intend to suggest that males do not
also fall victim to this process. My subject, however, is woman, and I must leave the study of
male victimization for another time.

28. Feminists often attribute this to another means of masculine oppression. The female
who is incapable of economic self-subsistence is more dependent, more obedient to the male,
and thus he, in turn, feels himself more "manly" for the "conquest."

29. In this respect, Puig's novel underlines the common idiomatic use of the verb *comer*—an
idiomatic use which Donoso takes quite literally and carries to its extreme in *Casa de campo*.

30. Fittingly, Herminia's notebook, which textually immediately precedes the letter, analyzes the word *lujuria* which is etymologically related to *lujoso*.

31. Derrida, of course, sees all language in this manner. See Jacques Derrida, *L'écriture et la
différence* (Paris: Seuil, 1967), p. 314.

I would also add that Jonathan Tittler's analysis of the novel offers a different and indeed
interesting reading of the male/female division within the text and the significance of each.
See "The Androgynous Text," in *Narrative Irony in the Contemporary Spanish-American Novel*
(Ithaca, N.Y.: Cornell University Press, 1984).

Chapter 7. José Donoso's *El obsceno pájaro de la noche*

1. The bibliography of works which study *El obsceno pájaro* is extensive. I list only a few of
those which have the greatest bearing on our topic. Alicia Borinsky, "Repeticiones y máscaras:
El obsceno pájaro de la noche," *Modern Language Notes* 88 (March 1973): 281–94; Guillermo Carnera, "*El obsceno pájaro de la noche*," *Cuadernos Hispanoamericanos* 87 (January 1972): 169–74;
Alexander Coleman, "Some Thoughts on José Donoso's Traditionalism," *Studies in Short
Fiction* 8 (Winter 1971): 155–58; John J. Hassett, "The Obscure Bird of the Night," *Review* (Fall
1973), pp. 27–30; Z. Nelly Martínez, "*El obsceno pájaro de la noche*: la productividad del texto,"
Revista Iberoamericana 46 (January–June 1980): 51–66; Z. Nelly Martínez, "Lo neobarroco en *El
obsceno pájaro de la noche* de José Donoso," *XVII Congreso del Instituto Internacional de Literatura
Iberoamericana: El barroco en América* (Madrid: Universidad Complutense de Madrid, 1978),
pp. 635–42; George R. McMurray, "José Donoso's Tribute to Consciousness: *El obsceno pájaro
de la noche*," *Chasqui* 3 (May 1974): 40–48; Anita L. Muller, "La dialéctica de la realidad en *El

obsceno pájaro de la noche," *Nueva Narrativa Hispanoamericana,* 2 (September 1972): 93–100; Juan Andrés Piña, "José Donoso: Los fantasmas del escritor," *Mensaje,* no. 246 (January–February 1976): pp. 49–53; Emir Rodríguez Monegal, "El mundo de José Donoso," *Mundo Nuevo,* no. 12 (June 1967): 77–85; Jaime Siles, *"El obsceno pájaro de la noche* y su técnica narrativa," *Cuadernos Hispanoamericanos* 87 (January 1972): 175–78; Charles M. Tatum, *"El obsceno pájaro de la noche:* The Demise of a Feudal Society," *Latin American Literary Review* 1 (Spring 1973): 99–105; Frances Wyers Weber, "La dinámica de la alegoría: *El obsceno pájaro de la noche* de José Donoso," *Hispamérica* 4 (nos. 11–12): 23–31; Zunilda Gertel, "Metamorphosis as a Metaphor of the World," *Review* (Fall 1973): 20–23; John Caviglia, "Tradition and Monstrosity in *El obsceno pájaro de la noche,"* *PMLA* 93 (January 1978): 33–45. See also the volume of essays entitled *The Creative Process in the Works of José Donoso,* ed. Guillermo Castillo-Feliú (Rock Hill, S.C.: Winthrop College, 1982).

The importance of the witch in other Donoso works has been noted by Howard M. Fraser, "Witchcraft in Three Stories of José Donoso," *Latin American Literary Review* 4 (Fall–Winter 1975): 3–8.

2. Severo Sarduy, *Barroco* (Buenos Aires: Sudamericana, 1974), p. 99. (English translations are my own.)

3. Only in the last few years, with the recent interest in the occult, has the stereotype of the witch as old been reconsidered.

4. See "Amidst the Illusory Depths of the First-Person Pronoun and *El obsceno pájaro de la noche,"* *Modern Language Notes* 93 (March 1978): 267–84; *"El obsceno pájaro de la noche:* Fiction, Monsters, and Packages," *Hispanic Review* 45 (Autumn 1977): 413–419; "From *El obsceno pájaro de la noche* to *Tres novelitas burguesas:* Development of a Semiotic Theory in the Works of Donoso," in *The Analysis of Literary Texts: Current Trends in Methodology,* ed. Randolph Pope (Ypsilanti, Mich.: Bilingual Press, 1980), pp. 224–35; "The Baroque, the Picaresque and *El obsceno pájaro de la noche,"* *Hispanic Journal* 2 (Spring 1981): 81–93.

5. All Spanish quotations are from the Seix Barral edition (Barcelona, 1971). English quotations are from the Hardie St. Martin and Leonard Mades translation, *The Obscene Bird of Night* (Boston: Nonpareil, 1979).

6. See my study on "The Baroque," cited in n. 4 above. Throughout this study I am forced, in seeming contradiction to my other studies, to speak of the text *as if* it had as its referent some extratextual event and *as if* there were varying levels of discourse, some more valid than others. I do this merely to facilitate the discussion.

7. Ultimately, of course, this is a triple masking, since a bridal nightgown, by implication, is a mask whose destiny is merely removal—a covering designed to conceal and reveal simultaneously.

8. This was the main thrust of an oral presentation, "A Transmutation Device in Certain Texts of José Donoso," which was presented at the Fourth Winthrop Symposium on Major Modern Writers and published in *The Creative Process in the Works of José Donoso,* pp. 118–28.

9. It is a fact that at least since the surge of the bourgeoisie, the household servant has almost always been female. Whether she takes the role of paid servant or wife and mother, the person charged with cleaning up after others is almost inevitably female.

10. William Woods, *A History of the Devil* (New York: Berkley, 1975), p. 202.

11. It seems less likely that an upper-class woman, accustomed to being served, would convert herself into a servant of the Devil.

12. The first woman executed by the Inquisition (1275) for copulating with the Devil bore a monstrous child with the head of a wolf and the tail of a serpent. See R. E. L. Masters, *Eros and Evil* (Baltimore: Penguin, 1974) p. 46. Significantly, too, witches, like the Devil, apparently took the form of animals. See Masters, p. 76.

13. Quoted by Edward Peters, *The Magician, the Witch, and the Law* (Philadelphia: University of Pennsylvania Press, 1978), pp. 170–71. Significantly, too, the major treatise on witchcraft, *Malleus Maleficarum,* was commissioned by this same pope.

14. Margaret Murray, in several books on witchcraft, suggests that witches were actually

the continuation of ancient religions. See, among others, *The God of the Witches* (New York: Oxford, 1952). Similarly, Julia O'Faolain and Lauro Marines note that the cult of witchcraft was a heretical, erotic cult largely in the hands of women. See *Not in God's Image* (New York: Harper, 1973), p. 207.

15. Merlin Stone, *When God Was a Woman* (New York: Harcourt Brace Jovanovich, 1978), also points out that many of the charges in witchcraft trials were related to sexual behavior.

16. The fact that the old woman was tied to a stake and floated down a river and the daughter sent to a convent also points to the implications of sexuality.

17. Obviously, the other major ellipsis in the text is Humberto's book, which, if ever finished within the framework of the fiction, certainly is never shared with us except for the few pages.

18. See *O* (Barcelona: Seix Barral; 1975), pp. 61–70.

19. My references to the English term are not gratuitous, inasmuch as Donoso himself is completely knowledgeable and fluent in English and wrote much of *El obsceno pájaro* while living in the U.S.

Many of my observations on the etymology of the terms are identical to those of Gloria Durán in her study "La bruja de Carlos Fuentes."

20. Mary Nelson's essay, "Why Women Were Witches," in *Women: A Feminist Perspective*, ed. Jo Freeman (Palo Alto, Calif.: Mayfield, 1975), pp. 335–50, which came into my hands after the completion of this chapter, offers a complementary economic explanation for women as witches.

Chapter 8. Women, Language, and Cats

1. Luisa Valenzuela (Argentina, b. 1938) is the youngest of the novelists studied here, the only female and perhaps the least well known of the group, although increasingly popular and important. I have included *El gato eficaz* for precisely these reasons and because I believe that the quality of *El gato eficaz* easily matches that of the other novels. This said, let us focus no longer on the gender, age, or fame of the novelist. The concern here is the texts.

2. The credence in the ability of the "poet" to see relationships hidden to the rest of the world is longstanding and has been perpetuated by most literary schools. It has been maintained by Dámaso Alonso, *Poesía española* (Madrid: Gredos, 1950) and Carlos Bousoño, *Teoría de la expresión poética*, 5th ed. (Madrid: Gredos, 1970), among others. See also Michel Foucault, *Les mots et les choses* (Mayenne: Gallimard, 1966). Octavio Paz makes similar statements about the function of the metaphor in *Conjunciones y disyunciones* (Mexico: Mortiz, 1969).

3. All page numbers refer to the 1972 edition (Mexico: Mortiz). Translations are my own.

4. I develop this notion more fully in *"El obsceno pájaro de la noche:* Fiction, Monsters, and Packages."

5. See "La structure, le signe et le jeu dans le discours de sciences humaines," *L'écriture et la différence.* Here Derrida specifically notes, "Ce centre avait pour fonction non seulement d'orienter et d'équilibrer, d'organiser la structure . . . mais de faire surtout que le principe d'organisation de la structure limite ce que nous pourrions appeler le *jeu* de la structure" (p. 409).

6. Sophocles, *Oedipus the King*, trans. and ed. Thomas Gould (Englewood Cliffs, N.J.: Prentice-Hall, 1970), pp. 18–19.

7. See Henry Chichester Hart, *Animals Mentioned in the Bible* (London, 1888) and Peter Farb, *The Land, Wildlife, and People of the Bible* (New York: Harper & Row, 1967).

8. See Claude Lévi-Strauss, *Le Cru et le cruit* (Paris: Plon, 1964).

9. See Carlos Fuentes, *Aura;* Julio Cortázar, *Rayuela;* Ernesto Sábato, *Sobre héroes y tumbas.*

10. It is ultimately impossible to separate those "original" points of contact between women

and animals which produced the metaphor and the connotations imposed upon each today as a result of that metaphor.

11. Writing as corruption is a common contemporary belief perhaps most fully developed by Claude Lévi-Strauss in *Tristes tropiques*. See "Leçon d'écriture."

12. Even Victor Goti, Augusto Pérez's friend in Unamuno's *Niebla*, equates thirst for knowledge and eroticism. He states, "es el instinto metafísico, la curiosidad de saber lo que no nos importa, el pecado original, en fin, lo que le hace sensual al hombre" (Madrid: Espasa-Calpe, 1968, p. 14) ("it is a metaphysical instinct, the curiosity to know what doesn't concern us, thus, original sin, which makes man sensual," my translation).

13. *Le Texte du roman* (Paris: Mouton, 1970). Derrida has also labeled representation as death in "Freud et la scène de l'écriture," "*L'écriture et la différence*, p. 335.

14. Derrida notes, "L'écriture est dangereuse dès lors que la représentation veut s'y donner pour la présence et le signe pour la chose même" (*De la grammatologie*, p. 207).

15. "Mais le supplément supplée. Il ne s'ajoute que pour remplacer" (*Grammatologie*, p. 208).

16. I list but a few of the many expressions in Spanish which are based on the word *gato* or some form of it: buscar tres pies al gato, gatillo, gatillazo, cuatro gatos, dar gato por liebre, llevar el gato al agua, gato encerrado. The word *gato* itself, of course, depending on the geographic location, can mean jack, moneybags, a clamp, etc.

17. My sources of information regarding the game of chess are the following: Elliot M. Avedon and Brian Sutton-Smith, eds., *The Study of Games* (Huntington, N.Y.: Krieger, 1979); Henry A. Davidson, *A Short History of Chess* (New York: David McKay, 1949); Harry Golombek, *Chess: A History* (New York: Putnam, 1976).

18. Nevertheless, there are also versions of the origin of the game which have nothing to do with a woman. Norman Reider, whose study "Chess, Oedipus and the Mater Dolorosa" is included in the Avedon collection (*Study of Games*, pp. 440–64), notes seven principal themes in the myths, but only two of those have a woman as a central focus point.

19. A great deal has been written about these myths. See *Bulfinch's Mythology* (New York: Avenel, 1979), Helen Diner (*Mothers and Amazons*), M. Esther Harding (*Woman's Mysteries*), among others.

20. The connections between the two myths become even more manifest when one realizes that the invention of chess is often attributed to Philometer, who killed his father, cut the body into 300 pieces, and threw them to the vultures, with the result that the game was invented to cure his madness (Reider, "Chess," p. 449). In an almost identical manner, it is said that Typhon, son of Isis, killed Osiris, her husband and son, cut the body into 14 pieces and threw them everywhere. Apparently, the soul of Osiris inhabits the body of a bull.

21. Whether the society of the "original" situation was matriarchal or patriarchal is not relevant to this discussion. If the powers of the father passed directly to the son upon the death of the former, there would be no need for the latter to marry the queen, and it is this marriage which interests me.

22. Lewis Spence, *Myth and Ritual in Dance, Games, and Rhyme* (London: Watts, 1947), p. 2.

23. Jorge Luis Borges, "Ajedrez I" and "Ajedrez II," in *Obras completas de Jorge Luis Borges*, ed. Carlos V. Frías (Buenos Aires: Emece, 1974), p. 813.

24. The homosexual overtones also imply metaphoric death (for her he is "dead").

25. Some experts insist that the word "checkmate" or *jaque mate*, a word which signals the conclusion of the game as well as the end of this novel, means that the king has died; others theorize that it is only a warning that the king has been surrounded or surprised. Whether or not one accepts the virtual death of the king, the important fact is that the word implies his death.

26. This notion leads us back to my comments on *Artemio Cruz* in Chapter 4 of this study. In that novel I noted that the *chingada* was viewed as responsible for the violation of which she was in fact a victim.

27. Quoted by Davidson, *Short History of Chess*, p. 26.

28. There is an etymological link between Prometheus and *pramantha*, which is what one uses to produce fire and which is also linked with the sexual act. See Diner, *Mothers and Amazons*, p. 210.

29. This was Valenzuela's declaration during an oral presentation which took place as a part of the Primer Congreso Internacional de Literatura Hispanoamericana Contemporánea in San Juan, Puerto Rico, on 18 September 1980.

30. The myth of the Phoenix, like that of Isis, has as its principal theme the periodic rejuvenation or rebirth and, according to the version noted by Bulfinch (*Mythology*, pp. 310–12), is related to the theme of the son who replaces the father.

Conclusion

1. Puig, particularly, in his various works has often drawn very approbatory and sensitive depictions of women. In *La traición de Rita Hayworth*, Mita is a relatively positive representation. Similarly, Donoso's Inés is a strong woman, determined to get what she wants, and the women in Vargas Llosa are generally shown to be neither more nor less reputable or despicable than their male counterparts.

Throughout this section page numbers are taken from the same editions of the novels used in the rest of this study.

2. A vacuum is an empty space, a space from which all else has been removed. It must be contained or it will pull into itself all that surrounds it.

3. I recognize fully that some of the neo-Freudians and followers of Lacan would express this as the search for the misplaced phallus. Nevertheless, such an approach to literature (or psychoanalysis) is merely more patriarchal myth making, designed once more to emphasize the male center and denigrate anyone who happens to lack that organ. It is precisely this form of linguistic misuse I am trying to debunk here.

4. Obviously, doña Bárbara's name is not arbitrary within the context of the novel, but rather carefully selected by Gallegos for its evocative qualities. What I am suggesting, however, is that were Bárbara a being in the world whose name had indeed been arbitrarily assigned (as it presumably was within the fiction of the novel), the same associations might have surfaced, just as our terms Mother Nature and Mother Earth (although no doubt intended as metaphors) cause us to associate women and nature.

5. Without a doubt, the one female character I have studied who closely approximates this portrayal of inner conflict is doña Bárbara, and ironically it is her readers, rather than Gallegos, who have insisted on seeing her as the unidimensional, "bad" character, much as it was and is biblical readers who insist on Eve's unequivocal culpability.

6. At the same time, however, it may be just this lack of duality, just this singularity of options, which produces the necessary inner conflict and thus encourages the creation of memorable characters.

7. Dorothy Dinnerstein, *The Mermaid and the Minotaur* (New York: Harper & Row, 1977).

8. According to the criteria I have suggested, Agata should have been a memorable character since she is the product of inner conflict and struggle. Nevertheless, there can be no denying that she is not. Why? I suggest that it is due to the mundane nature of her goals. Agata seeks to realize her full potential not through herself but through another human being who will provide all she needs. Don Quijote seeks to right the wrongs of the world; Emma Bovary is torn between the world of reality and the world of literature and like Quijote tries to live her fantasy. Agata wants to get married and have children, wants to find someone to provide ready-made happiness and fulfillment for her—indeed not memorable goals.

9. Octavio Paz, of course, has discussed at length the typical Mexican tendency to see the

world in terms of the *gran chingón* or the *chingada*. See *El laberinto de la soledad*, particularly the chapter entitled "Los hijos de la Malinche."

10. I definitely do not mean to suggest that a female writer, merely because she is a female, is necessarily more capable of recognizing these myths. Although the demystification found in Valenzuela *might* have been found in other women writers, it indeed cannot be found in all of them. At the same time, Manuel Puig has made great strides in debunking these female-oriented myths, particularly in *Pubis angelical*.

Bibliography

Aguero, Luis, et al. "Sobre *La ciudad y los perros.*" *Casa de las Américas* 5 (May–June 1965): 63–80.

Alonso, Dámaso. *Poesía española.* Madrid: Gredos, 1950.

Alonso, Martín. *Enciclopedia del idioma.* Vol. 1. Madrid: Aguilar, 1958.

Anderson Imbert, Enrique. *Historia de la literatura hispanoaméricana.* Vol. 2. Mexico: Fondo de cultura económica, 1970.

Añez, Jorge. *De "La vorágine" a "Doña Bárbara."* Bogotá: Imprenta del Departamento, 1944.

Araujo, Orlando. *Lengua y creación en la obra de Rómulo Gallegos.* Caracas: Ministerio de Educación, 1962.

Arciniegas, Germán. *Genio y figura de Jorge Isaacs.* Buenos Aires: Eudeba, 1970.

Avedon, Elliot M., and Brian Sutton-Smith, eds. *The Study of Games.* Huntington, N.Y.: Krieger, 1979.

Barthes, Roland. *S/Z.* Paris: Seuil, 1970.

Bastos, María Luisa, and Sylvia Molloy. "La estrella junto a la luna: Variantes de la figura materna en *Pedro Páramo.*" *Modern Language Notes* 92 (March 1977): 246–68.

Befumo Boschi, Liliana. "La mujer en *Pedro Páramo.*" In *La mujer símbolo del mundo nuevo,* edited by Vicente Cicchitti, 138–52. (Buenos Aires: Fernando García Cambeiro, 1976).

Bell, Alan S. "Rulfo's *Pedro Páramo:* A Vision of Hope." *Modern Language Notes* 81 (March 1966): 238–45.

Holy Bible. Revised Standard Version. New York: Thomas Nelson, 1953.

Blasco Ibáñez, Vicente. *Blood and Sand.* Translated by Mrs. W. A. Gillespie. New York: Dutton, 1922.

———. *Sangre y arena.* Buenos Aires: Espasa-Calpe, 1968.

Boldori, Rosa. *Mario Vargas Llosa y la literatura en el Perú de hoy.* Santa Fe, Argentina: Colmegna, 1969.

Booth, Wayne. *The Rhetoric of Fiction.* Chicago: University of Chicago Press, 1961.

Borges, Jorge Luis. *Obras completas.* Edited by Carlos V. Frías. Buenos Aires: Emece, 1974.

Borinsky, Alicia. "Repeticiones y máscaras: *El obsceno pájaro de la noche.*" *Modern Language Notes* 88 (March 1973): 281–94.

Bosch, Juan. "De *Don Quijote* a *Doña Bárbara.*" *Humanismo* (Mexico) 3 (August 1954): 31–35.

Bousoño, Carlos. *Teoría de la expresión poética.* 5th ed. Madrid: Gredos, 1970.

Boyd-Bowman, Peter. *Léxico hispanoamericano del siglo XVI.* London: Tamesis, 1971.

Brooks, Peter. "Freud's Masterplot: Questions of Narrative." *Yale French Studies*, nos. 55–56 (1977): 280–300.

Brown, Donald F. "Chateaubriand and the Story of Feliciana in Jorge Isaacs' *María.*" *Modern Language Notes* 62 (1947): 326–29.

Bulfinch's Mythology. New York: Avenel, 1979.

Bull, William. "Nature and Anthropomorphism in *La vorágine.*" *Romanic Review* 39 (December 1948): 307–18.

Burton, Julianne. "Sexuality and the Mythic Dimension in Juan Rulfo's *Pedro Páramo.*" *Symposium* 28 (Fall 1974): 228–47.

Cabrera Infante, Guillermo. *O.* Barcelona: Seix Barral, 1975.

Callan, Richard J. "The Jungian Basis of Carlos Fuentes' *Aura.*" *Kentucky Romance Quarterly* 18 (1971): 65–76.

Carnera, Guillermo. "*El obsceno pájaro de la noche.*" *Cuadernos Hispanoamericanos* 87 (January 1972): 169–74.

Carreras González, Olga. "Tres fechas, tres novelas y un tema: Estudio comparativo de *La vorágine, Canaima y Los pasos perdidos.*" *Explicación de Textos Literarios* 2:169–78.

Carvajal, Mario. *Vida y pasión de Jorge Isaacs.* Santiago de Chile: Ercilla, 1937.

Castanien, Donald G. "Introspective Techniques in *Doña Bárbara.*" *Hispania* 41 (1958): 282–88.

Castellanos, Rosario. *El eterno femenino.* Mexico: Fondo de cultura económica. 1975.

Castex, Eusebio R. *Tópicos lexigráficos.* Buenos Aires, 1927.

Castillo-Feliú, Guillermo, ed. *The Creative Process in the Works of José Donoso.* Rock Hill, S.C.: Winthrop College, 1982.

Castro, Américo. *La peculiaridad lingüística rioplatense.* Buenos Aires: Losada, 1941.

Caviglia, John. "Tradition and Monstrosity in *El obsceno pájaro de la noche.*" *PMLA* 93 (January 1978): 33–45.

Chasca, Edmundo de. "El lirismo de *La vorágine.*" In *Recopilación de textos sobre tres novelas ejemplares,* edited by T. Pérez, 114–35. Havana: Las Américas, n.d.

Christ, Carol P., and Judith Plaskow, eds. *Womanspirit Rising.* New York: Harper & Row, 1979.

Cicchitti, Vicente. "María y su magnificat." In *La mujer símbolo del mundo nuevo*, 11–18. Buenos Aires: Fernando García Cambeiro, 1976.

Coester, Alfred. "Maelstroms, Green Hells and Sentimental Jungles." *Hispania* 16 (March 1933): 43–50.

Coleman, Alexander. "Some Thoughts on José Donoso's Traditionalism." *Studies in Short Fiction* 8 (Winter 1971): 155–58.

Colina, José de la. "Susana San Juan, el mito femenino en *Pedro Páramo*." *Universidad de México* 19 (April 1965): 60–66.

Corominas, Joan, and J. A. Pascual. *Diccionario crítico etimológico castellano e hispánico*. Vol. 2. Madrid: Gredos, 1980.

Correa, Gustavo. "El mundo metafórico de *Doña Bárbara*." *Actas del Sexto Congreso del Instituto Internacional de Literatura Iberoamericana*, 227–33. Mexico: Imprenta Universitaria, 1954.

Costa Roa, Narciso. "El mundo novelesco de *Pedro Páramo*." *Revista chilena de literatura* 11 (April 1978): 23–84.

Curcio Altamar, Antonio. "Un nuevo mensaje." In *Recopilación de textos sobre tres novelas ejemplares*, edited by T. Pérez, 136–49. Havana: Las Américas, n.d.

Daly, Mary. *Beyond God the Father*. Boston: Beacon, 1973.

———. *The Church and the Second Sex*. New York: Harper & Row, 1975.

Dauster, Frank. "Aristotle and Vargas Llosa: Literary History and the Interpretation of Reality." *Hispania* 53 (May 1970): 273–77.

Davidson, Henry A. *A Short History of Chess*. New York: David McKay, 1949.

Davis, Elizabeth Gould. *The First Sex*. New York: Penguin, 1971.

Derrida, Jacques. *L'écriture et la différence*. Paris: Seuil, 1967.

———. *De la grammatologie*. Paris: Minuit, 1967.

Diez, Luis A. *Mario Vargas Llosa's Pursuit of the Total Novel*. Cuernavaca: Centro intercultural de documentación, 1970.

Diner, Helen. *Mothers and Amazons*. Translated and edited by John Phillip Lundin. New York: Doubleday, 1973.

Dinnerstein, Dorothy. *The Mermaid and the Minotaur*. New York: Harper & Row, 1977.

DiVirgilio, Paul. "*La muerte de Artemio Cruz*: The Relationship between Innovation in the Role of the Personal Pronouns in the Narrative and Reader Expectancy." *Revista Canadiense de Estudios Hispánicos* 5 (Fall 1980): 93–100.

Donoso, José. *Tres novelitas burguesas*. Barcelona: Seix Barral, 1973.

———. *El obsceno pájaro de la noche*. Barcelona: Seix Barral, 1971.

———. *The Obscene Bird of Night*. Translated by Hardie St. Martin and Leonard Mades. Boston: Nonpareil, 1979.

Durán, Gloria. "La bruja de Carlos Fuentes." In *Homenaje a Carlos Fuentes,* edited by Helmy F. Giacoman, 242–60. Long Island City, N.Y.: Las Américas, 1971.

Dworkin, Andrea. *Woman Hating.* New York: Dutton, 1974.

Englekirk, John. *Doña Bárbara,* Legend of the *Llano.*" Hispania 31 (1948): 259–70.

Escobar, Alberto. "Impostores de sí mismos." In *Homenaje a Mario Vargas Llosa,* edited by Helmy F. Giacoman and José Miguel Oviedo, 125–33. Long Island City, N.Y.: Las Américas, 1971.

Espronceda, José de. "Canto a Teresa." In *Presentación y antología de los siglos XVIII y XIX españoles,* edited by Lucía Bonilla and Juan Agudiez, 1:251. New York: Las Américas, 1966.

Farb, Peter. *The Land, Wildlife, and People of the Bible.* New York: Harper & Row, 1967.

Fidalgo, José Antonio. "Criollismo e ideología en Gallegos." In *Recopilación de textos sobre tres novelas ejemplares,* edited by T. Pérez, 461–70. Havana: Las Américas, n.d.

Firestone, Shulamith. *The Dialectic of Sex.* New York: Bantam, 1971.

Ford, Richard. "El marco narrativo de La vorágine." *Revista Iberoamericana* 42 (July–December 1976): 573–80.

Foucault, Michel. *Les mots et les choses.* Mayenne: Gallimard, 1966.

Fraser, Howard M. "Witchcraft in Three Stories of José Donoso." *Latin American Literary Review* 4 (Fall–Winter 1975): 3–8.

Freeman, Jo, ed. *Women: A Feminist Perspective.* Palo Alto: Mayfield, 1975.

Freud, Sigmund. *Civilization and Its Discontents.* Translated by James Strachey. New York: Norton, 1962.

———. *Das Ungluck in der Kultur.* Vienna: Internationaler Psychoanalytischer Verlag, 1930.

Frye, Northrop. *Anatomy of Criticism.* Princeton, N.J.: Princeton University Press, 1957.

Fuentes, Carlos. *Aura.* Mexico: Era, 1970.

———. *The Death of Artemio Cruz.* Translated by Sam Hileman. New York: Farrar, Straus and Giroux, 1964.

———. *La muerte de Artemio Cruz.* Mexico: Fondo de cultura económica, 1970.

Gallegos, Rómulo. *Doña Bárbara.* Buenos Aires: Espasa-Calpe, 1964.

———. *Doña Bárbara.* Translated by Robert Malloy. New York: Peter Smith, 1948.

Gertel, Zunilda. "Metamorphosis as a Metaphor of the World." *Review* (Fall 1973): 20–23.

Ghiano, Juan Carlos. *Constantes de la literatura argentina.* Buenos Aires: Raigal, 1953.

Giacoman, Helmy F., ed. *Homenaje a Carlos Fuentes.* Long Island City, N.Y.: Las Américas, 1971.

Giacoman, Helmy F., and José Miguel Oviedo, eds. *Homenaje a Mario Vargas Llosa.* Long Island City, N.Y.: Las Américas, 1971.

Girard, René. *Violence and the Sacred.* Translated by Patrick Gregory. Baltimore: Johns Hopkins University Press, 1979.

Goldenberg, Naomi. *Changing of the Gods.* Boston: Beacon, 1979.

Golombek, Harry. *Chess: A History.* New York: Putnam, 1976.

González, Alfonso. "Onomastics and Creativity in *Doña Bárbara* and *Pedro Páramo.*" *Names* 21:40–45.

González Echevarría, Roberto. "*La muerte de Artemio Cruz* y Unamuno: una fuente de Fuentes." *Cuadernos Americanos,* no. 177 (July–August 1971): 197–207.

———. *The Pilgrim at Home.* Ithaca, N.Y.: Cornell University Press, 1977.

Graham, Lloyd M. *Deceptions and Myths of the Bible.* New York: Bell, 1975.

Graves, Robert. *Adam's Rib.* New York: Yoseloff, 1958.

Green, Joan R. "La estructura del narrador y el modo narrativo de *La vorágine.*" *Cuadernos Hispanoamericanos,* no. 205 (January 1967): 101–8.

Grieben, Carlos F. *Eduardo Mallea.* Buenos Aires: Editoriales Culturales Argentinos, 1961.

Grimm's Fairy Tales. New York: Pantheon, 1944.

Gyurko, Lanin A. "The Image of Woman in Two Novels of Carlos Fuentes." *Research Studies* 43:1–18.

———. "Women in Mexican Society: Fuentes' Portrayal of Oppression." *Revista Hispánica Moderna* 38 (1974–75): 206–29.

Hall. Linda B. "The Cipactli Monster: Woman as Destroyer in Carlos Fuentes." *Southwest Review* 60 (Summer 1975): 246–55.

Hancock, Joel. "Animalization and Chiaroscuro Techniques: Descriptive Language in *La ciudad y los perros.*" *Latin American Literary Review* 4 (Fall–Winter 1975): 37–48.

Harding, M. Esther. *Woman's Mysteries.* New York: Putnam, 1971.

Hart, Henry Chichester. *Animals Mentioned in the Bible.* London, 1888.

Hassett, John J. "The Obscure Bird of the Night." *Review* (Fall 1973): 27–30.

Hellerman, M. Kasey. "The Coatlicue-Malinche Conflict: A Mother and Son Identity Crisis in the Writing of Carlos Fuentes." *Hispania* 57 (December 1974): 868–75.

Isaacs, Jorge, *María.* Buenos Aires: Losada, 1966.

———. *Maria.* Translated by Rollo Ogden. New York: Harper, 1890.

Janeway, Elizabeth. *Man's World, Woman's Place.* New York: Dell, 1971.

Jespersen, Otto. *Language: Its Nature, Development and Origin.* New York: Norton, 1964.

Johnson, Ernest A. "The Meaning of *Civilización* and *Barbarie* in *Doña Bárbara*." *Hispania* 39 (1956): 456–61.

Karson, Sonia. "La estructura de *María* de Jorge Isaacs." *Revista Hispánica Moderna* 34 (July–October 1968): 685–89.

Kermode, Frank. *The Sense of Ending*. New York: Oxford University, 1970.

Kolb, Glen L. "Aspectos estructurales de *Doña Bárbara*." *Revista Iberoamericana* 28 (January–June 1962): 131–40.

———. "Dos novelas y un solo argumento." *Hispania* 46 (1963): 84–87.

Kolbenschlag, Madonna. *Kiss Sleeping Beauty Good-bye*. New York: Doubleday, 1979.

Kristeva, Julia. *Le Texte du roman*. Paris: Mouton, 1970.

Lafforgue, Jorge. "*La ciudad y los perros*, novela moral." In *Homenaje a Mario Vargas Llosa*, edited by Helmy F. Giacoman and José Miguel Oviedo, 99–123. Long Island City, N.Y.: Las Américas, 1971.

Lakoff, Robin. *Language and Woman's Place*. New York: Harper & Row, 1975.

Lastra, Pedro. "Un caso de elaboración narrativa de experiencias concretas en *La ciudad y los perros*." In *Homenaje a Mario Vargas Llosa*, edited by Helmy F. Giacoman and José Miguel Oviedo, 37–44. Long Island City, N.Y.: Las Américas, 1971.

Leavitt, S. E. "Sex versus Symbolism in *Doña Bárbara*." *Revista de Estudios Hispánicos* (Alabama) 1 (May 1967): 117–20.

Lederer, Wolfgang. *The Fear of Women*. New York: Harcourt Brace Jovanovich, 1968.

Lévi-Strauss, Claude. *Le Cru et le cruit*. Paris: Plon, 1964.

———. *Tristes tropiques*. Translated by John Russell. New York: Atheneum, 1972.

Lichtblau, Myron I. *El arte estilístico de Eduardo Mallea*. Buenos Aires: Juan Goyanarte, 1967.

Llerena, Mario. "Función del paisaje en la novela hispanoamericana." *Hispania* 32 (1949): 499–503.

Loveluck, Juan "Aproximación a *La vorágine*." *Atenea* 39 (July–September 1962): 92–117.

Luchting, Wolfgang. "Los fracasos de Mario Vargas Llosa." *Mundo Nuevo*, nos. 51–52 (1970): 61–72.

MacAdam, Alfred. "Manuel Puig's Chronicles of Provincial Life." *Revista Hispánica Moderna* 36 (1970–71): 50–65.

———. *Modern Latin American Narratives: Dreams of Reason*. Chicago: University of Chicago Press, 1977.

McGrady, Donald. "Función del episodio de Nay y Sinar en *María* de Isaacs." *Nueva Revista de Filología Hispánica* 18 (1965–66): 171–76.

McMurray, G. R. "Form and Content Relationships in *La ciudad y los perros.*" *Hispania* 56 (September 1973): 579–86.

McMurray, George R. "José Donoso's Tribute to Consciousness: *El obsceno pájaro de la noche.*" *Chasqui* 3 (May 1974): 40–48.

Magnarelli, Sharon. "Amidst the Illusory Depths of the First-Person Pronoun and *El obsceno pájaro de la noche.*" *Modern Language Notes* 93 (March 1978): 267–84.

———. "The Baroque, the Picaresque and *El obsceno pájaro de la noche.*" *Hispanic Journal* 2 (Spring 1981): 81–93.

———. "From *El obsceno pájaro de la noche* to *Tres novelitas burguesas:* Development of a Semiotic Theory in the Works of Donoso." In *The Analysis of Literary Texts: Current Trends in Methodology,* edited by Randolph Pope, 224–35. Ypsilanti, Mich.: Bilingual Press, 1980.

———. "Juego/fuego de la esperanza." *Cuadernos Americanos* 247: 199–208.

———. "Gatos, lenguaje y mujeres en *El gato eficaz* de Luisa Valenzuela." *Revista Iberoamericana* 45 (July–December 1979): 603–11.

———. "Humor and Games in Luisa Valenzuela's *El gato eficaz:* The Looking-Glass World Re-visited." *Modern Language Studies* 13 (Summer 1983): 81–89.

———. "*El obsceno pájaro de la noche:* Fiction, Monsters, and Packages." *Hispanic Review* 45 (Autumn 1977): 413–19.

———. "*The Time of the Hero:* Liberty Enslaved." *Latin American Literary Review* 4 (Spring-Summer, 1976): 35–46.

———. "Women, Violence, and Sacrifice in *Pedro Páramo* and *La muerte de Artemio Cruz.*" In *Los mundos de Juan Rulfo,* edited by Coddou and Servodidio, *INTI,* nos. 13–14 (Spring–Fall 1981): 44–54.

Mallea, Eduardo. *All the Green Shall Perish.* Translated by John B. Hughes. New York: Knopf, 1969.

———. *Todo verdor perecerá.* Mexico: Espasa-Calpe, 1951.

Marban, Hilda. *Rómulo Gallegos: el hombre y su obra.* Madrid: Playor, 1973.

Mármol, José. *Amalia.* Mexico: Porrúa, 1974.

Martin, J. L. *La narrativa de Vargas Llosa, acercamiento estilístico.* Madrid: Gredos, 1974.

Martínez, Z. Nelly. "Lo neobarroco en *El obsceno pájaro de la noche* de José Donoso." *XVII Congreso del Instituto Internacional de Literatura Iberoamericana: El barroco en América.* Madrid: Universidad Complutense de Madrid, 1978.

———. "*El obsceno pájaro de la noche:* la productividad del texto." *Revista Iberoamericana* 46 (January–June 1980): 51–66.

Massiani, Felipe. *El hombre y la naturaleza venezolana en Rómulo Gallegos.* Caracas: Ministerio de Educación, 1964.

Massón de Gómez, Valerie. "Las flores como símbolos eróticos en la obra de Jorge Isaacs." *Thesaurus* 28:117–27.

Masters, R. E. L. *Eros and Evil.* Baltimore: Penguin, 1974.

Matthews, Robert P. "Las ideas de Carlos Fuentes: Desde lo mexicano hasta lo universal." *Revista Nacional de Cultura* 201 (November–December 1971): 47–60.

Maturo, Graciela. "La virgen, anunciadora del tiempo nuevo." In *La mujer símbolo del mundo nuevo* edited by Vicente Cicchitti, 11–18. Buenos Aires: Fernando García Cambeiro, 1976.

Mehlman, Jeffrey. "Introductory Note" to translation of Jacques Derrida, "Freud and the Scene of Writing." *Yale French Studies*, no. 48 (1972): 73–74.

Mejia B., William, S. J. "La mujer en la obra riveriana." *Boletín Cultural y Bibliográfico* 10 (1967): 158–63.

Menton, Seymour. "La estructura dualística de *María*." *Thesaurus* 25 (1970): 251–77.

Merrell, Floyd. "Communication and Paradox in Carlos Fuentes' *The Death of Artemio Cruz*: Toward a Semiotics of Character." *Semiotica* 18 (1976): 339–60.

Michalski, A. "*Doña Bárbara*, un cuento de hadas." *PMLA* 85 (October 1970): 1015–20.

Miller, Casey, and Kate Swift. *Words and Women.* Garden City, N.Y.: Anchor, 1977.

Morinigo, Mariano. "Civilización y barbarie en *Facundo y Doña Bárbara*." In *Recopilación de textos sobre tres novelas ejemplares,* edited by T. Pérez, 412–39. Havana: Las Américas, n.d.

Moss, Jennifer, ed. *Snow White and the Seven Dwarfs.* New York: Prestige, 1976.

Muller, Anita L. "La dialéctica de la realidad en *El obsceno pájaro de la noche*." *Nueva Narrativa Hispanoamericana* 2 (September 1972): 93–100.

Murray, Margaret. *The God of the Witches.* New York: Oxford, 1952.

Nelson, Mary. "Why Women Were Witches." In *Women: A Feminist Perspective,* edited by Jo Freeman, 335–50. Palo Alto, Calif.: Mayfield, 1975.

O'Faolain, Julia, and Lauro Marines. *Not in God's Image.* New York: Harper & Row, 1973.

Olivera, Otto. "El romanticismo de José Eustacio Rivera." *Revista Iberoamericana* 17 (December 1952): 41–61.

Ortega y Gasset, José. *La deshumanización del arte.* Madrid: Revista de Occidente, 1967.

Oviedo, José Miguel. *Mario Vargas Llosa: la invención de una realidad.* Barcelona: Barral, 1970.

Paz, Octavio. *Claude Lévi-Strauss o el nuevo festín de Esopo.* Mexico: Mortiz, 1967.

————. *Conjunciones y disyunciones*. Mexico: Mortiz, 1969.

————. *El laberinto de la soledad*. Mexico: Fondo de cultura económica, 1959.

Peña, Margarita. "El diablo, aliado y socio en *Doña Bárbara*." *Mundo Nuevo*, no. 48 (June 1970): 65–69.

Pérez, T., ed. *Recopilación de textos sobre tres novelas ejemplares*. Havana: Las Américas, n.d.

Peters, Edward. *The Magician, the Witch, and the Law*. Philadelphia: University of Pennsylvania Press, 1978.

Piña, Juan Andrés. "José Donoso: Los fantasmas del escritor." *Mensaje*, no. 246 (January–February 1976): 49–53.

Pope, Randolph. "*La vorágine:* Autobiografía de un intelectual." In *The Analysis of Literary Texts: Current Trends in Methodology*, edited by Randolph Pope, 256–67. Ypsilanti, Mich.: Bilingual Press, 1980.

Porras Collantes, Ernesto. "Interpretación estructural de *La vorágine*." *Thesaurus* 23 (May–August 1968): 241–79.

Posada Delgado, Ernesto. "El paisaje en *María* y en *La vorágine*." *Boletín Cultural y Bibliográfico* (Bogotá) 10 (1967): 880–84.

Promis Ojeda, José. "Algunas notas a propósito de *La ciudad y los perros*." In *Homenaje a Mario Vargas Llosa*, edited by Helmy F. Giacoman and José Miguel Oviedo, 287–94. Long Island City, N.Y.: Las Américas. 1971.

Puig, Manuel. *Betrayed by Rita Hayworth*. Translated by Suzanne Jill Levine. New York: Avon, 1973.

————. *La traición de Rita Hayworth*. Barcelona: Seix Barral, 1971.

Pupo-Walker, C. Enrique. "Relaciones internas entre la poesía y la novela de Jorge Isaacs." *Thesaurus* 22 (1967): 45–59.

Ramos Calles, Raúl. *Los personajes de Gallegos a través del psicoanálisis*. Caracas: Monte Avila, 1969.

Reider, Norman. "Chess, Oedipus and the Mater Dolorosa." In *The Study of Games*, edited by Elliot M. Avedon and Brian Sutton-Smith, 440–64. Huntington, N.Y.: Krieger, 1979.

Reik, Theodor. *The Creation of Woman*. New York: McGraw-Hill, 1960.

Rivera, José Eustacio. *La vorágine*. Buenos Aires: Losada, 1972.

————. *The Vortex*. Translated by Earle K. James. New York: Putnam, 1935.

Rodríguez Monegal, Emir. "Madurez de Vargas Llosa." *Mundo Nuevo*, no. 3 (1966): 62–72.

————. "El mundo de José Donoso." *Mundo Nuevo*, no. 12 (June 1967): 77–85.

Rogers, Katharine. *The Troublesome Helpmate*. Seattle: University of Washington Press, 1966.

Rulfo, Juan. *Pedro Páramo*. Mexico: Fondo de cultura económica, 1969.

————. *Pedro Páramo*. Translated by Lysander Kemp. New York: Grove, 1959.

Sánchez, Porfirio. "Aspectos bíblicos de *Todo verdor perecerá.*" *Romance Notes* 14 (1972): 469–75.

Sarduy, Severo. *Barroco*. Buenos Aires: Sudamericana, 1974.

Siles, Jaime. "*El obsceno pájaro de la noche* y su técnica narrativa." *Cuadernos Hispanoamericanos* 87 (January 1972): 175–78.

Sophocles. *Oedipus the King*. Translated and edited by Thomas Gould. Englewood Cliffs, New Jersey: Prentice-Hall, 1970.

Southard, David. "Betrayed by Manuel Puig: Reader Deception and Anti-Climax in His Novels." *Latin American Literary Review* 4 (Fall–Winter 1976): 22–28.

Spence, Lewis. *Myth and Ritual in Dance, Games, and Rhyme*. London: Watts, 1947.

Stone, Merlin. *When God Was a Woman*. New York: Harcourt Brace Jovanovich, 1978.

Tatum, Charles M. "*El obsceno pájaro de la noche:* The Demise of a Feudal Society." *Latin American Literary Review* 1 (Spring 1973): 99–105.

Teja, Ada. "*Pedro Páramo:* Dialéctica e historia." *Chasqui* 4 (February 1975): 51–59.

Tittler, Jonathan. *Narrative Irony in the Contemporary Spanish-American Novel*. Ithaca, N.J.: Cornell University Press, 1984.

Todorov, Tzvetan. *Littérature et signification*. Paris: Larousse, 1967.

Trible, Phyllis. "Eve and Adam: Genesis 2–3 Reread." In *Womanspirit Rising*, edited by Carol P. Christ and Judith Plaskow, 74–83. New York: Harper & Row, 1979.

Unamuno, Miguel de. *Niebla*. Madrid: Espasa-Calpe, 1968.

Valente, José Angel. "La naturaleza y el hombre en *La vorágine* de José Eustacio Rivera." *Cuadernos Hispanoamericanos*, no. 67 (July 1955): 102–8.

Valenzuela, Luisa. *El gato eficaz*. Mexico: Mortiz, 1972.

Vargas Llosa, Mario. *La ciudad y los perros*. Barcelona: Seix Barral, 1971.

———. *The Time of the Hero*. Translated by Lysander Kemp. New York: Harper, 1966.

Wagner, M. L. "Eusebio R. Castex' *Tópicos lexigráficos.*" *Revista de Filología Española* 20:176–77.

Woods, William. *A History of the Devil*. New York: Berkley, 1975.

Wyers Weber, Frances. "La dinámica de la alegoría: *El obsceno pájaro de la noche* de José Donoso." *Hispamérica* 4, nos. 11–12:23–31.

Index

rator, 80; witch, 148. *See also* Cova, Arturo

Vortex, The. See *Vorágine, La*

Witch: and baroque writer, 149; and ellipsis, 155–58, 162; and eroticism, 154–55, 158–59, 163; as female, 148–49, 152; inexplicable, 157; and knowledge, 164–65, 166; as linguistic creation, 157–58; and power, 148–49, 155–56, 164–65, 166, 167–68; as projection, 167; as reflection, 166–67; as self-referential, 158; and silence, 158; as symbol, 166–67

Woman: as absence, 45, 103–7, 140–41, 186–88; attenuation of threat, 108; and authority, 88–90, 95–96; as barrier to desire, 89–90, 99–100, 201; as beloved, 29; as by-product, 11–12; and cats, 172–73, 177–78; as center, 147; as composite, 188; conferrer of manliness, 113–14; as contamination, 114; as creation, 13, 14–15, 79; as creator, 114; and death, 80–81, 86–88, 90, 173, 174–75; as decay, 205; as desirable and despicable, 113–14; as destruction, 79; disparaged, 14–15; and dreams, 87–88; and economics, 109–10, 113, 143, 144–45, 148, 166; as ellipsis, 154–55; and eroticism, 148, 156, 160, 162, 164, 174; and evil, 38, 183–85, 186; as exchangeable signifier, 116; as exchange medium, 109–10, 203; fear of, 126; on fringes of society, 94, 151–52; and golden age, 103–4, 105–6; hidden role, 178; and honor, 159; and knowledge, 166; and language, 14, 16–17, 107, 109, 139, 172, 183, 186–88; as life and death, 86, 90; as linguistic creation, 186–88; and magical powers, 70–71; and moon, 70–71, 199; as mother, 29, 79, 99–100; as motivation, 45, 102–3; as myth, 54–56, 79, 172; and nature, 70–71; as object of desire, 89–90; and Oedipus complex, 180–81; as other, 13–14, 173, 176, 187, 191; and paradise, 99; as past, 103–4; and polarity, 88–89, 184, 187; populates land of illusion, 82; and power, 70–71, 95–96, 98, 99–100, 114, 148–49, 151–52, 164–65, 173, 180–82, 189–92; as projection of male, 186, 188, 191; as property, 56; as re-creation, 141; as reflection, 186–87; as reflector, 202; as repetition, 13, 54–55, 107, 116; as representation, 175; as reproduction, 13–14, 114; and sacrifice, 92–93, 100–101; as sacrificial victim, 91–92, 94, 96–97; as scapegoat, 71; as servant, 208; as sign, 107; and silence, 57, 158–60, 166; and sin, 202; and substitution, 181–82; as supplement, 22, 116, 142–43, 175–76, 182, 186–87, 187; as threat, 53, 113–14, 163–64; as transformable, 177–78; as translation, 13; and violence, 96, 100–101, 180–81, 185; worshiped, 14–15

Writing, 13–14; as exorcism, 191; as rite of passage, 35